The
Wolves
of
Mount
McKinley

Adolph Murie
Biologist, Fish and Wildlife Service

University of Washington Press
Seattle and London

Published in association with
Alaska Natural History Association

The Wolves of Mount McKinley was originally published in 1944 by the U.S. Government Printing Office as no. 5 in the series "Fauna of the National Parks."

University of Washington Press paperback edition published 1985
Fifth printing, 2001
Printed in the United States of America

Library of Congress Cataloging-in-Publication Data
Murie, Adolph, 1899–1974.
  The wolves of Mount McKinley.
  Reprint. Originally published: Washington: U.S. G.P.O., 1944
(Fauna of the National Parks of the United States. Fauna series; no. 5)
  Bibliography: p.
  Includes index.
  1. Wolves—Behavior. 2. Mammals—Behavior. 3. Mammals—Alaska—Denali National Park and Preserve—Behavior. 4. Denali National Park and Preserve (Alaska). I. Title.
QL737.C22M77   1985   599.74'442   84-22017
ISBN 0-295-96203-8

The paper used in this publication is acid-free and recycled from 10 percent post-consumer and at least 50 percent pre-consumer waste. It meets the minimum requirements of American National Standard for Information Sciences—Permanence of Paper for Printed Library Materials, ANSI Z39.48-1984. ⊛ ♲

Contents

➤➤❖◀◀

CHAPTER 3. Dall Sheep

CHAPTER 4. Caribou

VII

Chapter 5. Moose

Chapter 6. Grizzly Bear

Chapter 7. Red Fox

Chapter 8. Golden Eagle

Chapter 9. Conclusions

References

Index

Illustrations

➤➤❖◀◀

FRONTISPIECE: A Mount McKinley wolf

x

Foreword

>»❖«<

IN RECENT YEARS there has been widespread concern over the increase of wolves and coyotes in Alaska. Special efforts have been made to control the wolf, especially in areas occupied by domestic reindeer, and there has been some apprehension concerning the welfare of the big game herds elsewhere in Alaska. Since Mount McKinley National Park lies in the heart of the Alaska wolf range and carries its proportionate quota of the general wolf population, park administrators were uncertain as to what should be the policy toward the wolves in this particular area. What, for instance, is the total effect of the wolf preying on the big game species in this national park? What is the relationship between the wolves of the park and the general wolf population of Alaska? How do such predators as the golden eagle, fox, grizzly bear, and lynx affect the hoofed animals, and how does the wolf affect these predators? In short, what is the ecological picture centering about the wolf of Mount McKinley National Park?

In one form or another wolves have been found throughout the Old and New Worlds. In North America they ranged from the Arctic regions to Mexico. In the time of Lewis and Clark wolves were abundant all through the western United States. But the wolf is a powerful animal, and a cunning one, and unfortunately has run counter to the economic interests of man in settled regions. The war against the wolf on our western plains, when cattle replaced the buffalo and the wolf became a serious menace to the livestock industry, is an interesting phase of early western history. It was, of course, necessary that the wolf should go from those regions.

Aside from economic necessities, however, many persons wish to retain the wolf somewhere in the North American fauna, perhaps in the more remote parts of the continent, in wilderness areas where there will not be interference from economic interests.

In the December 1942 issue of *American Forests*, Stanley P. Young has expressed the heartfelt wish of naturalists, numerous outdoors men, and other interested persons throughout the land when he concludes:

> Where not in conflict with human interests, wolves may well be left alone. They form one of the most interesting groups of all mammals, and should be permitted to have a place in North American fauna.
>
> Fortunately, wolves still exist in many areas where there is no conflict with human interests. Such areas, it is believed, will perpetuate the existence of these interesting mammals, unless they are crowded out by further development. This will not be for a long time to come, if ever.

Many feel that our national parks and monuments are fitting places for just such a purpose. Congress has set aside these areas to preserve, among other things, the native fauna. Mount McKinley National Park is the only national park in which wolves occur in numbers.

It is not always possible to maintain the primitive picture without some human interference, since man's activities impinge upon the animal life even in such reservations. For instance, it has been found necessary to control the size of the Yellowstone elk herds, which had come to exceed the carrying capacity of their environment.

The question persisted—Is it feasible to permit moderate representation of the wolf in the fauna of Mount McKinley National Park? There is a wise provision of long standing in the policy of the National Park Service that no disturbance of the fauna of any given national park shall be made until a proper scientific appraisal of the question has been made. It was my good fortune to be given the assignment to study the wolves of Mount McKinley National Park.

ADOLPH MURIE.

October 4, 1942.

XIV

Summary

-»>❖«<-

A FIELD STUDY of the wolf-Dall sheep relationships in
Mount McKinley National Park was begun in April
1939, and was terminated in August 1941. Other animals
included in the study are the caribou, moose, grizzly, fox,
and eagle.

For several years preceding 1926, wolves were scarce in the
park. Their noticeable increase in 1927 and 1928 coincided
with a general increase of wolf numbers in interior Alaska.
From about 1928 to 1941, wolves have been common in the
park as well as over interior Alaska, and apparently their numbers have not varied much in the park during this period. It
is not unlikely that the fluctuations in wolf numbers are due
to diseases such as distemper, rabies, and mange.

A wolf family at a den on East Fork River was closely observed during two denning seasons. In 1940 there were five
adult wolves at the den—the parents, two males, and a female.
After these animals left the den, two other males joined them.
In 1941 the den was occupied by the same pair; the second
female mated with one of the extra males and had her own den.
She later brought her pups to the original den and the two
families lived together. The wolves generally rested at the
den during the day and hunted at night, but some hunting
was also done during the day. Food was brought to the den
by the parents and the other adults. The wolves were unusually friendly among themselves, and the pups played with
all the adults.

The 1940 group of seven adults and five pups traveled
together during the fall and winter. They were last seen
together on March 17, 1941. None of the 1940 young was

observed at the 1941 den. They traveled readily over a home range known to be at least 50 miles in diameter.

Two other wolf families were observed. In one of these there were three adults with the pups.

A wolf pup which was raised in captivity became tame and friendly. It did not come in heat until it was almost 2 years old. Another captive female wolf crossed with a dog and had young when she was 2 years old.

The feeding habits of the wolves were determined by field observations and the analysis of 1,174 scats. The principal food was caribou and mountain sheep, but ground squirrels, marmots, and mice were sometimes utilized to an important extent. Snowshoe hares were scarce, so there was no opportunity to learn the extent to which, when plentiful, they furnish food for wolves.

An exceptionally large Dall sheep population was greatly reduced by starvation during the winters of 1929 and 1932 because of the deep and crusted snow conditions. No doubt there was also heavy wolf predation at that time. Since 1932 the sheep population appears to have been rather stable.

The sheep breed in the latter half of November and early December, and the young are usually born in May. A single lamb is the rule.

Part of the sheep population migrates to a summer range near the main crest of the Alaska Range, but many sheep remain on the winter ranges all year. Migrations to and from the summer range take place in early summer and early fall. Grass is the staple food the year round, but much willow and a variety of herbs are eaten, especially in summer.

A disease which appears to be actinomycosis is common among the sheep. A heavy infestation of lungworm was found in one yearling.

The lynx is a casual predator on the sheep and has little effect on their numbers. The effect of the golden eagle on the sheep is unimportant.

XVI

The wolf preys extensively on sheep. Several hunting incidents are described. Wolves apparently chase many sheep before they find one that they can catch. Artificial intrusions such as roads increase predation.

To determine the types of sheep killed by wolves, sheep skulls were collected. These skulls were classified into four groups as follows: lamb, yearling, prime (2 to 8 years), and old (9 years and older). The skull studies showed that very few sheep in the 2- to 8-year class died, and that the majority of casualties in this class were severely diseased. The largest number of skulls belonged to the old-age group. There was a heavy mortality among young sheep in their first winter. Because so few sheep died in their prime, it is obvious that any wolf predation affects mainly the weaker animals.

The wolves restrict the sheep to the rougher country. It appears that during the period from 1932 to 1941 the sheep population was held in check by the wolves. It is the predation on the yearlings which seems to be most important in controlling sheep numbers.

During three seasons, counts were made of the lambs, yearlings, and ewes. In 1939 there was a large lamb crop and a large survival of yearlings from the 1938 lamb crop. The 1940 counts showed a heavy winter mortality in the 1939 lamb crop and an extremely small lamb crop. In 1941 yearlings were scarce, but the lamb crop was large. A 50-percent lamb-ewe ratio (2-year-old ewes classified as adult ewes) appears to constitute a good lamb crop. A survival of 50 percent of these lambs to the yearling stage probably is sufficient to increase the population. The summer losses among lambs were extremely light. These classified counts showed that during some years the survival of lambs is so small that there is a drop in the population.

Wolf predation probably has a salutary effect on the sheep as a species. At the present time it appears that the sheep and wolves may be in equilibrium.

XVII

A herd of caribou numbering from 20,000 to 30,000 live in Mount McKinley National Park and adjacent regions. They make annual migrations which may vary in minor or major particulars from year to year. They breed in late September and during most of October and the calves are born about the middle of May. Wolves feed extensively on the calves which, when available, constitute the main food supply. Several hunts are described in detail. The calves are captured in open chase. Usually the victim is one of the calves which drops behind the others, so that it appears that the weaker animals are eliminated by the wolf. Adult caribou are also run down, but when the calves are young the adults are seldom taken. In interior Alaska the caribou furnishes the main food of the wolf. When caribou are in the vicinity of sheep hills they are a buffer between the wolves and the sheep, thus materially reducing the wolf predation on sheep.

The caribou are subject to attack by the warble fly and the nostril fly; they also appear to suffer from actinomycosis.

About half of the cows above yearling age are followed by calves. In 1939 the yearling-cow ratio was 22 percent, signifying a loss during the first year of about 50 percent. In 1940 and 1941 the counts indicated similar losses of calves during the first year.

Under natural conditions the caribou herds are no doubt adjusted to the presence and pressure of the wolf.

Moose are common in suitable habitat. Their principal food at all seasons is willow. The rut begins in early September and continues for 3 or 4 weeks. The young are born in late May. Twins are common. In the presence of a large wolf population in recent years, moose have increased in the park and the region adjacent. The moose range is in good condition.

The grizzly bear is common in Mount McKinley National Park. Its food habits were studied by analyzing 201 scats and making numerous observations of feeding grizzlies. The food

XVIII

habits change as the seasons progress. In May and early June the principal food consists of roots; during most of June and July the main food is grass (mainly *Calamagrostis langsdorfi*), and *Equisetum arvense;* during late July, August, and September, blueberries and other berries make up the bulk of the food. Ground squirrels form a small part of the food at all seasons, and carrion is always acceptable. Grizzlies were seen feeding on caribou calves but probably are unable to catch the calves after they are a few days old. The bears mate during May and June, not oftener than every 2 years.

Some bears confined their movements to a rather definite range. One female was generally found in an area about 9 miles in diameter. There was considerable overlapping of ranges. The grizzlies frequently rob the wolves of their kills. Once a family invaded the vicinity of a wolf den in search of food scraps. The wolf will attack the grizzly but is unable to close in on him.

Foxes flourished despite the presence of wolves. No evidence was found in Mount McKinley National Park to show that wolves are harmful to foxes. In the fox-wolf interrelations the fox may be the gainer since the wolf often makes food available to him. Adult foxes have a year-long home range. The food habits were studied by analyzing 662 summer scats and 124 winter scats. The principal summer foods were mice and ground squirrels, and the principal winter foods were mice and blueberries. The snowshoe hare was rare so was scarcely available to the foxes.

The food habits of the golden eagle were studied by making observations at 13 occupied and 13 unoccupied nests, and by an analysis of 632 eagle pellets. The main food of the eagle is the ground squirrel which was found in 86 percent of the pellets. Most of the calf caribou eaten was carrion. The predation of the golden eagle on Dall sheep lambs and on the fox appears to be negligible. The economic status of the eagle was found to be favorable.

"The mountains are a part of me,
I'm fellow to the trees."

Robert Service

CHAPTER ONE

❮❮❮-

Introduction

❮❮❮-

Outline of the Study

IN 1939 I WAS REQUESTED to make a study of the relationships between the timber wolf (*Canis lupus pambasileus*) and the Dall sheep (*Ovis dalli dalli*) in Mount McKinley National Park, Alaska. I arrived in the park on April 14, and 3 days later was taken 22 miles into the park by dog team and left at a cabin on Sanctuary River where I started my field work. The next morning I climbed a mountain and saw a ewe and yearling on a grass slope, the first white sheep I had seen for 16 years, and a little later, through the field glasses, I "picked up" a beautiful ram resting on a ledge, the graceful curved horns silhouetted against a spring-blue sky. A strong cold wind was blowing on top so I slipped on my parka. During the day 66 sheep were classified, 20 of which were yearlings. Wolf tracks were seen and a wolf dropping, containing sheep hair, was found. The long, slow process of gathering data had begun.

In order to avoid accumulating only a number of miscellaneous observations I directed my efforts along the most promising lines and kept in mind the main points on which it was desirable to get quantitative data.

First it was necessary to learn what the wolves were eating. Killing the wolf to examine the stomach contents, in this case, was too much like killing the goose that laid the golden eggs. A dropping tells almost as much, so, to learn the food habits, wolf droppings were gathered, and of course observations of the wolves in action were made whenever possible. From the analysis of many droppings, some notion of the extent of the feeding on mountain sheep was obtained. The next point to determine was to what extent the sheep eaten represented carrion. It could, of course, all have been carrion. Some of it certainly was. But if it were learned that sheep are commonly run down and killed by wolves then it would be necessary to learn what kind of sheep are killed. Were they the ailing, the aged, and the young, or were all classes being taken indiscriminately? These were points difficult to determine. A thorough search of the sheep hills yielded skulls of 829 sheep. These skulls showed in what types of animals the mortality in the population lay and brought up fundamental problems concerning the natural role of the predator.

Another obvious line of attack was to classify the white sheep population to determine the size of lamb crop and the survival of yearlings in order to learn the losses during the first year—a critical period. Classifications were made in most parts of the range at every opportunity. Besides these salient points, all other available information on the wolves and sheep was gathered. The food habits and range of the sheep were of special interest, for adequate range is often an important factor in predatory problems. Historical data on the wolf and sheep populations were sought, for such data are frequently enlightening.

Involved in this same problem were other animals which required study to determine what part they play in regard to the sheep and to the wolf. The caribou is a basic food supply of the wolf in interior Alaska, so it had an important bearing on the wolf-sheep relationships. There were questions such as the extent that the caribou serve as a buffer species for the mountain sheep. The caribou were studied in much the same man-

ner as were the sheep. It is at least a tradition that the golden eagle who shares the high country with the sheep is one of its principal enemies. Perhaps the golden eagle was levying too heavy tribute on the sheep or perhaps it was a valuable citizen. Therefore, the food habits and actions of this bird required attention. Another animal on the agenda was the grizzly bear, known to be fond of caribou and sheep meat. The wolf has been accused of being destructive to foxes, so it seemed important to make what observations I could on this point. Furthermore, since foxes are a potential enemy of the lambs, their food habits required study. The moose was present in some numbers and, since it is generally considered a source of food for wolves, some attention was also given to this species. I had hoped to make observations of the coyote in the sheep hills but it was too scarce for study. Coyotes are more plentiful adjacent to the park in the rabbit country, a fact which may in itself be significant. Other animals like the porcupine, marmot, ground squirrel, snowshoe hare, mouse, and ptarmigan have been considered in their relationships to the larger forms.

This in brief gives the scope of the study which is reported in this paper. A chapter is devoted to each of the animals which has an important bearing on the problem. Some information not bearing directly on the problem is included in these chapters in order to round out the general ecological picture. Much of the data on the wolf is discussed in chapters dealing with its prey species.

In 1939 the field work, begun in April, was continued to the end of October. In 1940 I returned to the park in April and for the next 15 months remained in the field. The field observations were thus made over a period including most of three spring and summer seasons, two autumns, and one winter. In 1922 and 1923 I had spent several months in Mount McKinley National Park on other work, so when I undertook the present assignment I was already familiar with part of the area and some of the early wildlife conditions there.

In 1940 and 1941 I worked alone, but in 1939 I was ably assisted by two enrollees of the Civilian Conservation Corps. One of the enrollees, Emmett Edwards, was especially suited for the work as he had climbed many of the major peaks in the West. Irwin Yoger helped in the field work and drove the automobile when necessary.

An automobile road, 89 miles long, leads from the railroad to a little beyond Wonder Lake. This road passes through the heart of the sheep ranges. In a relatively short time I was able to drive in summer to any point along the road and from there cover the limits of the adjoining sheep hills in a day's tramp. In order to reduce the amount of back-tracking and thus cover more territory, I often had someone drive me to a place on this road from which I would hike in a semicircle and be picked up in the evening 10 or more miles from the starting point.

The work necessitated a large amount of hiking and climbing. In 1939 I walked approximately 1,700 miles. The following two summers the work still required much climbing but fewer long hikes. During the winter I traveled on skis. At this season a bedroll and food were carried in most cases and relief cabins were used for shelter.

In the summers of 1939 and 1941 I camped at Igloo Cabin and in 1940 at the East Fork cabin, 34 and 44 miles, respectively, by road, west of Park Headquarters.

Acknowledgments

I am deeply indebted to a number of persons for their help and support. To Harry J. Liek, Superintendent of Mount McKinley National Park when I first arrived, and later to Supt. Frank T. Been I am grateful for many favors, such as the use of an automobile, quarters, and various kinds of equipment. In fact, the entire park staff was of great assistance. Former Chief Ranger Louis M. Corbley and Ranger John C. Rumohr supplied considerable information on early conditions and were most helpful at all times. Ranger Raymond W. McIntyre accompanied me on several winter trips. Harold R. Herning, William H. Clemons, Jess Morrison, Charles Peterson, and Andrew Fluetsch cooperated in many ways, and were out on trips with me. Former Ranger Lee Swisher made a special trip to the park to tell me of his experiences there with big game in previous years, and of his trapping north of the park more recently. I also had the use of one of his relief cabins. Trapper John Colvin furnished much information and several specimens. L. J. Palmer of the Fish and Wildlife Service spent 2 weeks with me studying vegetation. Personnel of the Alaska Road Commission employed in the park cooperated in numerous ways. Mr. and Mrs. J. W. Rust drove me to Livengood and to Eagle Summit to see captive wolves and caribou range. Prof. Otto W. Geist of the University of Alaska gave much valuable assistance. Former Warden Sam White made available various reports on the wildlife in interior Alaska. Dr. and Mrs. Aven Nelson of the University of Wyoming kindly identified much plant material. Dr. Carl P. Russell of the National Park Service and Clifford C. Presnall of the Fish and Wildlife Service strongly supported the field work at all times. I am especially indebted to Director Ira N. Gabrielson and to Dr. W. B. Bell of the Fish and Wildlife Service for furthering the field work and making arrangements for me to write this publication; to Victor H. Cahalane, in direct charge of the project, for helpful cooperation from the beginning of the field work to the completion of the manuscript; and to my brother, O. J. Murie, who assisted me in many ways, and contributed the wolf sketches made from descriptions given to him.

My first expedition to Mount Mc-Kinley National Park to study wolf-sheep relationships was made in 1939 and was sponsored by the National Park Service, and the second, made in 1940–41, was supported jointly by the National Park Service and the Fish and Wildlife Service.

Climate

The region north of the Alaska Range is colder and has less snowfall than the region south of the range which is benefited by the warm ocean current. But on the north side of the range there is considerable difference in temperature between the lowlands of the interior and the mountain region of Mount McKinley National Park. The summers in the park are definitely cooler and the winters warmer than at inland points such as Nenana and Fairbanks. Strong south winds often prevail in the park in winter. Precipitation in summer varies considerably, at least so it seems to one in the field. In 1939 for a month and a half it rained some almost every day. In 1940 the rainfall was moderate, and satisfactory weather prevailed, but in 1941 June and July were again rainy and cloudy although many clear days were reported for August. The yearly precipitation is about 15 inches. Snow in September is to be expected, and may fall in August, but usually at this time it quickly melts in the valleys and on south-facing slopes. The winter snow on the foothills has largely disappeared by the first of June, although some drifts last far into the summer.

TABLE 1.—*Temperature (° F.) and precipitation (inches) at McKinley Park Station, Nenana, and Talkeetna, Alaska (Capps, 1932)*

MONTHLY MEAN TEMPERATURE

Station	No. of years' record	January	February	March	April	May	June	July	August	September	October	November	December	Annual
McKinley Park	6	1.6	6.4	13.6	24.0	42.1	54.3	56.1	53.9	43.1	28.9	15.6	0.7	28.4
Nenana	8	−5.9	3.0	8.2	27.6	50.0	57.6	61.5	58.0	44.6	26.7	3.4	−7.9	27.2
Talkeetna	11	8.4	16.7	21.6	32.9	45.5	54.6	58.1	55.2	39.9	34.7	20.6	9.7	33.2

DAILY MEAN MINIMUM TEMPERATURE

Station	No. of years' record	January	February	March	April	May	June	July	August	September	October	November	December	Annual
McKinley Park	5-6	−7.8	4.1	3.5	14.3	30.8	40.4	44.3	42.1	33.6	19.7	6.6	−6.3	18.8
Nenana	5	−23.5	−6.6	−2.3	14.3	34.6	46.6	51.1	46.6	35.0	18.3	−6.0	−15.7	16.0
Talkeetna	8	−0.8	3.6	10.8	20.5	31.6	40.9	45.4	44.0	35.0	26.7	12.3	0.2	22.5

LOWEST TEMPERATURE OF RECORD

Station	No. of years' record	January	February	March	April	May	June	July	August	September	October	November	December	Annual
McKinley Park	6	−52	−47	−28	−33	4	25	31	28	2	−15	−34	−54	−54
Nenana	6-7	−63	−51	−50	−26	18	35	37	30	15	−17	−49	−56	−63
Talkeetna	11	−48	−33	−24	−23	20	27	31	27	20	−8	−30	−41	−48

MONTHLY AND ANNUAL NORMAL PRECIPITATION

Station	No. of years' record	January	February	March	April	May	June	July	August	September	October	November	December	Annual
McKinley Park	6	.50	.57	.59	.93	1.31	2.31	2.25	1.83	1.80	.92	.45	.63	14.09
Nenana	8	.38	.51	1.04	.36	.66	1.50	2.63	1.98	1.58	.80	.26	.30	12.00
Talkeetna	11	1.68	2.18	1.85	.91	.95	1.63	3.84	4.50	4.80	4.00	1.54	1.81	29.69

MONTHLY AND ANNUAL SNOWFALL

Station	No. of years' record	January	February	March	April	May	June	July	August	September	October	November	December	Annual
McKinley Park	4-6	11.3	9.1	7.5	1.9	Trace	0	0	0	2.3	6.5	7.6	9.2	55.4
Nenana	8	5.9	5.3	9.6	3.4	1.2	0	0	Trace	.3	7.7	4.5	4.0	41.9
Talkeetna	6-8	22.9	23.2	28.4	13.4	.5	0	0	0	2.6	10.3	15.8	24.6	141.7

Physiography

In the central part of the Alaska Range, extending westward some 105 miles from the Alaska Railroad, lies Mount McKinley National Park. From the crest of the range, and within the park boundaries, rise several massive mountains, including Mount McKinley which is 20,300 feet in altitude. Most of the park lies on the north slope of the range, with its long axis parallel to the range. It is from 30 to 35 miles in width and contains 3,030 square miles.

In the eastern part of the park high lateral ridges run northward from the main range for distances up to 10 miles before sloping down into low rolling terrain, from which again rises a foothill range. As far westward as Sanctuary River this "outside" range is a single ridge. West of Sanctuary River this foothill range broadens out into an irregular mass of mountains that approach the main range so closely that the intervening lowland is squeezed into narrow low passes. These outside mountains have elevations from 4,000 to 6,000 feet, and rise from river beds 2,500 to 3,000 feet in altitude. Several glacial streams flow northward from the main range and have cut deep canyons through the foothills, thus creating excellent mountain sheep habitat. Westward from Mount Eielson the foothills disappear and the main Alaska Range rises abruptly from the interior Alaska lowlands.

Much of the area is sedimentary rock, but there is a considerable amount of igneous material scattered throughout (Capps, 1932). The terrain is varied, with talus slopes and rounded summits, as well as cliffs and rugged contours. Most of the streams are of glacial origin. They are swift and braided, flowing over broad gravel bars. There are numerous small ponds and lakes, suitable for waterfowl breeding places.

Vegetation

Mount McKinley National Park lies largely above timber line, which occurs at 2,500 to 3,000 feet altitude. Narrow strips of timber extend varying distances along the river bottoms. This limited forest growth consists chiefly of white spruce (*Picea canadensis*), with some black spruce (*Picea mariana*) in wet situations. Many of the plant species found in the treeless areas also occur in various degrees and combinations among the trees. There is a scattering of cottonwoods

On opposite page: Map of the Eastern Portion of Mount McKinley National Park. The present summer and winter ranges of Dall sheep in Mount McKinley National Park are outlined. The obliquely lined areas show winter range; this range is also occupied by sheep during the summer. The stippled areas indicate summer range only. As only sheep concentration areas are outlined, the ranges appear to be disconnected. Actually, the ranges are continuous since sheep move readily from one favorite locality to another and a few may be found on the less rugged slopes outside the outlined areas. When the sheep were more abundant, many of the lower slopes, lying between the rugged areas, were also much used. A few sheep are present in the Windy Creek region but their range is not indicated on the map. Arrows show the general direction of sheep migration from various sections of the winter range to the summer range.

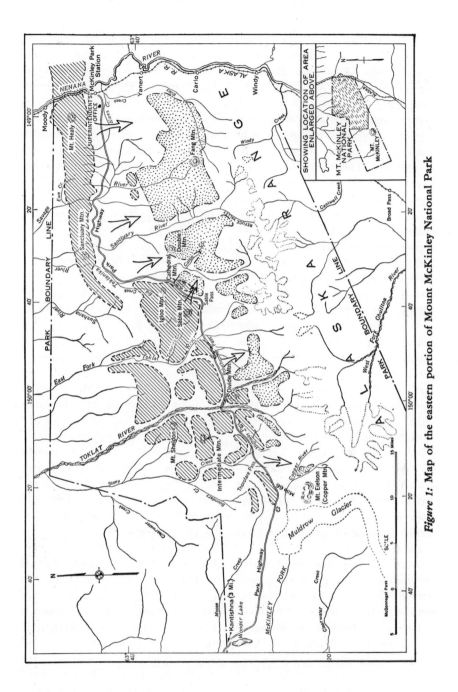

Figure 1: Map of the eastern portion of Mount McKinley National Park

(*Populus trichocarpa*), and aspen (*Populus tremuloides*) in suitable places. White birch (*Betula papyrifera*), so common in interior Alaska, is almost completely absent, being found only in the extreme eastern end of the park.

In the open lowland areas shrubs constitute a major feature of the vegetation. These shrubs consist largely of dwarf Arctic birch (*Betula nana*), several species of willow (*Salix* spp.), and blueberry (*Vaccinium uliginosum*). The dwarf birch and blueberries generally are knee high or less, and the willows vary from the dwarf creeping varieties to tall growths, sapling size. The taller willows are generally found along streams and draws. Alder (*Alnus fruticosa*) is plentiful in some areas. Much of it was found on the lower north slopes of the outside range. Buffaloberry (*Shepherdia canadensis*) is abundant over many gravel beds. Other common shrubs are crowberry (*Empetrum nigrum*), lowbush cranberry (*Vaccinium vitis-idaea minus*), Labrador tea (*Ledum groenlandicum*), rhododendron (*Rhododendron lapponicum*), and *Arctous alpina* in the open and *Arctous rubra* in the woods. Most of these shrubs occur in the timber as well as in the open.

Grasses, sedges, and wood rushes are dominant in a great many lowland situations and are found throughout the park. Bordering the highway and in some of the old trails *Calamagrostis canadensis* forms dense stands. Cotton grasses (*Eriophorum* spp.) are conspicuous in the wet tundra. Leaf lichens are abundant, and over wide areas of rolling lowland, species of *Cladonia* and *Cetraria* occur in varying degrees, in some places forming thick carpets. The family Leguminosae is well represented by species of *Hedysarum* (found abundantly on old river bars), *Oxytropis*, *Astragalus*, and *Lupinus*. Some of the conspicuous flowers are coltsfoot (*Petasites*), fireweed (*Epilobium angustifolium*), willow herb (*E. latifolium*), *Pedicularis* (several species), *Mertensia*, *Polemonium*, *Saxifraga* (a number of species) *Boykinia richardsoni*, poppies (*Papaver*), moss campion (*Silene*), *Delphinium*, and *Anemone*.

Perhaps the most characteristic plant on the mountain slopes is *Dryas*, which forms mats over vast areas and in other places is mixed with grasses and other vegetation. Species of *Dryas* also form mats over many old river bars. Many species of plants found in the open lowlands also occur on the ridges, but the associations on the ridges are somewhat different. The commonest grasses are species of *Poa* and *Festuca* which form low bunchy growths. *Hierochloe alpina* occurs widely, and sedges (*Carex*) and woodrushes (*Luzula*) are abundant; dwarf willows (*Salix*) of several species are common. The vegetation on many ridges is so short and dense that it has the appearance of a well-kept lawn. On south exposures or where erosion is active, the vegetation is sometimes sparse. An herbaceous cinquefoil (*Potentilla*) was conspicuous on some of these south slopes. There are many talus slopes where vegetation is scant.

CHAPTER TWO

Wolf

Physical Characteristics

I WAS A LITTLE UNCERTAIN about the identification of the first wolf I saw in Mount McKinley National Park. I was not sure whether it was a wolf or a coyote. The animal was some distance away, on a ridge parallel to the one from which I was watching, so that size was not a good criterion for identification and the color was about the same as that of a coyote. But it was noted that the legs appeared exceptionally long and prominent, and that there was something about the hind quarters which was peculiar, giving the animal just a suggestion of being crouched. On the slope it appeared more clumsy in its actions than a coyote. Its ears were more prominent than I had expected in a wolf. These characteristics were later found to be typical. The behavior of this wolf was of special interest so I checked my identification by an examination of the tracks which were approximately 5 inches long. After becoming familiar with the wolves, there generally was no difficulty in making identifications, but still on a few occasions a distant gray wolf could have been mistaken for a coyote.

There are some northern sled dogs which resemble wolves closely enough so that it would be hard to identify them correctly if they were running wild. Some years ago I drove a sled dog which was so similar to a wolf that even on a leash it could be mistaken for one. However, this animal was supposed to be a quarter-breed wolf. The wolf is lankier and has longer legs than the average sled dog. His chest is narrower so that the front legs are much closer together than those of the usual broad-chested sled dog.

There is much individual variation in wolves, especially in regard to color. They are usually classified as white, black, and gray, but among these types there is an infinite amount of variation. The wolves referred to as gray are sometimes a brownish color similar to that of a coyote. One type of animal is whitish except for a black mantle over the back and neck. In some, the fur on the neck is strikingly different from the rest of the coat. Some gray wolves have a striking silver mane. The tail is tipped with black. The black wolves often have a sprinkling of rusty or yellowish guard hairs which create a grizzled effect, and many are characterized by a vertical light line just back of the shoulder. Further description of their colors is given in the discussion of a family of wolves living at East Fork (see p. 25).

The black and gray wolves were present in about equal numbers in Mount McKinley National Park. Dr. E. W. Nelson (1887), reporting on his sojourn in Alaska from 1877 to 1881, states that at the head of the Yukon River the black wolves predominated

Figure 2: Tracks of front foot (at bottom) and hind foot (at top) of a wolf in soft mud. The front foot track is always noticeably broader than that of the hind foot. [*East Fork River, August 26, 1940.*]

and that the gray wolves were most abundant near the Bering Sea. I do not know if there is any dominance of color in different regions of Alaska at the present time but I expect that in most regions both color types are present.

I know of few weights of Alaska wolves but judge that the adult male in good flesh generally weighs approximately 100 pounds. Estimates have been made as high as 150 pounds and more. There is much variation in size, so that exceptionally large animals could be expected. Judging from the wolves that I saw, the females are smaller than the males.

Tracks

The tracks of a wolf can easily be distinguished from those of a coyote by their large size, and the long stride, but probably would often be indistinguishable from those of the large northern sled dog.

The front foot measures larger than the hind foot, being definitely broader and usually slightly longer. The width of the track, of course, varies according to the speed at which the wolf is traveling. When the animal is running fast or galloping the foot spreads considerably.

Tracks of a pup, on August 26, when it was about 3½ months old, measured as follows: Front foot, 4 inches long, 2⅞ inches wide; hind foot, 3½ inches long, 2⅝ inches wide.

The measurements of a 4½-month-old captive wolf pup (see page 45), a sister of the above wild pup, on

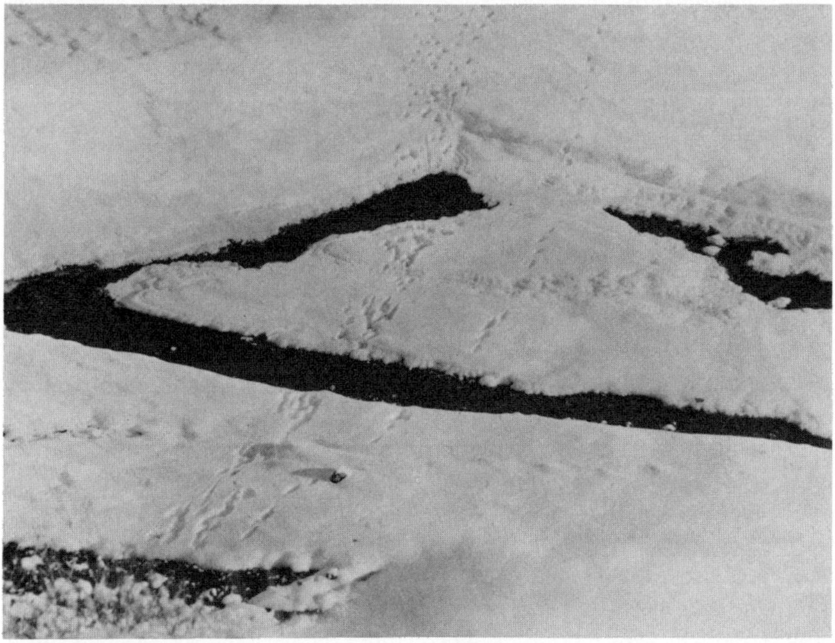

Figure 3: **Tracks of five wolves crossing a river bar in the snow. [*East Fork River, October 22, 1939.*]**

September 24, were as follows: Front foot, 4¾ inches long, 3¾ inches wide; hind foot, 4½ inches long, 3 inches wide.

The following measurements of tracks in moist mud are typical and show some of the variations. In most cases the animal had apparently been trotting.

Foot of animal	Length	Width
	Inches	*Inches*
Front	5⅛	3⅜
Hind	4⅝	3
Front	4⅞	[1] 3½
Hind	4⅜	3⅛
Front	5¼	4¼
Hind	5	3½
Front	5¼	3¾
Hind	4⅝	3

[1] Tracks of black female.

The pace of the wolf in walking and trotting on the level varies from 25 to 38 inches. In 7 inches of snow the pace measured between 27 and 30 inches. The pace of a track, in 6 inches of snow, probably made by a trotting animal, averaged 29 inches. A series of consecutive paces on a gravel bar measured 32, 34, 30, and 32 inches. In climbing a steep slope of about a 45-degree angle, in a few inches of snow, the pace of a band of wolves averaged about 16 inches. (By pace is meant the distance between the tracks of the two hind feet or the two front feet. A full stride would be twice the pace.)

In traveling through snow a band of wolves will often go single file, stepping in one set of tracks. The hind foot in such cases falls in the tracks of the front foot. At other times the hind foot may or may not fall in the track of the front foot. In order to avoid deep, soft snow the wolves often follow a hard packed drift or the edge of a road where the snow is more shallow.

Flecks of blood frequently seen in the trails in winter indicated that the wolves were subject to sore feet. In the case of the sled dog traveling in snow, especially in any kind of crusted snow, the hide on the toes is often worn off, sometimes causing the dog to limp considerably. If the crust is severe it may become necessary to protect the feet with moccasins. The feet of the wolves are probably affected by the snow in the same manner as are those of the sled dog, but possibly to a lesser degree. In summer a wolf would occasionally develop a limp and later recover.

History of Wolves in Mount McKinley National Park

Wolves no doubt have been a part of the present Alaska fauna for hundreds of years. Fossil remains are present in the Pleistocene fauna and it is probable that the wolves have persisted in Alaska since that time. The wolf then is not a new animal finding its niche in the fauna, with the possibility of upsetting existing relationships or exterminating some species. It is true that the effects of man's activities may be such as to bring the wolf into new associations with the native fauna, but as yet man's activities have probably not altered conditions sufficiently to seriously change the natural relationships.

The history of the wolves in Mount McKinley National Park during the last 25 years is, in a general way, quite well known. There is also considerable information on the prevalence of the wolf in interior Alaska, although much of this information is conflicting. There is often a tendency to report a great increase of the animals if any are noted, so that during a period when wolves were much less numerous than at present there are many reports of their abundance and great increase. Sometimes the caribou, the principal wolf food, shifts its range and brings wolves along with it into new territory where they are noticed and commented upon. I suppose that the history of the wolves varies a little in different parts of interior Alaska but that the general pattern is similar throughout. Since there are 586,400 square miles in Alaska, and 3,030 square miles in Mount McKinley National Park, which lies near the center of the Territory, it can perhaps be assumed that in its broad aspects the status of the wolves in the park has corresponded rather closely with their status in interior Alaska as a whole.

According to E. W. Nelson (1887) wolves were plentiful over much of Alaska during his sojourn there from 1877 to 1881. At that time wolves were scarce along the west coast due to the absence of caribou. Previously, when the caribou were plentiful there, before the advent of modern firearms among the natives, the wolves were also abundant. In 1880 they were reported most numerous toward the headwaters of the Kuskokwim and Yukon Rivers, which coincides roughly with the limits of the caribou range. At St. Michael, Dr. Nelson examined several thousand wolf skins which were handled by the trading post, and he reported the presence of many wolves inland among the caribou.

Wolves were apparently still plentiful in the early 1900's, and I have no information indicating that they were scarce between 1881 and 1900. An old-timer told me that between 1898 and 1903 wolves were abundant on the Stewart River. Charles Sheldon (1930) found wolves in the Mount McKinley region in 1907 and 1908, but just how prevalent they were it is hard to say. He found little evidence of wolves among the sheep hills along the Toklat River, but found these animals "very abundant" among the caribou at the edge of the mountains on Toklat River. In one night the wolves completely devoured a caribou bull he had shot.

Some time after 1908 the wolf population in the Mount McKinley region and perhaps also in other parts of the interior of Alaska was considerably reduced, probably as a result of natural causes. An old-timer who had hunted sheep in the McKinley region in 1916 and 1917

told me that he saw no wolves or wolf tracks there at that time. In 1920 and 1921 O. J. Murie visited a number of localities in interior Alaska in his travels by dog team and found wolves absent or scarce in most localities. In a trip through Rainy Pass and into the Kuskokwim country in the spring of 1922 he saw no tracks. Mr. Joe Blanchell at Farewell Mountain on the north side of Rainy Pass said that wolves were formerly common in that locality but had now disappeared. There were caribou all through this area so ample wolf food was present. In the past, about 1916 and 1917, a few wolves had destroyed some of Mr. A. H. Twitchell's reindeer herd near Ophir but no wolves were reported in the locality in 1922. This region lies just to the west and north of Mount McKinley National Park.

One trip was made by O. J. Murie through the caribou country between Chatanika and Circle in the spring of 1921, and the Chatanika region was again visited in the fall. No sign of wolf was found in the spring, and in the fall only one was seen, and wolves were heard howling only once. Part of this region was used the year round by caribou. A year or two before wolves had been reported more plentiful.

In March and April 1921, O. J. Murie traveled by dog team from Fairbanks to Tanana Crossing but saw no wolf tracks en route. He found that although wolves were not abundant, they did occur in the upper Tanana region in somewhat greater numbers than they did in the Chena and Chatanika regions nearer Fairbanks, and other regions visited. The upper Tanana region was inhabited by caribou at least for part of the year. In 1921 some wolves were reported on the north fork of the Forty Mile River.

On one trip which O. J. Murie and I made in the winter of 1922–23 we started from Nenana in November and traveled to Kokrines, where we visited a reindeer herd, crossed to Alatna, and traveled to the sheep hills in the Endicott Mountains at the head of the Alatna River; visited Bettles and Wiseman on the upper Koyukuk; came down the Chandalar River, where caribou were wintering, to the Yukon; continued to Fort Yukon and Circle, then west through the heart of the caribou country, arriving at Fairbanks on April 26. During the entire winter we saw not a single wolf track, which would indicate that wolves over much of interior Alaska were scarce at that time.

In 1922 and 1923 my brother and I spent considerable time among the sheep hills in Mount McKinley National Park. No tracks and no wolves were seen and none were reported by others.

In more recent years wolves have been more plentiful near Chatanika, where they had been so scarce from 1921 to 1923. During that period wolves had been even scarcer in Mount McKinley National Park.

In 1925, according to reports of the Superintendent, wolves had increased in Mount McKinley National Park to the extent that some tracks were seen in all parts of the park. [According to Soper (1942, p. 132) wolves began to increase in Wood Buffalo Park, Canada, about 1925 and since that time have continued to increase.] In 1927 is was reported that the wolves were becoming more numerous. A band of 11 was noted by one of the rangers. From 1928 to the present time wolves have been reported each year as plentiful in the park. From the records available, it appears there were no large fluctuations in the population during the period from 1928 to 1941.

The increase of wolves in the park coincided with a general increase in interior Alaska. There are no data to show that wolves are more abundant in Mount McKinley National Park than they are in other favorable localities in interior Alaska. Robert Marshall (1939) found wolf sign common in the Endicott Mountains in 1939. Wolves were reported plentiful in the Wood River country in the fall of 1940.

Since the recovery of the population the actual number of wolves in the sheep hills of the park has never been accurately determined. Estimates vary from 50 to 100. The wide ranging of the wolves and their movements in and out of the park make it extremely difficult to conduct any accurate census. My work did not take me over all the park, but within the sheep hills I would estimate the number of wolves to be between 40 and 60, perhaps nearer the first figure

To summarize, there have been two periods of wolf abundance and one of scarcity in Alaska in relatively recent years. Records available to me show that wolves were quite abundant in 1880, and probably from 1900 to 1908. Sufficient data, however, are not available to be sure of the exact status for the latter part of this period. Some time after 1908 the population declined and apparently wolves were generally scarce in 1916 and 1917 and up to about 1925, when they again increased. Since 1927 they have remained plentiful over much of interior Alaska. There is no doubt but that wolves were scarce during a period centering in the early 1920's and that since then they have increased and become common.

Causes of Fluctuation in Wolf Numbers

The causes of the scarcity of wolves in interior Alaska between 1916 and 1925, and perhaps some years preceding 1916, are not known. During this period of wolf scarcity the caribou herds, the main food supply, were large so that there was not a shortage of food. There was considerable trapping in the Territory at this time, but judging from the effect of trapping on the present wolf population in Alaska it is doubtful that this had much to do with the scarcity of wolves. Today there is extensive trapping in the interior of Alaska but apparently it has not caused any noticeable reduction in wolf numbers.

Intraspecific intolerance may hold a population in check but would probably not operate to cause a scarcity of the animals. If it operated at all it probably would tend to hold the animals at an optimum level which would be rather high.

The most probable cause of a drastic decimation of the wolves is disease. Mange, distemper, and rabies are some of the diseases which may affect them. Alexander Henry (1897) in his journal refers to scab in wolves. On March 5 (1801) at Pembina, N. Dak., he writes: "A large wolf came into my tent three times, and always escaped a shot. Next day, while hunting, I found him dead about a mile from the fort; he was very lean and covered with scabs."

R. M. Anderson (1938) writes as follows concerning mange in coyotes: "One young male coyote shot by Warden J. E. Stanton when the writer was with him in Cascade Valley early in September was very mangy, being so nearly devoid of hair from nose to tip of tail that the scabby and vesicular skin was plainly visible on every part of the body. Most of the half dozen coyotes seen in this area appeared to be afflicted with mange, and several wardens stated that many of the mangy coyotes lived through the winter, but that the worst cases usually died in the spring. This disease, and perhaps other causes, seems to keep the numbers down, and the reports of the superintendent of the park show that coyotes have decreased in numbers in recent years."

Warburton Pike (1892, p. 53) writes: "There was some sort of disease resembling mange among them (gray wolves) in the winter of 1889–90, which had the effect of taking off all their hair, and judging from the number of dead that were lying about, must have considerably thinned their numbers." This reference indicates that mange might destroy large numbers of wolves, especially in a large population where the conditions for the spread of the affliction would be optimum. Ernest Thompson Seton (1911, p. 351–352) says that in northern Canada mange is common at times. O. J. Murie tells me that he once lost a sled dog from mange.

Seton (1929, p. 288) says that rabies seems to break out among wolves at times. Alexander Henry (1897) as early as 1800 relates the killing of a wolf at camp which was thought to have rabies. Seton gives several instances in which wolves seemed to have had rabies. This disease probably could cause a drastic reduction in a population.

A disease like distemper could no doubt spread rapidly in a large wolf population, especially since the animals travel in packs. Distemper has been known to wipe out entire dog teams and it might affect wolves even more severely. Although the young animals are most susceptible to distemper, older wolves not having been in contact with the disease might be more vulnerable than old dogs which generally are considered immune. In 1924, O. J. Murie lost an entire dog team after he had traveled from Nenana to Hooper Bay, Alaska. Another team made up of older dogs was not affected. In that year a large number of dogs in interior Alaska are reported to have died from the disease, so apparently it was present in epizootic proportions. During April 1934, an outbreak of distemper is said to have prevailed in various sections along the Yukon and Tanana Rivers.

In an article in *Field* for December 1939, it is pointed out that distemper among dogs in England becomes much more prevalent and more severe in form when the dog population is high. During World War I, when few dogs were kept, there was hardly any distemper and it was nearly always mild. When the dogs were bred up again after the war, there were a great many deaths from distemper. Perhaps the disease was so destructive because the dogs came suddenly into contact with it and had no opportunity to become immunized in any degree. This occurrence suggests a possible threat to any large wolf population.

Three cases of wolves which may have died a natural death came to my attention. However, I found no evidence of disease among the wolves in Mount McKinley National Park.

The last reduction in wolf numbers may have been due to the large number of dogs that were brought into the wolf territory for transportation purposes and spread distemper or some other disease. The decrease in dog travel today may be an element favorable to the wolves. In addition, current trapping operations may be just sufficient to keep the wolf numbers from reaching a peak where they would be more susceptible to drastic reduction. This is, of course, theoretical, but seems worthy of consideration.

In connection with the problem of control of the wolf population it is of interest to consider the coyotes in Yellowstone National Park. During the long period that one or two hundred coyotes were destroyed annually in the park the coyote numbers remained high. When artificial control of the coyotes was stopped in 1935 many persons expected a great increase in their numbers. They did continue to be common, but apparently were no more plentiful than when artificial control was exercised. Now, in 1942, 7 years after control was stopped, there appears to have been a slight drop in the coyote population, judging from reports that have reached me, so that there may be fewer coyotes now than when artificial control was practiced. It is apparent that some natural controls, possibly disease, among others, are operating on these coyotes to hold their numbers in check. In a similar manner wolf numbers in Alaska may be subject to drastic natural controls and the population may again be greatly reduced through some natural factor like disease.

Breeding

In Mount McKinley National Park the young of wolves apparently are born in early May. Three litters of which the approximate time of birth was known had been born in early May. According to Bailey (1926, p. 155) this is more than a month later than in the Northern States. The gestation period of about 63 days (Seton, 1929, p. 274) would place the mating season early in March. Two females in the park each had four pups, and three had six pups.

A captive female which I raised and which was later kept at Mount McKinley National Park Headquarters, did not come in heat the first year but did so in early March in her second year and was in heat about 2 weeks. This agrees with the statement by Bailey (1926, p. 155) that wolves do not breed until they are 2 years old. Another captive female owned by Mrs. Faith Hartman of Fairbanks likewise did not come in heat the first year but bred with a dog the second year. The first 2 weeks that this wolf was in heat she fought off the dog but mated each day during the third week (March 9 to March 15). The male continued to pursue her on the following 3 days but there was no further mating after the fifteenth. She whelped four pups on May 15. The first one was born at 12:30 p. m., and the others at intervals of 45 minutes to 1½ hours. This observation placed the gestation period between 60 and 66 days.

Home Life

In 1940 and 1941 wolves were found denning on Toklat River but extensive observations on these Toklat wolves were not made. In 1940 a few notes were made regarding a family on Savage River, but in 1940 and 1941 much time was devoted to observing a family at a den on the East Fork of the Toklat River (known locally and hereafter referred to as East Fork or East Fork River). These three wolf groups will be discussed separately.

TOKLAT RIVER DEN

In 1939 no special effort was made to find dens because there were so many other phases of the field work which could not be neglected. The finding of dens sometimes seems simple, and at other times most difficult. To illustrate, in 1940 ex-trapper Frank Glaser, Agent of the Fish and Wildlife Service, and Wildlife Ranger Harold Herning of the National Park Service spent all their time from early March to early August in search of dens in Mount McKinley National Park. During this period they worked hard but found only one family of wolves and that was in a Toklat River den which was known to have been occupied on at least two previous occasions. Of course, their inability to find more may have indicated a scarcity of dens.

In a letter to O. J. Murie, former Ranger Lee Swisher gives an interesting description of his efforts to find this particular den on the Toklat River: "This past season I had great difficulty in locating a den. On two occasions, I saw (with the aid of binoculars) an old wolf carry meat

from a sheep carcass in Polychrome Pass, then go down Toklat River. I spent many days searching over the country where it seemed the den should be. There was a well-beaten trail for over 5 miles along the Toklat bars, then onto a bench where I could follow it no more. One morning while scouting along this bench close to the timber through some weeds I had no difficulty in following this trail which kept in the timber for about 2 miles where it then emerged onto the river bars again for another 5 miles or more where I located the den on a small timbered island along the river. I estimated that this wolf was carrying food to its young over 12 miles."

The Toklat River family was living about 12 miles north of the highway and 2 miles north of the sheep hills, on an island of spruces about 1 mile long and a third of a mile or less in width. Gravel bars surround this spruce island and sometimes the numerous channels of the Toklat River flow on both sides of it. The general level of the island rises only 2 or 3 feet above the gravel bars.

Following directions given me by former Ranger Lee Swisher, I first visited the den in the fall of 1939. It was located about 20 yards from the edge of the timber, in sandy loose soil in which a few cottonwoods grew along with the spruces. The wolves had renovated a fox den for their own use. The foxes had, as usual, a number of entrances, there being eight or nine of them in an area 20 feet across. One of them, leading under the roots of a spruce. was enlarged by the wolves when they took possession. It led to a chamber in the center, about 3 feet below the surface. According to reports, this chamber had been exposed by a trapper about 1937, and seven pups and a gray female were destroyed. In 1940 the wolves had used the same entrance but had dug 10 feet at right angles to the former burrow. Four pups were inadvertently removed from the den before I had an opportunity to observe it. There was no nest material in the chamber. The entrance was 16 inches high and 21 inches wide.

A narrow trail through the woods, 7 to 9 inches wide and 280 yards long, connected this den with another which also had been first occupied by foxes and later was taken over by wolves. It was located in a sandy rise in which a few cottonwoods grew with the spruces. One of the many holes had been enlarged and there was a large mound of dirt at its mouth. The entrance was 15 inches high and 20 inches wide. At least five well-defined trails led out in different directions. In 1940 this den showed some use, but this may have been in connection with the den from which the four pups were taken. Later in the summer it was evident that it had not been used after the first visit to it in May.

In 1941 the second den was occupied by a family on June 23. When I approached the den I saw four brownish pups playing near the entrance. The main burrow had been

enlarged some since the previous year, as had two or three of the smaller ones which were used by the pups. Along a wash in the woods 50 yards away there were five beds in the dirt, all dug out a little, one to a depth of 8 inches. It was not known how many adults were in the family. The den near this one, raided in 1940, was unoccupied.

SAVAGE RIVER WOLF FAMILY

In 1939 a pair of black wolves and some black pups were reported on Savage River and apparently the same pair was there the next year. Although it was evident that a wolf family was living on Savage River in the spring of 1940, I could not afford to take much time to search for its habitation since I was then busy making observations at a den on East Fork River. But on August 14, near the head of Savage River, I discovered the family. All along, on the gravel bars, wolf tracks had been plentiful. It was evident that pups and adults had traveled much up and down Savage River for a distance of 6 or 7 miles. In some stretches there was a definite trail in the gravel, and fresh trails had been made through vegetation, leaves and stems having recently been tramped down. Here and there a scat was found.

I first had a glimpse of the head of an adult black wolf on the edge of an extensive growth of willows bordering the bar. After watching me a few moments the animal disappeared, but by climbing a slope, I obtained a view of it running off, a half mile away. I continued up the bar to some old caribou corrals and, about 3 hours later, returned to the willows where I had seen the wolf. There were many pup tracks in the sand and a number of scats, so that the spot appeared to be a rendezvous. Presently I heard low growling in the willows just ahead of me. I knew it was a wolf or grizzly, but in either case I did not wish to disturb it, so I backed away cautiously, moved slowly toward a ridge nearby, and then climbed a short distance up the slope. Down river I heard a wolf howl, and a little later from the slope where I was screened by willows I saw a black wolf running. A half mile away it stopped to bark so I was sure the pups were near me. Presently a black pup passed an opening in the willows near the place where I had heard the growling and a short distance away on the bar other pups were discovered feeding on the remains of a large bull caribou. There were six pups, all of them black. Some were lying down, some feeding, some walking about aimlessly. One carried a piece of caribou across the bar, possibly to cache it. Two played briefly. Those walking about wagged their tails slowly. They seemed too full for much playing. Later another black adult joined the first one. Both barked, sometimes a series of barks, terminating in a long howl. The parents moved up a knoll across the narrow valley and watched. At 5 p. m. I departed, without disturbing the pups, which for 3 hours had been

oblivious of my presence about 200 yards from them.

The following day I hiked the 9 miles up the bar in hopes of getting moving pictures. Carefully I made my way to where I had watched the pups feeding on the caribou and arrived there at about 10:30 a. m. After watching a half hour I saw a black wolf galloping down a tributary on the other side of the valley. It was coming toward a knoll on which I saw another black wolf. The latter was lying about 30 feet above a narrow bar covered with willows 7 or 8 feet tall. After lying there for 15 minutes, frequently looking around, it moved out of sight. Soon the wolves howled in chorus.

I waited until 1:30 p. m. hoping the wolves would return to the carcass. At that time rapidly moving heavy clouds were rising above the horizon so I decided to approach the wolves for a picture before the sun disappeared. As I neared the mouth of the side stream where I had seen them a pup scurried across the gravel from one clump of willows to another. Two other pups scurried across openings. Continuing slowly through the willow-covered bar, I saw two adults and two pups running away in the distance. For a better view I climbed the knoll where the wolf had been lying. I continued climbing and presently saw the two adults returning toward me at a gallop. One was a large gray animal. They barked at me, then moved down to where the pups had been. Later I saw two black adults galloping downstream a half mile below me. The pups had dispersed; one of them I heard howling later 2 miles downstream.

During the winter a trapper saw a band of seven black wolves and one gray one on lower Savage River, not far from the park boundary, 17 or 18 miles north of where they were seen in the summer. These were probably the group I had observed at the head of Savage River. Somewhere along Savage River is a wolf den which apparently is used year after year.

The Savage River family was of special interest because of the presence of three adults, all concerned over the welfare of the pups. The sex and age of the extra adult was not known so its relationship was not determined. There could have been two families living together, but the uniformity in the appearance of the six pups indicates that they were of one litter. The extra wolf may have been a pup of the previous year, but judging from the relationships at the East Fork den, where there were extra adults, it seems likely that the extra wolf was not a yearling but was an adult living with the pair year after year.

EAST FORK RIVER DEN—1940

Finding the Den.—In front of our cabin at East Fork River, on May 15, 1940, wolf tracks were seen in the fresh snow covering the gravel bars. The tracks led in both directions, but since there was no game upstream at the time to attract the wolves, it ap-

peared that some other interest, which I hoped was a den, accounted for their movement that way. I followed the tracks up the bar for a mile and a half directly to the den on a point of the high bank bordering the river bed. In contrast to the Toklat den, which was located in the woods in a flat patch of timber, this one was 2 miles beyond the last scraggly timber, on an open point about 100 feet above the river where the wolves had an excellent view of the surrounding country. Apparently a variety of situations are chosen for dens for I was told of two others which were located in timber, and of a third which was in a treeless area at the head of a dry stream.

Foxes had dug the original den on the point, and wolves had later moved in and had enlarged a few of the burrows. It seems customary in this region for wolves to preempt fox dens. Former Ranger Swisher, who had found at least four wolf dens, said that all of them had originally been dug by foxes. There are many unoccupied fox dens available so it is not strange that they are generally used by the wolves. The soil at the sites is sandy or loamy, at least free of rocks, so that digging is easy. Only a little enlarging of one of the many burrows is required to make a den habitable for a wolf. Although the adult wolves can only use the enlarged burrow, the whole system of burrows is available to the pups for a few weeks. This advantage is incidental and probably has no bearing on the choice of fox dens as homes.

Figure 4: Locale of East Fork wolf den, which was on the promontory at left of picture (see arrow). The author's observation point was on the ridge directly opposite, between the two branches of the East Fork of the Toklat River. The mountains of the Alaska Range, on the skyline, are used in summer by sheep. [*May 5, 1940.*]

When I approached this den the black male wolf was resting 70 yards away. He ran off about a quarter of a mile or less and howled and barked at intervals. As I stood 4 yards from the entrance, the female furtively pushed her head out of the burrow, then withdrew it, but in a moment came out with a rush, galloped most of the way down the slope, and stopped to bark at me. Then she galloped toward the male hidden in a ravine, and both parents howled and barked until I left.

From the den I heard the soft whimpering of the pups. It seemed I had already intruded too far, enough to cause the wolves to move. As I could not make matters much worse, I wriggled into the burrow which was 16 inches high and 25 inches wide. Six feet from the entrance of the burrow there was a right angle turn. At the turn there was a hollow, rounded and worn, which obviously was a bed much used by an adult. Due to the melting snow it was full of water in which there was a liberal sprinkling of porcupine droppings. A porcupine had used the place the preceding winter. Its feeding signs had been noted on many of the nearby willows. From the turn the burrow slanted slightly upward for 6 feet to the chamber in which the pups were huddled and squirming. With a hooked willow I managed to pull three of the six pups to me. Not wishing to subject all of them to even a slight wetting, and feeling guilty about disturbing the den so much, I withdrew with the three I had. Their eyes were closed and they appeared to be about a week old. They were all females, and dark, almost black. One appeared slightly lighter than the other two and I placed her in my packsack to keep for closer acquaintance. The other two were returned to their chamber and I departed.

After my intrusion it seemed certain that the family would move, so the following morning I walked toward the den to take up their trail before the snow melted. But from a distance I saw the black male curled up on the point 15 yards from the entrance, so it was apparent that they had not moved away after all. In fact, they remained at the den until the young were old enough to move off with the adults at the normal time.

Figure 5: **The person (right center of the picture) is standing near one of the entrances to the East Fork wolf den. The lookout ridge is across the bar to the left, and sheep mountains above Polychrome Pass are on the skyline.** [*August 26, 1940.*]

Figure 6: **Five-year-old girl standing in the entrance of one of the burrows of the East Fork wolf den.** [*August 26, 1940.*]

On a ridge across the river from the den, about a half mile or less away, there were excellent locations for watching the wolves without disturbing them. There was also a view of the landscape for several miles in all directions.

Between May 15, when the den was discovered, and July 7, when the wolves moved a mile away, I spent about 195 hours observing them. The longest continuous vigil was 33 hours, and twice I observed them all night. Frequently I watched a few hours in the evening to see the wolves leave for the night hunt. Late in the summer and in the early fall after the family had left the den, I had the opportunity on a few occasions to watch the family for several hours at a time.

Composition of the East Fork Family.— So far as I am aware it has been taken for granted that a wolf family consists of a pair of adults and the pups.

Perhaps that is the rule, although we may not have enough information about wolves to really know. Usually when a den is discovered the young are destroyed and all opportunity for making further observations is thereby lost.

The first week after finding the East Fork den I remained away from its vicinity to let the wolves regain whatever composure they had lost when I intruded in their home. On May 26, a few days after beginning an almost daily watch of the den, I was astonished at seeing two strange gray wolves move from where they had been lying a few yards from the den entrance. These two gray wolves proved to be males. They rested at the den most of the day. At 4 p. m., in company with the black father wolf, they departed for the night hunt. Because I had not watched the den closely the first week after finding it I do not know when the two gray males first made their appearance there, but judging from later events it seems likely that they were there occasionally from the first.

Five days later, a second black wolf—a female—was seen, making a total of five adults at the den—three males and two females. These five wolves lounged at the den day after day until the family moved away. There may have been another male in the group for I learned that a male had been inadvertently shot about 2 miles from the den a few days before I found the den.

Late in July another male was seen

with the band, and a little later a fourth extra male joined them. These seven wolves, or various combinations of them, were frequently seen together in August and September. Five of the seven were males. The four extra males appeared to be bachelors.

The relationship of the two extra males and the extra female to the pair is not known. They may have been pups born to the gray female in years past or they may have been her brothers and sister, or no blood relation at all. I knew the gray female in 1939. She was then traveling with two gray and two black wolves which I did not know well enough to be certain they were the same as those at the den in 1940. But since the color combination of the wolves traveling together was the same in 1940 as in 1939, it is quite certain that the same wolves were involved. So apparently all the adult wolves at the den in 1940 were at least 2 years old. In 1941 it was known that the extra male with the female was at least 2 years old for he was an easily identified gray male which was at the den in 1940. The fact that none of the 1940 pups was at the 1941 den supports the conclusion that the extra wolves at the 1940 den were not the previous year's pups.

The presence of the five adults in the East Fork family during denning time in 1940 and three in 1941, and three adults in the Savage River family, suggests that it may not be uncommon to find more than two adults at a den. The presence of extra adults is an unusual family make-up which is probably an outcome of the close association of the wolves in the band. It should be an advantage for the parents to have help in hunting and feeding the pups.

Description of the Individual Wolves.— Wolves vary much in color, size, contour, and action. No doubt there is also much variation in temperament. Many are so distinctively colored or patterned that they can be identified from afar. I found the gray ones more easily identified since among them there is more individual variation in color pattern than in the black wolves.

The mother of the pups was dark gray, almost "bluish," over the back, and had light under parts, a blackish face, and a silvery mane. She was thick-bodied, short-legged, short-muzzled, and smaller than the others. She was easily recognized from afar.

The father was black with a yellowish vertical streak behind each shoulder. From a distance he appeared coal black except for the yellow shoulder marks, but a nearer view revealed a scattering of silver and rusty hairs, especially over the shoulders and along the sides. There was an extra fullness of the neck under the chin. He seemed more solemn than the others, but perhaps that was partly imagined by me, knowing as I did that many of the family cares rested on his shoulders. On the hunts that I observed he usually took the lead in running down caribou calves.

The other black wolf was a slender-built, long-legged female. Her muz-

The Dandy

Black Female

Gray Female

Figure 7: Wolf portraits.

Grandpa

Black Male

Robber Mask

Figure 8: Wolf portraits.

zle seemed exceptionally long, reminding me of the Little Red Riding Hood illustrations. Her neck was not as thick as that of the black male. This female had no young in 1940, but had her own family in 1941.

What appeared to be the largest wolf was a tall, rangy male with a long silvery mane and a dark mantle over the back and part way down over the sides. He seemed to be the lord and master of the group although he was not mated to any of the females. The other wolves approached this one with some diffidence, usually cowering before him. He deigned to wag his tail only after the others had done so. He was also the dandy in appearance. When trotting off for a hunt his tail waved jauntily and there was a spring and sprightly spirit in his step. The excess energy at times gave him a rocking-horse gallop quite different from that of any of the others.

The other gray male at the den I called "Grandpa" in my notes. He was a rangy wolf of a nondescript color. There were no distinctive markings, but he moved as though he were old and a little stiff. Sometimes he had sore feet which made him limp. From all appearances he was an old animal, although in this I may be mistaken.

One of the grays that joined the group in late July was a large male with a light face except for a black robber's mask over the eyes. His chest was conspicuously white. He moved with much spring and energy. The black mask was distinctive and recognizable from a distance.

The other wolf, which joined the group in August, was a huge gray animal with a light yellowish face. In 1941 he was mated to the small black female which had no young the preceding year.

All these wolves could be readily distinguished within the group but some of the less distinctively marked ones might have been confused among a group of strange wolves. The black-faced gray female, the robber-masked male, and the black-mantled male were so characteristically marked that they could be identified in a large company.

I suppose that some of the variability exhibited in these wolves could have resulted from crossings in the wild with dogs. Such crosses in the wild have been reported and the wolf in captivity crosses readily with dogs. Some years ago at Circle, Alaska, a wolf hung around the settlement for some time and some of the dogs were seen with it. The people thought that the wolf was a female attracted to the dogs during the breeding period. However, considerable variability is probably inherent in the species, enough perhaps to account for the variations noted in the park and in skins examined. The amount of crossing with dogs has probably not been sufficient to alter much the genetic composition of the wolf population.

Activity at the Den.—Many hours were spent watching the wolves at the den and yet when I undertake to write about it there does not seem to be a great deal to relate, certainly not an amount commensurate with the time spent observing these animals. There were some especially exciting and interesting incidents such as the times when the grizzlies invaded, and a strange wolf was driven away. The departure for the night hunt and the reactions of the wolves to caribou were always of interest. These special incidents are described on pages 43 and 204. But the routine activity at the den was unexciting and quiet. For 3 or 4 hours at a time there might not be a stir. Yet it was an inexhaustible thrill to watch the wolves simply because they typify the wilderness so completely.

The periods of watching were sufficiently long to yield behavior data of statistical value. I believe that the routine activity at this den was fairly well known.

Just as a laboring husband comes home to the family each evening after working all day, so do the wolves come home each morning after working all night. The wolf comes home tired, too, for he has traveled far in his hunting. Ten or fifteen miles is a usual jaunt for a hunt, and he generally takes part in some chases in which he exerts himself tremendously. His travels take him up and down many slopes and ridges. When he arrives at the den he flops, relaxes completely, and may not even change his position for 3 or 4 hours. Often he may not even raise his head to look around for intruders. Sometimes he may stretch and yawn, change his position, or shift his bed a few yards. Usually in summer he lies stretched out on his side, but occasionally may be curled up as in winter. Frequently a wolf will move over to a neighbor, perhaps sniff of him, getting for a response only a lazy indication of recognition by an up-and-down wag of the tail, and lie down near him. An animal may move from the point of the bluff down to the gravel bar, or while the overflow ice still remains on the bars, he may lie in the snow for a while. When the caribou grazed near the den a wolf might raise up a bit for a look, but generally a caribou was not sufficient reason for him to disturb his resting The female may be inside the den, or on the outside, for hours at a time. The five adults might be sleeping a few hundred yards apart or three or four of them might be within a few yards of each other. Of course all the adults were not always at home, one or two might be out for a short daylight excursion or fail to come home after the night hunt. That, in brief, is the routine activity at the den.

The first few weeks the gray female spent much time in the den with the pups, both during the day and at night. When she was outside she usually lay only a few yards from the entrance, although she sometimes wandered off as far as half a mile to feed on cached meat. When the rest of the band was off on the night hunt she remained at home, except on three occasions that I know of— June 1, June 8, and June 16. Each time she went off with the band she ran as though she were in high spirits, seeming happy to be off on an expedition with the others. On these three occasions the black female remained through the night with the pups.

The father and the black female were seen to enter the den when the pups were only a couple of weeks old. Later, when the pups were old enough to toddle about outside, the father and the two females were very attentive to them. The two gray males often sniffed at the pups which frequently crawled over all five wolves in their play. Sometimes the pups played so much around an adult that it would move away to a safe distance where it could rest in greater peace.

The attentiveness of the black female to the pups was remarkable. It seemed at times that she might have produced some of them and I do not absolutely know that she did not. But her absence from the den the first 10 days (so far as I know), the uniformity in the size of the pups, and the greater concern and responsibility exhibited by the gray female, strongly indicates that the gray one had produced all the pups. The companionship of these two adults suggests that two females might at times den together, although having pups in one den would be somewhat inconvenient. Rather, one would expect them to den near each other as these two females did in 1941.

Wolves have few enemies and consequently are frequently not very watchful at the den or elsewhere. Often I approached surprisingly close to the wolf band before being discovered. Several times I was practically in the midst of the band before I was noticed. Once, after all the others had run off, one which must have been sound asleep got up behind me and in following the others passed me at a distance of only about 30 yards. These wolves were scarcely molested during the course of the study, so they may have been less watchful than in places where they are hunted. But their actions were probably normal for primitive conditions. When alert their keen eyes do not miss much.

Before the vegetation changed from brown to green the gray wolves, when curled up or when only the back showed, were especially difficult to see against the brown background. But if they were stretched out so as to expose the light under parts they were plainly visible. The black ones were usually more conspicuous but under certain conditions of poor light or dark backgrounds the gray wolves were the more conspicuous. At the den all the wolves were sometimes difficult to see because of slight depressions in which they lay, and the hummocks hiding them. Once when all five adults were lying on the open tundra slope above the den not one could be seen from my lookout. Often only two or three of the five could be seen until some movement showed the position of the others.

The strongest impression remaining with me after watching the wolves on numerous occasions was their friendliness. The adults were friendly toward each other and were amiable towards the pups, at least as late as October. This innate good feeling has been strongly marked in the three captive wolves which I have known. Undoubtedly, however, wolves sometimes have their quarrels.

Food Brought to the Den.—It is likely that all the wolves brought food to the East Fork den. It was necessary to bring food for the pups, and for the female remaining with them. The gray female, the black male, and the mantled male were all observed carrying food. Some of the food was brought directly to the den where the young were often seen feeding on it. Much of it was cached 100 or 200 yards away, and some of it as much as a half mile away. The wolf remaining at home during the night was seen to go out to these food caches, and occasionally one of the other wolves might eat a little from them during the day. The wolves that hunted probably ate their fill near the kill.

Relatively few bone remains were to be found at any of the dens. At the Lower Toklat den, there was the skin of a marmot, four calf caribou legs, leg bones of an adult caribou, and 300 yards away the head of a cow caribou. Remains, mainly hair, of an adult caribou were found on the bar about a quarter of a mile from this den. At the East Fork den there were scarcely any bones around the den after the family left, and there were only a few where they lived after leaving the den. At this den, where the food was mainly calf caribou, probably most of the long bones were eaten. Former Ranger Swisher told me that at a den he had found several years ago there were a number of legs of mountain sheep.

Departure for the Night Hunt.— There was considerable variation in the time of departure for the night hunt. On a few occasions the wolves left as early as 4 p. m., and again they had not left at 9 or 9:30 p. m. They were seen departing for the hunt 11 times. Five of these times they left between 4 p. m. and 5:45 p. m., and six times they left between 7 p. m. and 9:30 p. m. Usually the hunting group consisted of the three males, but sometimes one of the females was in the group. The wolves hunted in a variety of combinations—singly, in pairs, or all together. In the fall the adults and young traveled together much of the time, forming a pack of seven adults and five pups.

Usually the wolves returned to the den each morning, but three wolves which left the den at 4 p. m. on May 26 had not returned to the den the following day by 8 p. m. when I left the lookout, after watching all night and all day. The wolves had probably spent the day near the scene of their hunt. These wolves were again at the den on May 28.

Considerable ceremony often precedes the departure for the hunt. Usually there is a general get-together and much tail wagging. On May 31 I left the lookout at 8:30 p. m. since the wolves seemed, after some indications of departure, to have settled down again. But as I looked back from the river bar on my way to camp I saw the two blacks and the two gray males assembled on the skyline, wagging their tails and frisking together. There they all howled, and while they howled the gray female galloped up from the den 100 yards and joined them. She was greeted with energetic tail wagging and general good feeling. Then the vigorous actions came to an end, and five muzzles pointed skyward. Their howling floated softly across the tundra. Then abruptly the assemblage broke up. The mother returned to the den to assume her vigil and four wolves trotted eastward into the dusk.

On June 2 some restlessness was evident among the wolves at 3:50 p. m. The two gray males and the black male approached the den where the black female and some pups were lying. Then the black male lay down near the den; the mantled male walked down on the flat 100 yards away and lay down, and Grandpa, following him, continued along the bar another 150 yards before he lay down. At 6:45 p. m. the mantled male sat on his haunches and howled three times, and in a few minutes he sent forth two more long mournful howls. Grandpa stood up and with the mantled male trotted a few steps toward five passing caribou. Then the mantled male howled six or seven times, twice while lying down. The gray female trotted to the gray males, and the three of them stood together wagging their tails in the most friendly fashion. The mantled one howled and they started up the slope. But before going more than 200 yards they lay down again. A

Figure 9: "All together."

few minutes later, at 7:15 p. m., the mantled male howled a few times and walked to the den followed by Grandpa. The latter seemed ready to go whenever anyone decided to be on the move. At the den the black female squirmed and crouched before the mantled male, placing both her paws around his neck as she crouched in front of him. This hugging with the front paws is not an uncommon action.

Later the two gray males and both black wolves were in a huddle near the den entrance, vigorously wagging their tails and pressing against each other. The gray female joined them from up the slope and the tail wagging became more vigorous and there was a renewed activity of friendliness. At 7:30 p. m. the mantled male descended the slope to the bar and started to trot away. He was shortly followed by the black male and Grandpa. The black female followed the departing males to the bar, then returned to the gray female at the den. Both females remained at the den this time.

On June 8 at 7:15 p. m. Grandpa approached the mantled male, wagging his tail. The mantled male stood stiffly erect and wagged his tail slowly, with a show of dignity. The two walked over to one of the blacks and lay down. The mantled male turned twice around like a dog, before lying down, then rose and turned around again before settling down.

There was no movement until 9 p. m., when Grandpa rose, shook himself, and walked over to the mantled male. They wagged tails and were joined in the ceremony by the black female. The mantled male sniffed at the black male who was still resting. He rose and the tail wagging began again. The gray female hurried down the slope to the others and the tail wagging became increasingly vigorous. The friendly display lasted 7 or 8 minutes and, led by Grandpa, who seemed specially spry this evening, they started eastward. The black female followed a short distance, then stopped and watched them move away. A quarter of a mile farther on the four wolves commenced to play on the green flat. The black female trotted rapidly to them and joined in the play. After a few minutes of pushing and hugging the four again started off, this time abreast, spaced about 50 to 75 yards apart. The black female followed for a short distance and lay down. She appeared anxious to follow. After 15 minutes she returned to the den, and two or three pups came out to join her.

The gray female at first led the wolves up the long slope toward Sable Pass, but later the two gray males were in front, running parallel about 200 yards apart. They trotted most of the time, but galloped up some of the steeper slopes. On a snow field they stopped for a time to frolic. The black female remained at the den all night. The hunters returned at 9:15 the following morning. The gray female hurried unhesitatingly to the burrow, like a mother who has been absent from her child for a few hours. The black male flopped over on his side a short distance from the den and lay perfectly still and relaxed. About 1 mile north of the den the mantled male was stretched out on his side on a high point. The wolves had been away on the hunt about 12 hours.

At 4 p. m. on June 16 the two gray males, the black male, and the gray female left the den, led by the mantled male. Soon the female took the lead and she headed for a spot where some eagles were feeding. She nearly captured one of the eagles by jumping high in the air after it as it took off. These wolves went directly to Teklanika River some 7 or 8 miles from the den.

It was evident that by evening the wolves were rested and anxious to be off for the night hunting. The time of their departure for the hunt no doubt varied from day to day depending somewhat upon how soon they came in from the previous night's expedition. Theirs is not a lazy life for the nature of their food demands that they travel long distances and work hard for it, but they seem to enjoy their nightly excursions.

The Family Leaves the Den.—The extended wanderings of the pups below the den on the river bar, early in July, indicated that the family might soon move away. I had refrained from approaching close enough for taking pictures, but with their departure seemingly imminent I made a careful stalk to the bank opposite the den on July 8. I was a day late, for although I waited until evening not a wolf was seen.

In the evening I looked over at the den from Polychrome Pass. At 8 p. m. the mantled male came from the direction of Sable Pass. He stopped several times near the den and appeared to be howling but he was too far away to be heard. He moved to a knoll south of the den and sniffed about in a short ravine where the pups had often been seen. It appeared that the family had moved during his absence. He dropped down to the bar and followed southward along the bank for a half mile, then abruptly turned and climbed the bank at a gallop. Above, on the sloping tundra, he joined the female and the pups and for a time they wagged tails and romped together. The days at the den were over.

The following morning, July 9, I walked up the river past the wolf den and across the broad level bar covered with grass and dryas, toward the spot where I had seen the wolf family the previous evening. The gray female and both black wolves were with the pups and saw me when I came in view around the point on which the den is located. They sat on their haunches watching me approach. There had been no chance to make a stalk so I continued forward, hoping that the wolves would stay close enough to the pups to permit me to take some pictures. After watching me advance for about 200 yards the three adults ran up the long open slope, stopping at intervals to bark and howl. The black male, after angling up the slope, galloped along the hill in my direction, keeping his elevation above me and frequently stopping to bark. I continued forward and passed the three wolves which were now barking at me from directly up the slope. The gray female joined the black male, but the black female moved higher up. When I was almost opposite and within about a quarter of a mile of the pups (they had taken refuge in a burrow 10 feet long and open at both ends) the black male galloped down the slope to the bar, followed closely by the gray female. They came out on my trail and headed directly into the wind toward me at a gallop. The female took the lead and with noses to the ground they came on at a rapid, brisk trot. I set up the movie camera and saw them in the finder, running silently and swiftly. Their purposefulness and intent manner worried me some, and I began to wonder if they would turn aside. They were accustomed to seeing people, so lacked the timidity of most wolves. I wondered if the two grays and the other black might not join the two coming toward me. Generally I carried an automatic pistol in my packsack, and as I had not checked on the matter before starting out, I now hurriedly looked and was relieved to find it was there. By that time the wolves were about 100 yards away and, circling to one side, they commenced to bark. The female passed me and the male remained on the other side. Both continued howling and barking, about 200 yards away. After exposing my film I walked down the bar. The female remained opposite the pups,

howling at intervals, and the male kept abreast of me for a half mile as I went down the bar to camp. The black female remained on the slope, howling. When I returned to the spot an hour and a half later with more film, the wolves had all departed. The pups were not seen again until August 22, when they were found about 5 miles away. The adults in the interim were often seen, but the pups were not traveling with them. They apparently were at some rendezvous.

A Group of Adults Observed on July 30.—At 6 a. m. on July 30 deep howling was heard a short distance above our camp. With my camera I hurried toward the sound and came upon the mantled male on the flat below Sable Mountain. Presently he was joined by the gray female and Grandpa. They howled together and were answered by a wolf farther up the gentle slope. The three wolves moved nearer the base of Sable Mountain, where they joined the black-masked wolf. They lay on the tundra, in a depression just sufficiently deep to hide them from me.

Later the black male came from the west and joined them. His coming was heralded by the loud chirping of the ground squirrels all along his route. The black male walked slowly to the mantled male and was surrounded by the other wolves, all wagging their tails. The black male walked about 30 yards away and they all lay down again. Later they stood up and after some more friendly tail wagging lay down.

Early in the afternoon Ranger Harold Herning and I advanced cautiously toward the band for pictures, taking advantage of the shallow swale below the animals. We were about 100 yards from them when we noticed the black male peering over the rise and saw him trot to one side and watch us. The others, who had not seen us, trotted over to the black male. There was a slight altercation accompanied by a little growling and snarling when they came together. Grandpa lay down, but about that time all the wolves saw us. They watched us for a few seconds before trotting up the slope, still not much afraid. They continued over a rise and disappeared up the mouth of a short canyon. When we came in view again they were moving slowly up the canyon. Near its head they laboriously climbed a steep rock slope, using a switch-back technique. On top they followed the ridge along the sky line for some time before disappearing.

The black female was absent from the group; she probably was with the pups. The band was resting up for the night hunt and may not have been far from the pups. From this time on the black-masked male was frequently with the band.

The Pups Found Again.—On August 22, on the flat below Polychrome Pass, the pups were seen for the first time since they left the den on July 9, although some of the adults had frequently been seen. The wolves seemed to have been attracted to this vicinity by the refuse from a nearby road camp. The men at the road camp had been hearing the wolves howling for several nights so the family probably had been headquartering there for a few days before I saw them.

At 4 p. m. a wolf howled three times from a point southeast of the refuse heap, and an hour later the gray female, followed by a pup, appeared from behind a bench. She apparently was on her way to the refuse heap. Out on the flat the mantled male walked slowly into view from behind the same bench, followed by two black pups 100 yards to the rear. He walked slowly, with head down and tail held horizontally. Some distance to the west the two adults met and moved westward. The pups did not follow but returned to the east and lay down in sight of us.

The following day, with two companions I returned to Polychrome Pass and saw the wolves lying on the tundra among the dwarf birches and short willows. As we watched, a large gray wolf with a light face walked toward the others. He looked over the flat where the other wolves rested and lay down on the bench a short distance from them. This gray wolf was the second addition, so there were now seven adults in the band.

We stalked the wolves, coming first to the large gray one on the bench. He rose 50 yards or so ahead of us and loped away toward the others on the flat and aroused them. They ran off from in front of us, all headed southward. I hurried over the flat to get a picture of a black pup which was standing uncertainly watching the others run. While I was photographing the pup the mantled male got up behind me a short distance and ran close past me between me and my companions. He must have been sound asleep to be aroused so tardily. Five of the adults and some of the pups stopped on a knoll about a mile away. The parents hung back, barking at us, probably solicitous over some of the pups which had been left some distance behind. When I walked toward them they barked and howled and those on the knoll howled in the usual mournful chorus. Soon the parents hurried to join the others. The pups in the rear must have caught up with the band by this time. The green grass at the base of a bench near the place where the wolves had been lying was flattened and much worn, showing that the wolves had spent much time there. The bones of a fresh front leg of a large caribou were noted nearby, and several droppings were found.

Some Activities Observed September 17.—On September 17 the family was seen again on the flat below Polychrome Pass. At 8 a. m. three pups trotted briskly down a gravel bar. They stopped at one spot and sniffed zealously, apparently in search of morsels where they had feasted during the night. Nothing was there except rich sniffing. They climbed a bluff above the bar, scared an eagle from its perch, and sniffed about on a point of rock. They re-turned to the bar and hurried to the gray female and the black-masked male who were lying within a few feet of each other. The mantled male had just lain down on a bench above these two and was hidden in the dwarf birch. The three black pups, now almost the size of their mother, swarmed all over her, and later touched noses with the black-masked male who had joined the band after the pups left the den.

The mother led the way to the base of a bench and there uncovered some morsels of food which were at once eaten by the pups. They resumed their play all over the mother, after which they all lay down near the black-masked male, forming a circle. Another black pup who had been off by itself hunting mice approached the group and smelled of the black-masked male who sniffed at it, causing it to roll over on its back with diffidence. The pup then smelled of each of the others, who barely noticed the salutation by raising the nose a trifle. A yellow pup who had been hunting mice also joined the group. It first smelled noses with the black-masked male, who raised his nose to it and as he lay flat on his side, wagged his tail a few times. Then the pup, wagging its tail all the while, sniffed noses with each of the other pups, who were stretched out flat. The mother now trotted a mile to the east on some errand and returned a couple of hours later.

In the afternoon, some of the pups hunted mice. At 4 p. m. they all moved a mile out on the flat and lay down. An hour later grandpa showed up, sniffed around where the wolves had been resting, and continued southward on their trail.

Family Moves 20 Miles From Polychrome.—The wolf family was seen at Polychrome Pass on September 22, 23, and 24. But on September 28 it had moved to a point on Teklanika River 20 miles away.

My attention was first attracted by the yellow pup which disappeared in a fringe of trees. Later I heard the howling of several wolves and saw the yellow pup trot in the direction of the sound and join the four black pups. Soon they all galloped out of sight. I advanced cautiously and came upon the five pups, their parents, and grandpa, 140 yards from me. I exposed some motion-picture film, then dropped out of view to change film. While I was thus occupied they all howled and

there was considerable barking which resembled the yapping of coyotes. When I again peered over the rise all but the black male were moving away with much tail wagging and milling around. The black male saw me and trotted after the others, and all disappeared around the base of a low ridge. On my way back to the road I met the other four adults heading toward the spot where the wolves had howled. Apparently they had heard the noise too. The mantled male was quite surprised when he saw me 150 yards away and made several high jumps with head turned toward me. They all stopped to watch me, then slowly trotted on around the ridge after the others. This was about 9:30 a. m.; at 3 p. m. I found all the wolves resting near the base of a long slope about a mile away. They saw me approach in the distance and moved up the slope a short way from where they watched me. The following day I saw

Figure 10: "Siesta."

the band 4 miles to the north but I was unable to stalk them.

The East Fork Family Still Together March 17.—Although tracks, presumably of the East Fork family, had been seen during the winter, the wolves had escaped observation. But on March 17 I came unexpectedly upon the band at Savage River, 30 miles from the East Fork den site. I followed several fresh tracks which crossed my way and led out on an open flat where there were many bare spots made by the caribou in pawing for grass and lichens. One of the many spots appeared a little different than the others so I looked at it through field glasses and saw that it was a black wolf stretched out on its side. Searching the flat ahead of me, I made out two more black wolves. Off to one side of these a gray wolf sat up and, before curling up, looked about at random, without noticing me as I crouched about 300 yards away. To reach a strip of woods from where I could watch the wolves unobserved, I back-tracked cautiously but was discovered just as I was about to enter the woods. The black wolf which saw me aroused all the others when it howled. At least 10 wolves came to life and after a brief view of me hurried away, kicking up sparkling puffs of snow as they galloped.

Dispersal of Young.—I have little data on the dispersal of the young. The 1940 East Fork pups remained with the pack through the first winter until at least March 17, 1941, the last date I saw the pack together. On May 14 one of the pups was seen

2 miles from the den, and 3 days later another was seen at a similar distance from the old home. This was the last time I saw the 1940 pups. None of these young was ever seen at the 1941 den. Some of them may have been trapped during the winter, but at least three or four escaped the trappers.

East Fork River Den—1941

Same Pair Have Young at East Fork Den.—The East Fork den which was used in 1940 was again used in 1941. As in the previous season, the black male was mated to the gray female. On my first visit to the area on May 12 the black male was seen lying close to the den entrance. The mantled male headquartered at the den as he had done the previous year, but grandpa and the black-masked male were not seen all summer. Possibly they had been trapped during the winter. On June 21 four pups played on the bar and climbed over the father and the mantled male.

Black Female Has a Den.—The black female which helped the gray female take care of her young in 1940 was not seen at the old East Fork den early in the summer, but was several times noted in the region. On June 1 she and a large light-faced gray male that was with the band in the late summer of 1940 were traveling together on Igloo Creek. It was later learned that she was mated with this male, but her den was not found.

On June 30 two hikers saw the black female coming up East Fork River followed by a pup which, in crossing the river, was carried downstream some distance and treated a little roughly by the fast water. The hikers were able to run it down and catch it by the tail. They said that the mother barked at them from a point about 150 yards away. When they released the pup the mother continued up the river toward the den occupied by the gray female.

The following day I saw the black female coming down the bar but before I could take cover she had seen me. Instead of following down the bar she climbed a high ridge opposite me and then dropped down on the bar below me. I hoped she was on her way to her den, but if she were she changed her mind. After trotting down the bar one-third of a mile she climbed the bank, smelled about a knoll, then came back and climbed over a high ridge. I searched for her den, but did not find it. After reviewing the places where I had seen this wolf and tracks during the summer, it seemed certain that she had denned about 4 miles below the East Fork den occupied by the gray female.

On June 30 the black female and her pups were living at the den of her neighbor, the gray female. On July 9 the gray female and her mate had moved to a rendezvous a third of a mile above the den, where the pups spent much time in a clump of willows and the parents rested on the open bar nearby. On this day the black female was still using the gray female's den. On July 12 both families were together at the rendezvous. There were 10 pups—6 in one litter and 4 larger ones in the other. Gray and black pups were present in both litters.

The two families were living together at the rendezvous as late as August 3, the last day I visited the area. Besides the two pairs of adults there was one extra adult wolf at the rendezvous—the mantled male. In September a band of 15 wolves was seen about 3 miles from the den by a truck driver. These probably were the two families, still traveling together.

An incident in line with the observations on the East Fork wolves with respect to the association of two females is given by Seton (1929, vol. 1, p. 342) who writes as follows: "Thomas Simpson [1843, p. 275–76] while exploring the Arctic coast east of the Copper-mine, on July 25, 1838, encountered wolves at the mouth of a small stream near Hepburn Island, and thus refers to the incident: 'The banks of this river seemed quite a nest of wolves; and we pursued two females, followed by half a score of well-grown young. The mothers scampered up the highest rocks where they called loudly to their offspring; and the latter, unable to save themselves by flight, baffled our search by hiding themselves among the willows which fringe the stream. The leader of the whole gang—a huge, ferocious old fellow—stood his ground, and was shot by McKay.' "

Behavior When Disturbed.—On the morning of July 9 I approached the wolf den with a companion and managed, without being discovered, to gain a clump of willows on the bank 100 yards south of the den and at about the same elevation. The black female was later seen a few yards above the den. I do not know that she was aware of our presence, but she trotted to the den and nimbly entered one of the three burrows. A little later a black pup emerged from some brush and waddled up to a burrow. In the afternoon the large gray mate of the black female came trotting down the den knoll. He sniffed at a pup, which then followed him. A moment after arriving at the burrows he suddenly became alert and looked intently toward us. Apparently he had heard the motion picture camera. He took a step forward and stood with muscles tense, peering searchingly at us. Then he loped up the slope out of view above us. The pups continued to move about near the den, unaware of any danger. The male soon appeared on the bar below us, about 200 yards away, and for several minutes howled and barked. While he howled at us the very tip of his tail twitched back and forth, as it does on a cat when it is waiting to pounce on a mouse. When he retreated we walked up the bar toward the rendezvous where we had seen the other pair with their pups. The male we had disturbed went ahead of us to this pair and as we neared them they all ran up the slope and out of sight. Several pups were seen and we found two of them in a clump of willows and spent some time trying to approach them

for pictures, but they finally moved off and kept a respectable distance between us.

On July 12 the pups of both families were together among the willows at the rendezvous. We approached slowly, taking advantage of the scattered willow clumps along the way. When about 75 yards from the willow clump where we knew the pups to be, we saw the head of the black male near the willows. After looking in our direction he put his head down but raised it again almost at once. A second time he seemed assured but his uneasiness persisted and again he looked at us. I started my motion picture camera. He stood up to look and listen, then trotted diagonally toward us, examining us intently as he trotted nearer. Then he became certain of what we were and galloped out on the bar and began to howl and bark. The gray male was approaching in the distance, carrying what appeared to be a ground squirrel. A little later we failed to see the gray male but he no doubt was not far off. We frightened a number of pups from a clump of willows in which they had well-beaten trails and many beds in the tall grass. They disappeared in the brush along the bank, all except one which ran out on the bar toward the black male. During the hour or so that we were at the rendezvous, the black male howled and barked. He followed us up the bar when we searched for the pups.

In spite of our intrusions the two wolf families remained at the rendezvous. On July 31 a companion and I, with much crawling, managed to gain a gully adjacent to the flat where the wolves rested and played. We watched for some time from the creek which was bordered by tall willow brush. At about 1 p. m. we had planned to make a close approach on one of the wolves for pictures, only waiting for the sun to shine before starting. While waiting, the gray female appeared on the creek bank 25 feet away, passed behind some willows, and reappeared 15 feet away. She then saw us and bounded away. All the wolves were alarmed and 3 adults and 10 pups scattered over the bar. The general retreat was southward, but the pups crisscrossed so much that the bar seemed covered with wolves.

The following day the two families were again at the rendezvous, and 4 days later when the study was terminated and I left the park the wolves were still there.

Hunting Range

The East Fork wolves were known to move readily over a range at least 50 miles across. During the denning period their movements radiated from the den, and ordinarily the wolves traveled a dozen or more miles from it. But greater distances were readily traveled. In the spring of 1941, when a band of five or six thousand caribou calved some 20 miles away, the wolves traveled this distance nightly to prey on the calves.

In the winter of 1940–41 there were many caribou along the north boundary of the park, which attracted the East Fork wolves. The hub of their movements was shifted in that direction, but they continued at intervals to make trips back through the part of the range which they used most in summer. These trips were probably made in search of mountain sheep for there were no caribou along the route. Wolves seem to enjoy traveling, and these excursions may in part have been made because of their habit of being on the move. Wolves are often reported to have a circular route which they take a few times during the month, but the East Fork wolves on a number of occasions traveled both ways on the same route.

The family at Savage River lived the year round in that locality. They ranged westward 10 miles to Sanctuary River, which was normally the east boundary of the range of the East Fork wolves. I do not know how far to the east these Savage River wolves wandered, but possibly 12 miles to the Nenana River or farther. The east-west breadth of their range appeared to be less than that of the East Fork wolves, but the former may have wandered farther in a north-and-south direction. The center of the Savage River range was some 35 miles east of the East Fork den.

The Toklat River den was about 22 miles northwest of the East Fork den. Nothing was learned of the range of this family but it probably overlapped the range used by the East Fork wolves. Wolves lived the year round at Wonder Lake, about 40 miles west of East Fork.

The different wolf families seemed to have rather definite year-round home ranges which overlapped somewhat. It was significant that within the large range of the East Fork wolves almost every wolf seen was recognized as belonging to that band.

The winter distribution of the wolves in Mount McKinley National Park seems to be only locally influenced by the movements of the caribou. When the caribou winter along the north boundary the wolves spend most of their time among them, but in years when the caribou are absent the wolves desert this part of their range. Instead of moving off with the caribou they shift their attention to mountain sheep.

It is generally believed that the wolves follow the caribou herds but to what degree this is true is not well known. Since the caribou appear to be the main food supply of the wolves in interior Alaska it is to be expected that the wolves gravitate toward the caribou range and, in the presence of this food supply, flourish. When caribou make large permanent shifts in their ranges the wolf distribution probably becomes adjusted to the shift, but perhaps not all at once. The wolves probably do not as a rule follow particular herds and it seems likely that in general their movements on the caribou range are similar to those observed in Mount McKinley National Park. Local circumstances no doubt influence movements in each region. Where hares,

moose, or mountain sheep are available, there would be less need for the wolves to move with the caribou.

Intraspecific Intolerance

The only data bearing on intraspecific intolerance are a few incidents, which are only suggestive. Of course the rather definite home ranges that the wolf families appear to have, also suggest that an intolerance to strange wolves exists. A strange wolf, probably belonging to the Savage River family, was reported to have traveled up high on a mountain on one occasion in order to avoid five East Fork wolves at Teklanika River. Such behavior could occur, however, where there was considerable tolerance.

An incident at the East Fork den indicates the treatment that a strange wolf may receive. On May 31, 1940, all five adults were at home. Between 10 a. m. and noon the mantled male had been on the alert, raising his head to look around at intervals of 2 or 3 minutes. Several times he changed his position until he was about 200 yards above the den. Such prolonged watchfulness was unusual, but it was explained by later events. Shortly after noon the four wolves at the den joined the mantled male and they all bunched up, wagging tails and expressing much friendliness. Then I noticed a sixth wolf, a small gray animal, about 50 yards from the others. No doubt the presence of this wolf had kept the mantled male so alert during the preceding 2 hours.

All the wolves trotted to the stranger

and practically surrounded it, and for a few moments I thought that they would be friendly toward it for there was just the suggestion of tail wagging by some of them. But something tipped the scales the other way for the wolves began to bite at the stranger. It rolled over on its back, begging quarter. The attack continued, however, so it scrambled to its feet and with difficulty emerged from the snapping wolves. Twice it was knocked over as it ran down the slope with the five wolves in hot pursuit. They chased after it about 200 yards to the river bar, and the mantled male crossed the bar after it. The two ran out of my sight under the ridge from which I was watching.

Four of the wolves returned to the den, but the mantled male stopped half way up the slope and lay down facing the bar. Presently he walked slowly forward as though stalking a marmot. Then he commenced to gallop down the slope again toward the stranger which had returned part way up the slope. Back on the bar the stranger slowed up, waiting in a fawning attitude for the mantled male. The latter snapped at the stranger which rolled over on its back, again begging quarter. But the stranger received no quarter, so again it had to run away. The male returned up the hill, tail held stiffly out behind, slightly raised. When he neared the den the four wolves ran out to meet him, and there was again much tail wagging and evidence of friendly feeling.

The unfortunate stranger's hip and base of tail were soaked with blood. It was completely discouraged in its attempt to join the group, for it was not seen again. It may have been forced to leave the territory of this wolf family, for if it were encountered it probably would have been attacked again. Judging from the usual reaction of a group of dogs to a strange dog, such treatment of a strange wolf would seem normal. Small groups of wolves may be treated like this lone wolf, hence it is advantageous for minor packs to find territories where they are unmolested. Such rough treatment of individual wolves, if it is normal, would tend to limit the number of wolves on a given range.

The Wolf Pack

Wolves normally travel in packs. The smaller packs consist of a single family group, the larger ones perhaps of two or more families. E. W. Nelson (1887, p. 237) reported wolf packs in 1880 numbering as high as 50, but usually containing from 6 to 10 individuals. A trapper reported seeing tracks of a pack of 24 wolves north of Mount McKinley National Park in the winter of 1939–40. At Wonder Lake a few years ago a pack of 22 wolves was seen and another of 19 was reported by a Ranger.

In 1940 the East Fork pack consisted of 7 adults and 5 pups. In August 1941, it was made up of 5 adults, all part of the previous year's pack, and 10 pups, offspring of two pairs. In 1940 the Savage River pack consisted of 3 adults and 6 pups in August, and in December this same group was traveling together.

When there are 2 or more females in a group, the adults, plus the pups, might make a sizeable band. Three females could easily have 15 or 20 pups, and these, together with 6 or more adults, might make a pack of 20 or 25 wolves. When there is more than 1 female in a band it is probable that they den quite near each other as did the 2 females at East Fork in 1941.

Although the East Fork wolves often traveled together, at other times they traveled singly or in various combinations. Quite often a member went off alone for a time but rejoined the band daily, so far as I could tell. There is at times the "lone wolf" which lives by itself, at least for a period. In the winter of 1940–41 a lone wolf spent several weeks around Park Headquarters. It apparently picked up scraps at the garbage heap. During the day it often rested in the woods less than half a mile from headquarters.

Because wolves rely mainly on large animals, the pack is an advantageous manner in which to hunt. A lone wolf would ordinarily have difficulty in catching sheep, but several wolves working together can hunt sheep rather successfully. Adult caribou are sometimes brought down by a single wolf, but it is no doubt easier for two or more to hunt them.

The size of the pack may be limited by the law of diminishing returns. Beyond a certain size, advantages may disappear. A pack might be so large that, after the strongest members had finished feeding on a kill, there would be little or nothing left for the rest. In such a situation, hungry ones would go off to hunt again, and the strong ones, already fed, would remain where they were. There thus might result a natural division of a band which was too large to function advantageously for all its members. One would expect that where game is scarce the wolves would operate in smaller units than where food is abundant.

Wags, the Captive Wolf

The wolf pup removed from the East Fork den on May 15, 1940, was taken for the purpose of checking on the development of the pups at the den and familiarizing myself with wolf character. The pup was a dark furry female, so young that its eyes were still closed and it could only crawl about on its stomach. Because of her friendliness and tail wagging as she grew older, we called her Wags, a name she continued to merit. Her eyes did not open until May 23, so she was a week old or less when brought to the cabin. From the beginning she readily took evaporated milk, slightly diluted, from a nipple, and thrived. The first 4 days she was restless and whimpered softly much of the time, but then she quieted down and became contented. As she grew older her appetite increased. For instance, she drank 8½ ounces of milk on May 19 and 13 ounces on May 23. On June 2 she drank milk from an open dish. The nipple was dis-

Figure 11: **Female wolf pup, Wags, the day after she was taken from the den. She was about a week old, and her eyes had not yet opened.** [*East Fork River, May 16, 1940.*]

head, her stomach was distended and she could hold no more. She cleaned her jowls by rubbing them on the grass, and then went to sleep stretched out on her side. A magpie came along later and flew off with the rest of the ground squirrel, a division of the spoils common in the wilds.

On May 15, when Wags was about a week old, she had the following measurements: Total length 14⅝ inches, tail 3⅝ inches, hind foot, 2⅜ inches; ear, 1 inch. On July 12 she was 14½ inches tall at the shoulder; on August 6, 17½ inches; on September 5, 19½ inches; on October 23, 24 inches. By midwinter she had attained most of her growth. On December 17, 1941, when she was in her second year, she measured 27 inches at the shoulder (measurement made by Charles Peterson).

carded because she was having difficulty getting milk from it. Her mouth seemed too large. At this time she was able to walk around in a wobbly manner. The pups at the den were also now walking about outside their burrow. They were first seen outside on June 1. Wags howled for the first time on June 10.

On June 25 I fed the pup its first ground squirrel. She picked it up, growled, shook it, and repeated the growling and shaking several times. First she bit off the tip of the tail, then chewed off both front feet, a shoulder, ribs, and internal organs. She ate the stomach wall and part of the intestines, together with their contents of vegetation. On later occasions she often ate the stomach contents along with the stomach. The chewing was done far back in the mouth. When she had eaten all but the hind quarters, back, and

Figure 12: **Wolf pup about 3 weeks old, drinking condensed milk through a nipple.** [*East Fork River, June 2, 1940.*]

The pup was usually chained near the kitchen door but all summer she was permitted to run loose for a while almost every day. She enjoyed wading in the little camp stream and prowling through the grass. When I called or whistled she would return and was never hard to catch, although by fall she sometimes did not like to come near the chain, knowing that she would be tied up. She recognized strangers but was not very shy and usually came to them and permitted their petting.

The black female wolf on several occasions, and the black male once, were seen near our cabin at East Fork, apparently attracted there by the wolf pup. (We had no garbage pile.) They probably sometimes were at camp without our knowledge, especially at night when we were asleep and no ground squirrels were abroad to call the alarm.

On June 27, at 6 o'clock in the morning, the ground squirrels in the vicinity of the cabin were uttering alarm calls. When I looked outside I saw the black male wolf trotting off 100 yards away. It turned to look at me several times before leaving. I followed it to the highway in the car. Later it passed close to the cabin in returning to the den. At noon the squirrels were again giving the alarm and the black male was seen only 25 yards behind the cabin.

On August 11, at 7 o'clock in the evening, the wolf pup was heard whining softly. On looking out I saw the black female only a few yards from the pup. The following evening at 8 o'clock I heard the pup whining again and saw the black female with it. She traveled slowly and reluctantly up the slope, looking back repeatedly. The pup tried to follow and when it reached the end of the chain, kept jumping forward to be away. The black female trotted off to join three other wolves which were about 200 yards from the cabin. If the pup had been loose it surely would have gone off with the band.

Toward the end of the summer Wags would seize my hand in her jaws in play but she never pressed hard enough to hurt. By early winter her teeth were so long that I had to wear gloves when I played with her, and although she was careful not to clamp down, still her "tenderness" was a little too rough for my bare hand. By late spring she played less in this way. She often cowered in a friendly way when I approached her, just as a wild wolf often cowers when approaching another wolf.

Wags was not only friendly with people but also with dogs and liked

Figure 13: **Wolf pup at the age of about 7 weeks.** [*East Fork River, June 29, 1940.*]

THE WOLVES OF MOUNT MCKINLEY ✦ 47

Figure 14.: Wolf pup at the age of about 3½ months. [*East Fork River, August 24, 1940.*]

to play with them. In early November she was seen playing with a small Husky pup about half her size. She was gentle with him, pawed him lightly, and galloped vigorously around him. During the winter the pup approached her almost every day to play. Once while Wags was feeding on some bones the dog pup came along and began to feed on the scraps. He growled and snapped at Wags, who retreated, wagging her tail. She permitted the pup to eat all the scraps even though she was much more powerful than he and was very fond of the bones. In late winter when the dog was almost as large as the wolf, he often growled and snapped at her, but she never became angry and always was able to jump aside or, in some cases, protect herself by taking a position on top of him. It was surprising to me that she continued to be good tempered with the dog, and never harmed him, as she could so easily have done.

When I moved from Headquarters out into the park in the spring of 1941, Wags was placed in one of the dog pens. She was much more restless here than when she was chained near our cabin. During the summer I visited her when I came to Headquarters. She always recognized me and was beside herself with friendliness. The day I left the park I paid a last visit to the most friendly "dog" I have ever known.

In a letter of transmittal accompanying a wildlife report, Superintendent Frank Been wrote as follows about Wags on February 3, 1942, 6 months after I had left the park: "As Wildlife Ranger Andrew Fluetsch made reference to a wolf carrying away a door mat from the Superintendent's residence, explanation should be made that the culprit was Wags, the domesticated she-wolf which was raised from a pup. Wags has been permitted to exercise on the wire to which the dogs are fastened by leash. She broke the wire on two occasions and explored the Park Headquarters. She was as playful and gentle as a dog of the same age and enjoyed being near the people with whom she was acquainted."

In a memorandum to the Director of the National Park Service dated April 14, 1942, Superintendent Been discusses Wags' behavior during the breeding period as follows: "The wolf is surprisingly gentle and playful. She plays more roughly than a dog but does not bite. There has been only one incident that varies with this general rule of the animal's conduct. We had been chaining the wolf to the exercising wire, permitting her to run loose occasionally. One evening the caretaker was taking the wolf back to her kennel for the evening when she turned on him. The man claims that he had to climb on the kennel fence in order to get away from the animal which had torn one sleeve of his shirt. The caretaker was alone and could make no one hear his calls so that he eventually coaxed the animal into an open kennel without getting to the ground as he stated the wolf showed that she wanted to attack. Since that time we have had no trouble with her but we have discontinued moving her between the kennel and the wire.

"We believe that she was distracted as she was in heat and also reluctant to give up the freedom of the exercising wire for the confines of the kennel.

"Since the incident we have arranged a wire on which she has considerable freedom so that we do not have her in the kennel at all now. She appears to be happier and healthier where she has more leeway than in the kennel."

I was acquainted with two other captive wolves which were, so far as I could tell, similar in disposition to Wags. In 1939 I saw a male near Livengood which had been removed from a den along with five others. One pup had died early, but the

Figure 15: The tame wolf enjoyed playing with a malemute pup. She was always gentle, even when the pup, as it grew older, lost its temper at times and attacked her. [*Park Headquarters, November 1940.*]

Figure 16: Wags is waiting expectantly for a romp, but she is too rough for this little girl. [*Park Headquarters, February 1941.*]

other five were raised and became tame. When allowed to run loose they visited other miners in the region and became somewhat of a nuisance. At the time of my visit a black female, said to be the tamest of the lot, was away. The owner said she was remaining away because she did not want to come home and be chained. The male I saw on the chain permitted petting and handling by us strangers.

Another captive wolf, a female, owned by Mrs. Faith Hartman, was unusually tame. When Otto Geist and I visited Mrs. Hartman at Fairbanks her wolf was a year and a half old. When she unchained it and let it loose in the cabin it came to each of us like a pet dog, anxious to be friendly. This is the wolf that crossed with a dog and had pups when she was 2 years old.

Food Habits of Wolves

Data on the food habits of the wolves were acquired in different ways. Frequently wolves were observed chasing and killing their prey. Some carcasses on which they had fed were found, and when the snow was on the ground the tracks and signs in the snow recorded the story of their feeding activities. Data gathered by these methods were especially significant in considering the effect of food habits on prey species and have, for the most part, been discussed in those chapters dealing with the prey species.

The discussion of food habits in this section is primarily confined to the results obtained from the analysis of 1,174 wolf scats gathered on the sheep and caribou ranges. Field observations were extensive enough to give the general picture of the feeding habits of the wolves, but examination of the scat material brought out information not otherwise obtainable and placed the study on a quantitative basis. The data obtained from analysis of the scats supplement the other field observations on food habits.

Most of the scats contained the remains of only one food item. This is to be expected because so much of the prey consists of large animals which furnish food sufficient for a number of complete meals. When rodents were eaten, more than one food item was sometimes found in a scat. For instance, mice, ground squirrel, and caribou might all occur together. Except in the case of mice, usually only an individual of a species was present in a scat.

The scat data have been presented in Table 2, p. 53. The number of scats in which each food item was found have been tabulated and the data have been segregated according to the time and place that the scats

were gathered. Those found from May 1 to September 30 have been designated summer scats. (The collecting of the 1941 summer scats was discontinued in early August.) Scats gathered from October 1 to April 30 during the 3 years represent the winter period. Those picked up at the dens were segregated since they were definitely dated and gave the feeding habits during the denning period. Since there were no significant differences in the contents between the scats of old and young wolves at the den, they were not segregated. Those gathered at the dens represent the feeding habits from early May to early July. When the wolves left the den, they moved only a short distance away, but sufficiently far to give another collection of dated scats. The locality used after leaving the den, which has been called the rendezvous, was occupied in the second week of July 1940, and most of July 1941.

While scats gathered at the dens and at the two rendezvous are closely dated, as are many of the others, there are a number of them which were deposited some time before they were collected. This is true of those containing adult Dall sheep remains in 1940, and especially in 1941. Most of those containing sheep remains were deposited during the winter and represent a winter rather than a summer food.

Some of the data in the table are misleading due to the manner in which the scats were collected. The 1939 scats indicate an unusually heavy predation on sheep the preceding winter. As a matter of fact, I believe that the predation during that winter was less than that in the following winter of 1939–40. The explanation for the large number of 1939 scats containing sheep lies in an analysis of my 1939 itinerary. That summer I spent much time searching for remains of sheep carcasses and skulls, so covered a great deal of the territory where wolves had fed on sheep. As a result, I found many scats at and near the carcasses and these naturally contained sheep remains. If there had been a similar concentration on this phase of the work in 1940 and 1941 no doubt many more scats containing sheep would have resulted, or if caribou carcasses had been visited the data would have been weighted with caribou records.

The data on food habits gained from the scats are closely correlated with the observed field conditions. In 1940, for instance, calf caribou were plentiful near the wolf den and most of the scats at the den contained calf caribou remains. In 1941 calf caribou were readily available for most of the denning period, but their general absence from the den region for part of the period is reflected in a slightly higher frequency of marmot, ground squirrel, and mouse in the scats at the den. At the time the wolf families were occupying the rendezvous after leaving the den, both in 1940 and 1941, calf caribou were scarce within the hunting range of the wolves. This scarcity of calves

is reflected in the reduction of calf remains and the noticeable increase in the incidence of ground squirrel and marmot, and in 1940, of mouse also.

One more correlation should be mentioned. In 1939, 33 scats contained lamb remains and of those gathered during the next 2 years only 9 contained lamb. The heavier predation on lambs in 1939 is correlated with the absence of calf caribou during the midst of the lambing period. In the absence of calves the wolves hunted sheep.

Big game (caribou, sheep, moose) was found in 935 scats, and other food items including rodents, birds, etc., were found in 415. These figures seem to represent fairly well the general pattern of the food habits of the wolves. Big game is the preferred food, but smaller animals are also utilized in varying degrees.

DISCUSSION OF FOOD ITEMS IN WOLF DIET

Caribou.—The main food supply of the wolves in Mount McKinley National Park, as well as over interior Alaska in general, is the caribou (*Rangifer arcticus stonei*). Both young and old animals are taken. During the calving period greater attention is given to calves. Remains of adult caribou, including calves in their first winter, were present in 267 scats; calf remains were found in 313 scats. The remains include hoofs, foot bones, and pieces of the long bones.

TABLE 2.—*Classification of 1,350 individual food items found in 1,174 wolf scats collected in Mount McKinley National Park*

Food items	Number of scats in which each item occurred										Percent of occurrence in total number of food items
	Summer[1] 1939	Summer[1] 1940	Summer[2] 1941	Winter 1939–41[3]	East Fork Den, 1940	East Fork Den, 1941	East Fork Rendezvous, July 1940	East Fork Rendezvous, July 1941	Toklat Den, 1940, 1941	Total	
Number of wolf scats collected	259	134	79	167	108	87	101	156	83	1,174	
Caribou, adult, *Rangifer a. stonei*	25	28	21	75			64	35	19	267	19.78
Caribou, calf, *Rangifer a. stonei*	21	20	31		103	66	6	31	35	313	23.18
Dall sheep, adult, *Ovis d. dalli*	159	60	12	69	3		1			304	22.52
Dall sheep, lamb, *Ovis d. dalli*	33	5	3				1			42	3.11
Ground squirrel, *Citellus p. ablusus*	14	20	7	5	6	13	28	64	17	174	12.89
Marmot, *Marmota c. caligata*	8	9	5	3	1	12	7	58	11	114	8.44
Mouse (Microtine species)	10	2	10	6		9	21	9	6	73	5.47
Grass and sedge		3	3	8			6	1		21	1.55
Moose, *Alces gigas*	1	3		5						9	.67
Porcupine, *Erethizon e. myops*	4	4								8	.59
Ptarmigan, *Lagopus* spp			2	2			2			6	.55
Garbage, refuse							5			5	.37
Snowshoe hare, *Lepus a. macfarlani*		1		2						3	.22
Beaver, *Castor c. canadensis*		1	1							2	.15
Wasp	1						1			2	.15
Red fox, *Vulpes kenaiensis*		1								1	.07
Wolf, *Canis l. pambasileus*	1									1	.07
Bone fragments		1								1	.07
Bird, fledgling						1				1	.07
Leather							1			1	.07
Corn (garbage)							1			1	.07
Rag							1			1	.07
Total food items										1,350	

[1] Includes the period from May 1 to Sept. 30.

[2] Includes the period from May 1 to early August.

[3] Includes the period from Oct. 1 to Apr. 30 (April, October, 1939; April and October–December, 1940; January–April, 1941).

In the Mount McKinley National Park region there is a local caribou herd numbering at least 20,000 and possibly as high as 30,000. This herd as a unit has existed since the early 1900's and probably for a great many years before that. Its movements, which vary greatly over a period of time, are not known in detail but the animals inhabit an area which at one time or another includes Broad Pass, all of the park, and the Lake Minchumina district. At times they probably extend their range east of Broad Pass. Most of the animals move through the park over a period of a few weeks in May and June, at which time the resident wolves live mainly on the calves which they run down. The movements of the caribou and their hunting by wolves is discussed in detail in the chapter on caribou, beginning on p. 144. After the main bands have passed on, a few stragglers are always left behind. Often little groups and lone animals are up in the headwaters of the streams near the glaciers in the crest of the range. Although these stragglers are scarce the wolves seem to find them and continue to subsist mainly on caribou during the summer months after the large bands have moved westward.

In winter at least a part of the caribou herds generally are to be found along the north boundary, both within and outside the park. Those wolves living in the park then move down to the caribou to secure their food but still make occasional trips into the sheep hills. The park wolves in winter are not entirely dependent on the caribou, for sheep are also available to them. But when caribou are present among the sheep hills they probably furnish the bulk of the food supply.

Not all the animals eaten by wolves are killed by them, for caribou are frequently found that have died of other causes. However, it appears that most of the caribou eaten by wolves are killed by them. It is not known what proportion of the adults killed are weak, but it seems probable that the weaker animals are the first to be taken.

No doubt the caribou has been the main source of food for centuries and are adapted to hold their own in the presence of a wolf population under natural conditions. Wolf numbers might vary and perhaps cause the caribou numbers to fluctuate some but the relationship is old and tried.

Dall Sheep.—Remains of adult sheep (*Ovis dalli dalli*) were found in 304 scats, and those of lambs in 42.

Adult sheep were not preyed upon extensively during the summer. At three dens only four scats contained adult sheep and only one contained lamb. Probably more sheep remains were not found at the dens because in 1940 and 1941, when the dens were observed, calf caribou were readily available and formed the bulk of the food. If a den had been observed in 1939 no doubt more sheep remains would have been present, because in that year calf caribou were not available in the eastern half of the park until early June.

In 1940 and 1941, after the bulk of the caribou had left the vicinity of the den and only stragglers were available, the food of the wolves was supplemented by rodents rather than sheep. This would indicate that at this time the wolves were more disposed to capture rodents than to run down sheep, even though many sheep roamed the hills only a few miles from the dens. Further discussion of the predation of wolves upon sheep is given in the chapter on sheep beginning on page 62.

Ground Squirrel.—Ground squirrels (*Citellus parryii ablusus*) were found in 174 scats. At the rendezvous used by the East Fork wolf family during

July 1941, ground squirrels occurred in more than one-third of the scats. About one-fourth of the scats gathered at the rendezvous in 1940 contained ground squirrels. During these two periods, caribou were scarce which probably accounts for the heavy utilization of these rodents. Along with ground squirrels, marmots and mice were also utilized more than usual at this time.

Ground squirrels are abundant from low to high elevations. They are an important food supply to foxes, eagles, and gyrfalcons (*Falco rusticolus*), as well as, at times, to wolves.

Marmot.—A total of 114 scats contained remains of marmot (*Marmota caligata caligata*). Like ground squirrels, the marmots hibernate all winter and thus are available for food for only about 5 months. They are abundant, living usually among cliffs or loose rocks and boulders. Marmots weigh up to 17 or 18 pounds and therefore furnish considerable food even for the wolf. They can be methodically hunted by wolves with success, so in lieu of other game would furnish subsistence to a certain number of wolves. They are quite vulnerable to attack. I have frequently come upon marmots which I could have captured easily if I possessed the speed of a wolf or dog. They often range some distance from their holes. Once I saw a group of six large marmots move from one cliff to another about 200 yards away. In one place marmots often traveled 500 yards across an unprotected route. O. J. Murie reports that his Norwegian elk hound, which resembles a small Husky dog, captured a large marmot with little trouble, and I saw him run down another which he bit at but did not hold. This last one was almost captured, even though, along with some others, it had been scolding the dog that was approaching in plain sight. Their vulnerability is also indicated by the fact that coyotes have been known to subsist almost entirely on them in bighorn range in Wyoming.

The largest number of marmot remains were found at the wolf rendezvous at a time when caribou were scarce. The wolves at this time were resorting to marmots for an important part of their food supply. The predation on marmots tends to check their numbers and so moderate their consumption of vegetation among the cliffs used by sheep in winter. The extent of the control is not known. Probably the wolf's predation by itself would be ineffective, but combined with the activity of other predators it may play an important role in controlling marmot numbers.

Mouse.—Mouse remains were found in 73 scats. The mice available were the lemming (*Lemmus yukonensis*), red-backed mouse (*Clethrionomys*), and four kinds of meadow mice (*Microtus*) In analyzing the mouse contents no effort was made to segregate the species. Several scats were made up entirely of mouse remains, as many as six occurring in one, but often only traces of a single mouse were found.

When caribou are plentiful the wolves do very little mousing for they prefer to feed on the larger game animals. But even when feeding mainly on big game the wolves will sometimes turn aside to pounce on a mouse. In the fall considerable mousing by the pups and one or two adults was observed.

On May 3, 1940, an adult wolf on East Fork River was seen hunting a mouse in the snow. He pounced with legs stiff, much in the manner of a coyote, in order to break through the crust. After the pounce he dug in the snow but I could not be sure that the mouse was captured.

On September 10, 1940, at Polychrome Pass, an adult wolf was observed hunting mice for an hour on a flat grown up in dwarf birch and sedge. During this hour it made about 17 pounces. It then traveled briskly toward the Toklat River, turning aside occasionally to catch a mouse which it heard or smelled along the way. Usually in pouncing on a mouse it did not hop up in the air and drop on it, but pounced in a more nearly direct horizontal line, much as a dog would do. On one occasion it went up in the air more than usual and so vigorously that on landing it went off balance and its hind quarters swung to one side. Often it made a short run of five or six jumps before pouncing. Twice while it hunted it stopped to howl. When looking for a mouse— one for which it had pounced and not captured—it wagged its tail, the rate of tail wagging increasing with the rise of its excitement, which in turn was dependent upon the nearness of the mouse.

On the morning of September 17, 1940, I watched the East Fork family from a vantage point near Polychrome Pass. A black pup hunted mice by itself a half mile from the others for almost 2 hours. A yellowish pup hunting mice in some tall grass, played with one it had captured, tossing it in the air a few times and catching it. Apparently the pup was not hungry. The presence of magpies (*Pica p. hudsonia*) and an eagle, and the uncovering of a cached morsel by the gray female, were evidence that the wolves had finished a feed on larger game earlier in the morning. At 1:15 p. m., after a rest of 3 hours, the yellow pup went off hunting by itself. The usual method of pouncing was noted, but sometimes there was hardly any jump and only the forepaws would strike forward to press the mouse to the ground.

On the morning of September 23, 1940, three pups about a quarter of a mile apart were moving eastward over the broad flats at Polychrome Pass, probably to join the rest of the family. They were constantly attracted by mice to one side or the other, and they followed up grassy swales where the hunting was good. In about an hour one of them lay down in the open and the other two disappeared behind a slight rise in the tundra.

On September 24, 1940, the East Fork family was still at Polychrome Pass. While the others were resting, two pups hunted diligently for mice a half mile away. These two pups hunted from 8 a. m. until noon. In the afternoon one of the pups was again seen hunting mice. At this time, when the main caribou herds were elsewhere and only stragglers were available, the mice seemed to form an important supplement to the food supply, especially for the pups, but also for the adults. A number of sheep were only 2 or 3 miles from the rendezvous where the wolves were hunting but still were apparently not much molested.

Perhaps the wolf would feed more on the mice if it did not take so many of them to make a meal. Mice are large enough to serve as a staple diet for a 10-pound fox or a coyote, but are probably a little small for a 100-pound wolf to depend on, especially if the mice are not plentiful. I do not know how many mice would make a full meal for a wolf. As an average-sized field mouse weighs only a few ounces, many of them would be needed to furnish a meal of 7 or 8 pounds. One evening in September I tossed in quick succession to the tame wolf pup, which had a surplus of dried salmon and scraps available and was not especially hungry, 19 mice and 2 shrews. These were caught in the air and swallowed so rapidly that each one hardly stopped in the mouth. There was no evidence of satiety after the last mouse was swallowed. But when mice are plentiful a wolf would probably be able to subsist very well on them.

In winter I found little evidence of feeding on mice, but no doubt they are often eaten at this season, and in winters when the mice are exception-ally abundant, as in 1938–39, they probably feed considerably on them. Exceptionally deep snow would, of course, make mousing difficult.

Moose.—Remains of moose (*Alces gigas*) were found in nine scats. At Savage River some pieces of thick moose hide had been chewed. The evidence gathered indicates that moose are not readily taken by wolves. Probably at times under certain conditions moose may be preyed upon, especially if they are in a weakened state due to scarcity of food or disease. The majority of trappers interviewed were of the opinion that ordinarily wolves were not a menace to moose.

Porcupine.—Remains of porcupine (*Erethizon epixanthum myops*) were found in eight scats. In the woods at Toklat River where porcupines had killed many spruces I found the nearly complete hides of three porcupines turned inside out. Two wolf droppings found nearby contained only porcupine remains, including large stout spines. Other skins neatly turned were also found. It is well known that it is not uncommon for coyotes to kill and eat porcupines, and there are considerable data to show that the fox also feeds on them. A wolf shot May 10, 1940, contained porcupine quills under the skin of the muzzle and front legs.

Former Chief Ranger Louis Corbley had a Husky dog which a few years ago killed many porcupines. The technique used by the dog was to keep circling the animal and worrying it until an opportunity came to seize it by the nose. The dog kept his hold, then as the porcupine relaxed, a deeper hold on the head was taken, which usually was fatal. The dog deftly turned the porcupine over on its back, while still grasping its head, and if still alive, quickly killed it. The killing was so skillfully done that the quills were usually avoided. A wolf would be able to use a similar technique.

Back in 1927 there were unusual numbers of porcupines in the park. One could see dozens of them without any trouble, according to all reports. The animals are still fairly common. In places entire groves of trees have been killed by girdling. At timber line, where the growth is scattered, there are places where every tree is killed, thus serving as a pressure to push timber line down the valley. However, I have noticed many seedlings coming up in some of these areas so that these advance patches of timber are recovering.

Snowshoe Hare.—The snowshoe hare (*Lepus americanus macfarlani*) was represented in only three scats, a scarcity correlated with the extreme scarcity of hares. Only in a few spots along the north boundary was any appreciable hare sign noted.

According to the monthly wildlife reports for Mount McKinley National Park, the big die-off took place in the summer of 1927. Since that time the hares have remained rare over most of the park. In a memorandum accompanying the November 1942 wildlife report for the park, Chief Ranger Grant H.

Pearson states that when the hares were dying during the last epidemic, small blisters appeared all over their bodies under the skin, and that dead hares were to be seen everywhere. Some were even observed as they fell over and died. (The blisters were possibly caused by the larvae of the tapeworm *Multiceps serialis*.)

Although hares in Mount McKinley National Park have been scarce since about 1927, in other parts of Alaska they have become numerous since then and in some of these areas they have again disappeared. For instance, in 1939, from the railroad, I saw many dead hares near Fairbanks.

If hares were plentiful they would probably supplement the food supply of wolves considerably. In 1923, when I observed them in Mount McKinley National Park, I am sure they were plentiful enough to furnish subsistence for a number of wolves. E. A. Preble (1908, p. 212) reports that one band of wolves near Fort Simpson lived largely on hares, many of which were taken from the snares of the natives. J. F. Stanwell-Fletcher (1942, p. 138–139) reports wolves in British Columbia hunting snowshoe hares in late February when there was a firm crust on the snow. Earlier in the winter the hares had been able to escape the wolves in the soft snow. No doubt the abundance of the snowshoe hare is an important factor in wolf ecology.

Beaver.—The beaver (*Castor canadensis canadensis*) is widely distributed over the park but is not abundant.

Remains of beaver were found in two droppings. In 1941 a dead female, found by Wildlife Ranger Clemons, represented potential carrion.

Red Fox.—The red fox (*Vulpes kenaiensis*) is numerous in the park, but remains were found in only one scat. One trapper told me that wolves frequently ate foxes they found in his traps. All evidence points to the fact that in Mount McKinley National Park foxes are little molested by wolves.

Wolf.—Wolf remains were found in one scat. In the spring of 1939, remains of a black wolf were found which had been eaten by other wolves. A trapper told me that he knew of several wolf carcasses which had been eaten by wolves.

Ptarmigan.—Remains of ptarmigan (*Lagopus* spp.) were found in six scats. Ptarmigan are probably taken incidentally and possibly some represent carrion as they not infrequently fly into the telephone wires. There are three species of ptarmigan available but the willow ptarmigan (*Lagopus lagopus alascensis*) is the only one which becomes sufficiently abundant at times to be of some importance as a food. At the present time the willow ptarmigan is far from its peak of abundance but recovering somewhat from the low part of the cycle.

Grass and sedge.—Remains of coarse blades of either sedge or grass were found in 21 scats. Grass is eaten at all seasons. Some of the droppings containing grass also contained several round worms, so seemed to act

as a scour. On June 27 I saw a black male eat grass for a few minutes. He left a watery scat in the road which indicated his stomach was not quite normal. Later he vomited up some of the grass he had eaten.

Garbage.—Garbage remains were definitely recognized in five scats. Wolves seem to visit garbage dumps readily. The garbage dump of a road camp near Polychrome Pass was visited regularly by wolves during the summer of 1940, and they have often been seen at the Savage River Camp seeking garbage. During the winter, wolves have at times stayed around Park Headquarters seeking refuse.

CACHING

Wolves, in common with most flesh eaters, often cache excess food for future use. Once I noted a sheep horn which had been carried some distance and buried in the snow; another time the head of a ram was hidden in the snow; and again two pieces of sheep meat were cached only to be shortly consumed by foxes. But not always is the food cached. When there is an abundant supply the bother of caching the food is often omitted. I have found calf caribou on the calving grounds left untouched where killed. The wolves were seemingly aware that there was not much point in caching them since food was readily available on all sides.

A good example of provident caching was observed on July 19, 1941, after a wolf had killed a caribou calf on the bars of the East Fork River.

At this time the caribou herds had moved out of the region so that food was not readily available, and therefore was worth caching. The wolf was hungry for she ate voraciously for more than half an hour. Three times during the meal she walked to the stream for a drink. After feeding she got my scent, circled above me, barking and howling, then retreated toward the den, still not having seen me. I waited for almost an hour before I saw her coming down the river bar along the opposite shore. She trotted directly to the carcass and after feeding on a few morsels she chewed until a foreleg and shoulder had been severed. With this piece in her jaws she waded the stream and trotted about 300 yards up the bar. Here she stopped, and still holding the leg in her mouth, pawed a shallow hole in the gravel, and placed the leg in it. Then with a long sweeping motion of her head she used her nose to push gravel over the leg. The job was quickly completed and she trotted back to the carcass, chewed off the head, and buried it about 300 yards away without crossing the stream. On the third trip she carried another leg and cached it on the side of the river from where I was watching. When she returned to the carcass from this trip the wind shifted, bringing my scent to her. Without hesitating she trotted briskly across the stream and up the bar, not stopping until at least a half mile separated us.

Many of the caches made by wolves are utilized by bears, foxes, eagles, and other flesh eaters. These others probably use the caches about as much as do the owners.

Trapping Wolves

Many of the wolves in the park move back and forth across the north boundary in winter. When outside the park these wolves are roaming in territory that is being trapped, mainly for foxes. One trapper caught eight wolves in the winter of 1938–39 and three or four in the winter of 1940–41. He said that occasionally a trap-wise wolf is difficult to catch but that the average wolf is much easier to trap than a coyote. Wolves were continually springing his fox traps without getting caught because the jaw spread was too small. If he used bigger traps he was sure he could easily catch quite a number of wolves. On December 17, 1940, he showed me a black pup he had caught in a fox trap. Another wolf pup which he had captured that day was trapped by the tail and had dragged the toggle until it became tangled in the brush. On the same day, I saw tracks of still another wolf that had been dragging a trap and toggle. This trapper lost four wolves which had been caught in his traps. On December 2, 1940, along a wolf trail inside the park in Savage River Canyon, I found a trap with the toe of a wolf in it.

Another trapper caught an adult gray wolf which already carried a trap on one foot. He also had had many fox traps sprung by wolves.

Lee Swisher, trapping for foxes

north of the park on the Teklanika and Sushana Rivers, caught eight wolves in the winter of 1940–41. They were caught in No. 3 traps, though they had sprung many others without getting caught. Swisher said that if he had been using larger traps he could have cleaned the wolves out of his trapping territory. He also said that he thought wolves as a rule are easily trapped but that occasionally there is a trap-shy animal. He once tried to catch such a wolf which he said was more canny than a wise coyote.

One trapper told me that about 1935 he trapped between Eagle and Circle, Alaska. A band of about 30 wolves appeared about three times each month. He thought they traveled over a range 50 miles across. There were also a few odd wolves whose movements were local. He found the wolves hard to catch, because they ranged so far. Other trappers also reported wolves hard to trap. I suspect that when wolves are only passing through a region it would be more a matter of chance that any would be caught. It might be difficult to have the traps set in proper order at the time the wolves appeared.

Caribou may spring many traps set for wolves or foxes. One was caught and nearly tore the clothes off a trapper with its hoofs when the trapper endeavored to free it.

In the winter of 1940–41 about 19 wolves were known to have been taken by trappers along the north boundary of the park between Wonder Lake and the eastern border. Some of these had probably wandered out of the park. The number captured by these trappers varies from year to year.

CHAPTER THREE

⪻⪻⪻⪻⪻⪻⪻⪻⪻⪻⪻⪻⪻⪻⪻⪻⪻⪻

Dall Sheep

⪻⪻⪻⪻⪻⪻⪻⪻⪻⪻⪻⪻⪻⪻⪻⪻⪻⪻

Description

ALL THE ALASKA SHEEP have been referred to as *Ovis dalli dalli*, except those found on the Kenai Peninsula, which have been described as *Ovis dalli kenaiensis*. Only slight skull differences separate this latter form from *Ovis dalli dalli*.

The Dall sheep is smaller than the Rocky Mountain bighorn (*Ovis canadensis canadensis*), has more slender and gracefully curved horns, and is white in color. On a dark background Dall sheep appear to be pure white, but in the snow they are seen to be slightly yellowish. Live rams average slightly less than 200 pounds in weight and the ewes are not quite as heavy.

Distribution of Dall Sheep in Alaska

Dall sheep, found in Mount McKinley National Park, are widely distributed over the mountainous regions in Alaska. They are found throughout most of the Alaska Range, in the Nutzotin, Wrangell, and Chugach Mountains, on the Kenai Peninsula, in the Endicott Mountains north of the Arctic Circle, and a few still occur in the Tanana Hills. Their range extends into Yukon Territory where they intergrade with *Ovis d. stonei*, a subspecies which differs from the Dall sheep mainly in color. Locally, the sheep have been reduced in numbers, or eliminated by hunting, but still they are found over most of their ancestral ranges. Sheep are reported to be still plentiful in the Wood River and Mount Hayes district of the Alaska Range, in the Endicott Mountains and on the Kenai Peninsula. In some areas, such as Rainy Pass, they are reported less abundant than formerly. However, on most of their range the actual status of the sheep is not well known.

History of the Sheep in Mount McKinley National Park

The history of the Dall sheep in Mount McKinley National Park, so

far as we know, goes back over a stretch of many thousand years. It would be intensely interesting to know the detailed history of the sheep—the many vicissitudes during this long period. But through it all the sheep have survived. There probably have been many periods of sheep abundance, and many periods of sheep scarcity. During a series of easy winters, the population probably built up and overflowed the rough country into the lower gentle hills. Wolf populations may have had their own periods of scarcity and abundance, and, depending somewhat on the status of the caribou, preyed extensively upon sheep at times, or affected them little. When hares disappeared, leaving the lynx population stranded, no doubt the lynx in desperation

hunted sheep. The history is an ever-changing mosaic. It is to make possible the continuation of this natural course of events that Mount McKinley National Park has been established.

From 1906 to 1923, when I first visited Mount McKinley National Park, the sheep population was consistently high although there was considerable sheep hunting in the area up to 1920. Charles Sheldon (1930) found sheep abundant during his days there from 1906 to 1908. An "old-timer" told me that in 1915 and 1916, when he had hunted sheep in the area, they were very abundant, and that one winter he had sold 42 sheep carcasses. At this time several other market hunters operated in the region. Many sheep were apparently killed for the market and many were fed to the sled dogs used in hauling the meat. At an old crumbling cabin on East Fork River I found many old ram skulls, most of which were heaped in a pile. There were 142 horns, so at least 71 rams had been brought to this camp. The skulls had been split open, probably to make the brains readily available to the dogs.

O. J. Murie in 1920 observed a market hunter operating at Savage

River. The hunter had shot a number of sheep on these slopes. At that time many sheep were wintering on the ridges south of Savage Camp.

In 1922 and 1923 I observed sheep summering in considerable numbers at the head of Savage River where now scarcely any are to be found. In 1923 they were plentiful but probably not as plentiful as during the next few years because extensive market hunting had stopped only 2 or 3 years before.

From 1923 to 1928 there was a steady increase in the population. Some think the peak was reached in 1928. The numbers were estimated at 10,000 and upward. Two rangers estimated the population as 10,000

Figure 18: Heap of 142 ram horns at the ruins of a hunter's cabin on East Fork River. This indicates the extent of hunting in the early days before establishment of Mount McKinley National Park. [*July 1939.*]

and another member of the park force estimated it as 25,000. No organized counts were made so far as I know, so it is hard to evaluate the estimates. Nevertheless the population in 1928 was no doubt large. With so many sheep occupying the ranges there was not sufficient food for all among the cliffs so that many wintered on gentle slopes and down along the river banks 4 or 5 miles from the mountains. The animals were forced into the lower hills and valleys to feed. On some ridges there were patches of dead willow which I presumed had been killed during the high density of the population. I feel confident, from all the information I have been able to gather, that there were at least 5,000 sheep in the park during the peak. How much larger the figure was it is difficult to say, but it is possible that there were as many as 10,000, as some have estimated.

During this period the history of the wolves is briefly as follows: In 1906–8 Sheldon (1930) found wolves among the caribou herds but few among the sheep. He observed two different wolves hunting sheep in the Toklat River region. Possibly they hunted more to the east of Toklat River, but apparently there were only a few wolves among the sheep. John Romanoff, who hunted sheep in the park in 1915 and 1916, said he did not see a wolf track in the area at that time. In 1922 and 1923 my brother and I saw no wolf signs at Savage River, nor had my brother seen any wolf tracks on a trip up

Toklat River in December 1920.

Former Superintendent Karstens in his monthly report for December 1925, mentions the presence of wolves in the park and that they seemed to be on the increase. The wolves were not considered abundant in 1926 and 1927, but in 1928 it was felt that there had been a decided increase. From 1928 to the present time wolves have persisted in the sheep hills, apparently in fair numbers. No one knows what variation has taken place in the wolf population during this period. One ranger estimated 50 wolves in 1929–30 when he felt wolves were at their peak. I estimate the 1941 population at between 40 and 60 wolves in the sheep hills. The population may not have varied greatly from that figure during the last 10 or 12 years.

There apparently had been no severe winter during the time the sheep herd built up, although some sheep apparently were adversely affected by winter conditions at times. One of the rangers captured a ewe in the deep snows of Sable Pass in 1927 and the animal died a few days later. A weak ram found at the same time but not brought in was dead when seen again.

The snow conditions in the winter of 1928–29, according to reports, caused quite a large loss among the sheep. The Park Superintendent's report for March 1929, describes conditions as follows: "The winter has been a hard one on sheep with the deep snow and storms. They have been driven down from the ridges and into the deep snow of the flats in their effort to get feed. They were even noticed out on the flats near the north boundry 4 miles from the range."

In the April report the following statement is found: "The month of April proved to be the hardest one of the year for sheep. Very few places were kept blown bare by the wind. What few bare spots there were, were soon grazed off and the sheep ranged into the flats in search of feed. It is believed that many sheep starved to death. In the vicinity of Igloo the rangers picked up three rams and three ewes with lamb, though one of the ewes was too far gone to recover and died after a few days."

The account is continued in the July report for 1929: "Nyberg and Myers returned from a trip into the mountain [McKinley] on the 27th and reported that the wild sheep in the park look to be about as numerous as ever notwithstanding the hard winter and heavy snows, and report that most of the losses occurred in deep passes where they were marooned in the heavy snow and blizzards of March and April."

One ranger wrote me that the wolves had killed many sheep that winter, but that "the big jolt" had come in April, when heavy snows covered the food. For the part of the range he had investigated near Headquarters he estimated that a third of the sheep population had died. He said that those sheep that perished were mostly the old and the yearlings.

In the spring of 1929 there apparently was a fairly good lamb crop. The following two winters were not severe, but heavy wolf predation on the large sheep population was reported.

The most serious reduction among the sheep apparently took place in the winter of 1931–32, which was much more severe for the sheep than that of 1928–29. The Park Superintendent's report for December 1931 states that the rangers were experiencing difficulty in making patrols because of the heavy snows and that "from all indications the sheep are going to have a hard time finding forage this winter." The January 1932 report states that the month was very cold, that the sheep were all in good condition, but that the late snows had driven them well up toward the summits of the mountains. In February 1932 it was reported that all records for snowfall had been broken, that 72 inches had fallen in 6 days, and that the winter of 1931–32 would be remembered as the "year of the big snow." The Superintendent reported: "During the heavy snowfall which came on the 3d of the month, I was alone at headquarters and taxed to the utmost in shoveling snow from the roofs of the buildings. It was thought for a while that several would go down, as the snow was 4 feet deep in places. I called up on the phone to get a man from the station to come up and help me out. He left there at 8 a. m. and arrived here at 3:10 p. m. It took him just 7 hours to go the 2 miles notwithstanding the fact that he had on a good pair of snow-shoes. The heavy snows that came during the fore part of the month were followed by 2 days of rain, then below-zero weather, and a heavy crust was formed which has caused untold suffering amongst the wild animals of the interior of the park. This is especially true concerning the moose. Their legs from the knee down are worn to the bone, and each moose trail is covered with blood. It is possible to walk right up on a moose as they have not the courage or strength to run away."

In the April 1932 report, after some investigation of conditions among the sheep had been made, the following statements are found: "We have suffered a severe loss of mountain sheep during the winter as a result of the heavy snows; also the predatory animals have taken their toll. Ranger Rumohr counted 15 dead sheep while on his way in from Toklat. He examined many of the carcasses for evidence of wolf kills, but in most cases it appeared that the deaths were the result of starvation."

Former Ranger Lee Swisher wrote me that he found a great many dead sheep that spring which were not wolf kills. Dixon (1938, p. 231) reports that Ranger Swisher had told him in August 1932 that he did not believe there were more than 1,500 sheep in the park at that time as contrasted with an estimate of 10,000 to 15,000 he had made in 1929. In view of the deep snow and the severe crust, and the huge sheep population,

which quickly consumed the food available on the more favorable ridges, it is not surprising that such a catastrophe occurred.

The lamb crop in 1932, probably because of the hard winter, was very poor, so that deducting normal winter losses, the numbers must have been smaller in 1933. Ivar Skarland, anthropologist of the University of Alaska, told me that in a trip into the park in April 1931 he had counted 830 sheep. In 1934 he made the same trip in April and saw scarcely any sheep, which agrees with the other reports on the reduction of the population.

For the period from 1933 to 1939 variations in sheep populations are not well known. One ranger thought the ebb was reached about 1935 or 1936. In 1939 there was an excellent lamb crop and a good survival of the yearlings of the previous year. Another ranger said he thought there were more sheep in 1939 than there had been for 4 or 5 years.

The yearling losses were heavier in the winter of 1939–40, and in the spring of 1940 the lamb crop was far below par. These losses and the small lamb crop were a definite set-back to the population. The lamb crop in 1941 was excellent, but there were very few yearlings because of the few lambs the year before. The present population is estimated to be between 1,000 and 1,500 sheep, perhaps not far different from the population in the spring of 1932, when Lee Swisher estimated the number at not more than 1,500. It appears to me that since 1932 the sheep population has not varied greatly.

That, in brief, is the recent history of the sheep in Mount McKinley National Park, so far as I have been able to outline it from available records.

Distribution of Dall Sheep in the Park

The main ranges of Dall sheep in Mount McKinley National Park lie north of the backbone of the Alaska Range where the snowfall is much less than on the south slope. In an east-and-west direction, the sheep are found from the Nenana River to Mount Eielson, about 68 miles to the west. From Mount Eielson to the western boundary there are no sheep now except for some sporadic records. Scarcity of these animals west of Mount Eielson is apparently due to the absence of foothill ranges, there being too much snow on the short high spurs coming from the main range for much winter use. West of the park, hills occupied by sheep are again found in the Tonzana River region. Along the eastern border of the park, a few sheep occur between McKinley Park Station and Windy, near the Alaska Railroad. Eastward from the park boundary, sheep distribution continues on all suitable locations throughout the Alaska Range.

Because less range is used in winter than in summer, the winter and summer distribution will be discussed separately. (The areas of year-long use and purely summer use are marked on the map on page 7.)

WINTER DISTRIBUTION

In winter the sheep are found from the Nenana River to Mount Eielson, in suitable cliffs and slopes in the foothills and on the north end of a few of the spurs coming off the main range. From the Nenana River to Teklanika River sheep are largely confined to the long single "outside" or foothill ridge. The canyons through this ridge made by the Savage, Sanctuary, and Teklanika Rivers are especially suitable for winter range because of their ruggedness. Farther west, between Teklanika River and Stony River, the mountains available to sheep are a dozen miles in breadth. A depression a mile or more wide separates the "outside" range or foothills proper from the spur ridges coming off the main Alaska Range. At Savage River the tips of the spur ridges were formerly much used by sheep in winter, but this is no longer the case. Possibly the sheep had been too vulnerable to wolf attack there. At Toklat River the spur ridges which are separated from the foothills only by the gravel bars of the streams are still a part of the winter range.

The ridges on the winter range are mostly under 6,000 feet elevation and the sheep are usually found between 3,000 and 5,000 feet. When conditions are suitable they may range from a stream bed at 3,000 feet up the slope to 4,000 or 5,000 feet. At altitudes in excess of 5,000 feet food

becomes scarce. As a rule there is relatively little snow on the winter range, even on the flats, although deep snows do occur occasionally. Prevailing south winds, which often become strong, blow many of the ridges and slopes free of snow. Although the prevailing winds are from the south, many north slopes also are blown bare. Much snow is blown into gullies and ravines and thus may at times impede free travel from one slope to another.

SUMMER DISTRIBUTION

When the winter snows melt sufficiently to permit freedom of travel the range of the sheep expands greatly. Many then move nearer the

Figure 19: Double Mountain and Tek-lanika River. This mountain is much used by sheep in summer, but is fre-quented very little by them in winter. Many caribou use the pass between the two peaks in crossing between Sanctuary and Teklanika Rivers. [*May 17, 1939.*]

main Alaska Range, some going to the heads of glacial streams. In mid-winter the snow is too deep in these regions to permit their use. Not all the sheep make these movements, for during the summer some sheep may be found over much of the winter range. Thus, on the winter range near East Fork, between 100 and 200 rams and some ewes may be found throughout the summer. Many of these rams have moved into the area from other parts of the winter range. There is apparently considerable movement by those sheep which summer on the winter range. Sheep are found all year in some numbers on Sable, Cathedral, and Igloo Mountains, and on winter range along the Toklat River as far north as the last canyon. The exclusive summer ranges are slightly higher in elevation.

Migration

The movements to the summer range take place during much of June and sometimes as late as July. The return to the winter range begins in August, but most of the fall migration takes place in September. Stragglers have been seen migrating in early October.

Although many details concerning the migrations are not known, a number of observations were made of the general movements. Sheep wintering on the outside range near the Nenana River apparently summer in some of the mountains on the west side of Riley Creek. They were seen crossing to the winter range in late August at Mile 5. Some of the sheep at Savage Canyon cross a mile or more of low country and follow the ridges to the head of Savage

Figure 20: Some of a large group of rams that spent the summer on the hills along East Fork River. This is also a winter range. [*July 15, 1940.*]

River. Some of these sheep were seen moving southwest toward Double Mountain and others may go to Sanctuary River before going southward. Most of the sheep wintering in Teklanika and Sanctuary Canyons move south 9 or 10 miles to Double Mountain and points beyond. Some of the sheep wintering on the hills west of Big Creek go eastward to Double Mountain by way of Igloo and Cathedral Mountains. Sheep from the hills west of Sable Mountain and the head of Big Creek and possibly from lower East Fork River move eastward to Cathedral Mountain and cross the Teklanika River to Double Mountain and ridges between the forks of Teklanika River. This is a pronounced movement.

Some sheep summer at the head of the east fork of the East Fork River but I do not know where they come from. They could come from the East Fork or Toklat River winter ranges. Some of those wintering on the Toklat River move to the heads of the two forks of the Toklat 7 or 8 miles beyond the boundaries of the winter range. The few sheep on Stony

Figure 21: **Looking up to the head of the east branch of the Teklanika River. This is mountain sheep summer range. Vegetation, especially grass, is sparse in these mountains. [*May 17, 1939.*]**

Creek move to the head of the creek, and those wintering in the cliffs across from Mount Eielson move 8 or 9 miles to the vicinity of Sunshine Glacier.

Before venturing a crossing over low country the sheep may spend hours looking over the region from the slopes, apparently to be sure the coast is clear. Sometimes they may spend a day or two in watching before making the attempt. Often ewes and rams move across together in a compact band.

The sheep at Sanctuary and Teklanika Canyons have 3 or 4 miles of low, rolling country to cross to reach the hills adjoining Double Mountain, their immediate destination. Three or four well-defined migration trails lead across the low country.

On June 7, 1940, a band of about 64 sheep, both ewes and rams, crossed from Sanctuary Canyon to the low hills adjoining Double Mountain. They started crossing about 2 p. m., and did not arrive at the hills until 5:30 p. m. Most of the way the sheep traveled in a compact group, stopping frequently to look ahead. Through tall willows and scattered spruce woods they walked in single file. Just before reaching the first hills they fed for about 15 minutes on the flats at their base. They probably were all hungry and came upon some choice food. When they emerged from the woods to the open hills they were strung out considerably and galloped up the slope in high spirits, seeming relieved to have made the crossing.

On July 27, 1939, eight sheep made a belated migration from Sanctuary Canyon to the hills north of Double Mountain. From these hills I saw a group consisting of two old ewes, two lambs, and two yearlings, one 2 year-old ram, and a young ewe coming across the flats, alternately galloping and trotting, and occasionally stopping briefly to look both ahead and behind. I lost sight of them as they approached the hills to one side of me but presently I saw them cross a creek and climb a long slope to the south. They disappeared over the top but in a few minutes all eight sheep reappeared in precipitous flight and galloped down the slope with miraculous speed and abandon. The lambs kept up with the others. They passed within 30 feet of the place where I crouched in the willows so I could see clearly how they panted hard with open mouths. They climbed a slope north of me and stood above some cliffs surveying the terrain they had crossed. No pursuer was seen but it appeared they had been badly frightened. Later they regained their composure and fed and rested.

When sheep cross a valley they often follow an old rocky stream bed even though the travel would be much easier on the sod beside the stream. They probably have an instinctive feeling of safety when traveling among boulders even on level terrain since such terrain resembles the cliffs where they are safe. This instinct for seeking the boulder-strewn country on the level

would serve a good purpose if such areas were extensive enough so that an enemy could not follow on firm smooth sod close by, as they can along the stream beds. On one occasion two ewes which were captured by wolves might have escaped if they had not followed a rocky stream while the wolves ran on the firm sod alongside the rocks.

In migrating along ridges where there are cliffs the sheep move leisurely, frequently stopping in places for a day or longer to feed. Sometimes they may remain on a mountain along the way for a week or more. A band of about 100 ewes and lambs fed on Igloo Mountain for a week before continuing their migration. They moved slowly around the mountain in their feeding, some days going only 300 or 400 yards. Sometimes a band will retrace its steps a half mile or so before going forward again. The movements in both spring and fall are similar, although the fall migration may at times be hurried a little by snow. However, the sheep frequently begin their fall movements before the coming of heavy snows. Single animals, or bands containing up to 100, may be seen in migration.

The causes of migration are difficult to determine. Vegetation influences migration at least to the extent that it must be satisfactory on the range sought by the sheep. Grazing animals will often follow the snow line in spring as though they were seeking the tender new vegetation. This may be partly a cause-and-effect relationship, but, at least in part, it may be purely an incidental correlation; in following the snow line the animals may simply be driven by an urge to return to a remembered summer habitat, and not necessarily because of the seasonal stage of the plant growth. In Mount McKinley National Park it was not at all evident that the sheep were following very closely the appearance of new vegetation. Near the glaciers, where some of the sheep go, it is true the plant growth is much later than on parts of the winter range, but in many cases the growth stages of vegetation on winter and summer habitats are quite similar. On north slopes, especially, the growth on winter range is late and is green and succulent all summer. Indeed, in some respects the food on winter range seems better than on purely summer range. On winter range there is more grass and a greater variety and abundance of plant species. On the other hand, many of the species that are especially attractive to the white sheep occur on the purely summer ranges in quantity that is ample for their needs. If the migra-

tion were a complete one from winter to purely summer range, with no exceptions, one might conclude that the summer range was preferred and was not utilized in winter because of deep snows. This may still be true to some extent. A detailed study of the vegetation over all the ranges might reveal some interesting correlations.

We may assume that migratory habits had a beginning in the racial history of a species. At such an early period the sheep may have remained on the remote summer ranges until driven out by snow. Then, after such a movement had become habitual and more or less punctual, it is reasonable to assume that their fall migration might anticipate the coming of the snow. Or, the inception of the fall movement may be due to the deterioration of vegetation (by ripening and drying) on the purely summer range, for the sheep usually begin to move before the snow drives them out.

Insects are often stressed as a factor causing migration of big game and no doubt do at times influence local movements. Occasionally flies annoyed the sheep and caused them to seek the shade of cliffs, but usually the flies were not much in evidence, probably because of the cool breezes on the ridges. Since insects are relatively scarce on purely summer and winter ranges, it seems unlikely that any difference in their incidence would be sufficient to cause migratory movements. As suggested above, the insects might cause local movements such as from one side of a ridge to the other or from the sunshine into the shade.

One factor which may be of importance in explaining the migrations is the natural tendency of animals to wander. Let loose some horses and they will wander widely in their grazing. In any area the sheep wander about considerably over a period of days. Repeated wandering movements to certain localities may in time have established definite migration habits. In other words, the sheep may migrate simply because they like to travel.

The factors originally causing the movements of sheep may have disappeared, so that the animals may now be migratory largely because of habit which has no present-day use. When the population was excessively large, as it was in the late 1920's and often has been in the past, the sheep may have moved from an overgrazed winter range to the fresh pastures unavailable in winter. Now that there is no need for fresh pastures, the sheep may continue their treks because of a habit handed down to them.

The causes motivating sheep migration require more study and careful interpretation before any conclusions can be reached.

Figure 23: **Excellent all-year Dall sheep range along East Fork River.** [*July 15, 1940.*]

Food Habits

The general pattern of the food habits of the sheep was established by observing their feeding, examining the vegetation where they had fed, following their tracks in the snow, and examining stomach contents. A detailed study of the summer food habits was not made so that no doubt many minor food items are not here recorded. It was of interest to find that, although the main food consisted of grasses and sedges, considerable browse was eaten.

WINTER FOOD HABITS

Much of the information on the winter food habits was secured from the analysis of the stomach contents of sheep which had died on the range. The stomach contents of 75 sheep were analyzed. Of these, 54 had died in winter when no green grass was available, and 21 had died during the fall and spring, when a small amount of green grass was to be obtained. Since the only essential difference between the two series is the presence of some green grass in one of them, they have been combined in Table 3, page 76. Seventeen of the stomachs were from rams, 26 from ewes, 2 from lambs, 5 from yearlings, and 25 were undetermined.

Since most of the sheep from which these stomachs came were old or diseased it is possible that the contents are not entirely representative of the entire population. Healthy sheep might wander down in the bottoms more to feed on willow or sage, and weak animals probably would not move about a great deal in search of variety. However, the series of stomachs probably gives a fairly good picture of the winter food habits.

An annotated list of the foods

TABLE 3.—*Results of food analyses of 75 Dall sheep stomachs collected in Mount McKinley National Park, from animals that succumbed in autumn, winter, and early spring*

Plant species	Number of stomachs in which item occurred	Percentages	
		Average volume	Maximum volume
Grass and sedge	75	81.5	100
Equisetum arvense	4	48.0	96
Blueberry, Vaccinium uliginosum	8	14.9	60
Willow, Salix spp	63	10.2	75
Sage, Artemisia hookeriana	20	5.4	35
Cranberry, Vaccinium vitis-idaea minus	30	4.6	70
Crowberry, Empetrum nigrum	14	2.7	30
Dwarf willow, Salix reticulata	2	1.0	2
Lapland Rose-bay, Rhododendron lapponicum	1	1.0	1.0
Loco, Oxytropis spp	7	.8	5.0
Labrador tea, Ledum sp	3	.6	1.0
Dwarf Arctic birch, Betula nana	2	.5	1.0
Mountain avens, Dryas spp	19	.4	3.0
Lichen, Cladonia sp	4	.12	.5
Saxifrage, Saxifraga tricuspidata	13	.08	.5
Moss	2	Trace	Trace
Alpine azalea, Loiseleuria sp	2	Trace	Trace
Cinquefoil, Potentilla fruticosa	3	Trace	Trace
Leaf lichen	2	Trace	Trace
Alder, Alnus fruticosa	1	Trace	Trace
Bearberry, Arctostaphylos uva-ursi	1	Trace	Trace
Aster, Aster spp	2	Trace	Trace
Pyrola sp	1	Trace	Trace

Figure 24: Igloo Creek is in the foreground; the far mountains are on the other side of Teklanika River. Sheep frequently descend to the creek bottom to feed on the willows. The spruce in the middle distance is at timber line on Igloo Creek. [*September 1939.*]

known to be eaten by the sheep in winter follows:

Grasses and Sedges.—The principal winter food of the mountain sheep consists of grasses and sedges. Every stomach contained some grass, and the average amount present was 81.5 percent.

In the middle of September, when the ground was covered with 14 inches of snow, and again in October after a heavy snowfall, I noted, in following trails, that the sheep were feeding extensively on the seed heads of *Calamagrostis canadensis, C. langsdorfi, Festuca rubra, Agropyron latiglume,* and *Trisetum spicatum.* Heads of other grasses are perhaps also eaten. Such feed must be very nourishing. Considerable amounts of dry grasses were eaten by early October.

There is a good growth of grass and sedge on the winter range, and since the wind generally blows the snow off the exposed ridges, usually these foods are readily available. On the high ridges species of *Poa* and *Festuca* form much of the grass cover. Along with these highly palatable grasses there is a much-utilized short sedge (*Carex hepburnii*) which grows in solid stands.

Willow.—Willows (*Salix* spp.), both the tall and dwarf types, are eaten at all seasons. They were present in 63 stomachs and the average percentage in these was 10.2. The largest percentage found in any stomach was 75. The species of willow are not listed separately except in the case of one of the dwarf willows (*Salix reticulata*) which was noted in two stomachs. Some willows may be somewhat more palatable than others but several species among both the tall and dwarf varieties are highly relished.

Figure 25: **The ewe and ram are on one of the exposed grassy ridges which are grazed closely in winter.** [*Polychrome Pass, May 17, 1939.*]

Dwarf willows are widely distributed over the ridges, and the tall willows grow along the streams and in swales between the spur ridges, sometimes far up the slopes where the sheep can feed upon them without too much danger from wolves. Often in October and November sheep descended to creek bottoms to feed on willows. They also fed extensively on those growing in the swales between the ridges. Here in the fall they waded through 14 inches of snow in search of willow leaves that were still green. Dried leaves were also eaten at this time. Along with the leaves, twigs up to a quarter of an inch in diameter were eaten. Generally the leaves are picked off the sides of the twigs, sometimes down the twig a foot or

Figure 26: Ewes feeding in about 14 inches of snow. They pawed readily down to grass but fed mostly on the leaves and twigs of willows and grass heads protruding above the snow. [*Igloo Creek, September 19, 1939.*]

two. Because willow is eaten so much during the early winter, I expected a higher representation in the winter stomachs, but as the snow deepens in the swales, willow probably is not so readily available.

Horsetail.—Although horsetail (*Equisetum arvense*) was found in only four stomachs, it is nevertheless highly relished. The species is found in swales and wet spots, and sometimes in good stands quite high up the slopes. Because of its occurrence in swales it is probably not readily available in winter because of snow. At East Fork at the base of the ridges there is an extensive stand which had been closely cropped in the spring of 1941. There were many sheep drop-

pings on the area. In the fall after the snow appeared several places were noted where sheep had pawed for it through the snow. Two ewes killed by wolves on October 5, 1939, had been feeding in a swale on this plant when surprised. Their stomachs contained almost 100 percent *Equisetum.*

Sage.—There are at least three species of sage which are highly palatable. *Artemisia arctica* and *A. frigida* occur scatteringly and were nowhere found to be abundant.

These sages are probably eaten in winter although none was recognized in the stomach contents. In late fall they were found much eaten. The tall herbaceous sage, *Artemisia hookeriana*, is highly palatable at all times. It is most abundant along streams and reaches far up the slopes in the draws between ridges. It often grows in dense clumps. In September and October, when the leaves and stems were dry, the sheep frequently fed on this herbaceous sage in the creek bottoms. Tracks at Big Creek

showed that a band had crossed the creek and fed on a sage patch near the mouth of a ravine. In the high draws at East Fork this sage was uniformly closely browsed by spring. It was found in 20 of the stomachs and averaged 5.4 percent of the contents. The greatest amount of it found in a stomach was 35 percent of the contents.

Cranberry.—Cranberry (*Vaccinium vitis-idaea minus*) is an abundant evergreen widely distributed over the hills. Although eaten in only small quantities, it apparently is frequently sampled. It was found in 30 stomachs. Usually only a trace was noted, but in one stomach it made up 70 percent of the contents.

Figure 27: A swale, between lateral ridges of Igloo Mountain, where sheep often fed in the fall on the willow which protruded through the snow. [*September 19, 1939.*]

In October, when a variety of food was available, the sheep were several times observed feeding on cranberry.

Blueberry.—Blueberry (*Vaccinium uliginosum*) was found in eight stomachs, making up 60, 40, and 15 percent of the contents of three of them, and 1 percent of the contents in each of five others. The berries, leaves, and twigs were eaten, but the berries were especially sought. The stomach of a lamb which was killed on October 4, 1939, contained 40 percent blueberries. On that date a band had been feeding extensively on blueberries. On October 7 and 12 it was again noted that sheep had fed heavily on them. Some of the berries had been picked up from the ground. The deterioration of the berries as the season advances, and their reduced availability because of snow, probably is the explanation for the relatively few stomachs containing blueberry in the winter.

Crowberry. — Crowberry (*Empetrum nigrum*) was present in 14 stomachs, making up 30 percent of the contents of one stomach, but on the average comprising 2.7 percent of the contents. The twigs and leaves of this evergreen were found in the stomachs, but very likely the berries were also eaten. It was found browsed in early October. Perhaps it would be eaten more extensively if it were more abundant on high ridges and grew taller. Crowberry is most plentiful on the lower slopes.

Mountain Avens.—Mountain avens (*Dryas* spp.) was found in 19 stomachs, averaging 0.4 percent of the contents. There are about five species of dryas in the park. Some grow mainly on the old river bars where they form extensive mats, while others are found on the ridges. The principal cover of many slopes is dryas, consequently these slopes are poor winter range for sheep. Because it is much eaten in summer it has sometimes been referred to as an important winter food. However, in winter it becomes dry and brittle and loses much of its palatability.

Loco.—Loco (*Oxytropis*) was found in seven stomachs. Some species were highly relished in the fall while the leaves were still green. The remains found in the stomach contents consisted of the basal part of the plant nipped off at the root. Dry leaves may have been present in other stomachs and escaped detection.

Hedysarum.—Both *Hedysarum americanum* and *H. mackenzi* are highly relished in the fall but none was found in the stomachs. The seed pods were often noted eaten in September.

Dwarf Birch.—Dwarf Arctic birch (*Betula nana*) was found in only two stomachs. The leaves and fine twigs of dwarf birch were noted eaten in late September. It is not readily available on the high ridges.

The following species were found in the stomachs in small quantities: *Saxifraga tricuspidata, Ledum groenlandicum, Loiseleuria procumbens, Potentilla fruticosa, Rhododendron lapponicum, Alnus fruticosa, Arctostaphylus uvaursi, Aster* sp., *Cladonia* sp., leaf lichen sp., and moss.

The following species were found eaten in late fall: *Heracleum lanatum* (seed heads and leaves), *Delphinium* sp. (when dry), *Shepherdia canadensis* (mainly berries), and *Mertensia* sp.

SUMMER FOOD HABITS

In summer, as in winter, the principal food of the sheep consists of grasses, sedges, and willows. However, at this season much *Dryas* is also eaten, and a variety of other species are eaten in small amounts. Frequently sheep were seen feeding on the leaves of willow. For example, on June 11, 1940, 36 sheep fed steadily on two species of willow for 40 minutes, and on June 20, 1940, a band fed for a half hour on willows. On some of the higher slopes where the shrubby willows are absent there is an abundance of dwarf willows only a few inches high which are grazed extensively. Some species of *Oxytropis* and *Hedysarum* are much sought. The leaves and flowers of herbaceous cinquefoil, *Aconitum* sp., *Campanula lasiocarpa*, *Arnica*, and *Conioselinum* were eaten.

The contents of one stomach, that of a 2-year-old ewe that died on June 8 as a result of a snag injury, were available for analysis. The following determinations were made: green grass, 85 percent; willow, 14 percent; *Oxytropis* sp., trace; *Pyrola* sp., trace; and *Salix reticulata*, trace.

MINERAL LICKS

Sheep were often seen at licks, and well-defined trails led to some of them. A lick on Ewe Creek was much used, and two in Teklanika Canyon, similar to the preceding, were used extensively. On East Fork the sheep visited a lick on the side of the slope where water seeped out. The mud in this lick was black, while in some of the others the material was gray. On Double Mountain a lick was used by both sheep and caribou. On Toklat River two licks were also found in use.

Above the Ewe Creek lick many sheep droppings were found which were made up entirely of clay, so it is evident that considerable quantities of the earth are eaten at times.

Dixon (1938, p. 223) had samples of the Ewe Creek lick analyzed by Dr. G. L. Foster of the Division of Biochemistry, University of California. He reported that calcium and iron phosphate were the two minerals present in the lick which would be soluble in digestive fluids. Insoluble substances, chiefly magnesia and silicates, were also present.

Carrying Capacity of the Winter Range

After observing so many overgrazed big-game ranges in the States it was a pleasant experience to find the sheep range in Mount McKinley National Park not overutilized. By spring the grasses on the more accessible ledges are closely grazed but they are not harmed even in these places where grazing is concentrated. Willows are not now overutilized, although in years past, when sheep were more abundant, patches on the ridges were killed off by overbrowsing.

There are now from 1,000 to 1,500 sheep using the winter range which comprises an area of between 200 and 250 square miles. But of course not all of this area is a source of food. Many cliffs and rock slides support little growth; the vegetation on many slopes, ravines, and stream bottoms is deeply covered with snow; and extensive areas have a cover which is mainly *Dryas*, thus furnishing little winter grazing. Hence, without an extensive survey of cover types, it would be difficult to determine the amount of range actually available to the sheep in winter, and this amount would fluctuate from year to year because of varying snow conditions.

The carrying capacity of the winter range is several times the number of sheep now present in the park. As will be discussed later in detail, it is the wolf, rather than the food supply, that appears to be the chief factor limiting the size of the sheep population. The wolf reduces the size of the sheep range by confining sheep to the more rugged country where they are less vulnerable to wolf attack than elsewhere. In the rugged country, the wolf preys on the sheep sufficiently to keep them

Figure 28: Cathedral Mountain in foreground; south extension of Double Mountain on center sky line. Dryas predominates on so many slopes that Cathedral Mountain is a rather poor winter range for Dall sheep. [*September 1939.*]

below the carrying capacity of the range as determined by food supply. Thus the present sheep numbers apparently are dependent on the extent of cliff protection and the degree of wolf pressure.

Disease and Parasites

ACTINOMYCOSIS

From an examination of the skulls, it is obvious that the sheep are subject to two diseases, common among big game animals, which are known as actinomycosis and necrotic stomatitis. These ailments are described in detail on p. 117. Much of our information on necrotic stomatitis was secured among the elk in Jackson Hole, Wyo., where it was also found among the deer, bighorns, and moose. In the case of elk, many calves are subject to it. Death among them is often rapid, occurring before the lesions have affected the bone tissue. Many older animals which have recovered are often left with serious dental deformities or loss of teeth. The annual loss among the elk due to necrotic stomatitis apparently becomes more severe during years of food scarcity. The data available indicate that the Dall sheep may be affected by this disease in a manner similar to the elk. The annual loss due to this disease is not extensive.

LUNGWORM

In the lungs of a yearling collected April 24, 1939, and examined by Dr. Frans Goble, numerous eggs, larvae, and adults of a nematode were found which apparently belonged to the genus *Protostrongylus* or a close ally. (Goble and Murie, 1942.) This is the first record of lungworm in the Dall sheep, but the parasite is probably common among them. Lack of previous records is probably due to lack of material for examination. Lungworms might affect the health of some animals, but no data on this were secured. Coughing, so prevalent in the sheep in Yellowstone National Park and Jackson Hole, Wyo., was not observed.

SCABIES

No animals were seen which showed any evidence in the appearance of the coat that scabies existed among them. No mites were found in patches of hide examined. Scabies is quite prevalent among some of the Rocky Mountain bighorns.

A SICK LAMB

About the middle of June 1940, a sick lamb with its mother was seen by a ranger at a tributary of Igloo Creek on the east side of Sable Pass. The lamb was too weak to walk, and saliva drooled from its mouth. It was carried to the creek where it was seen the following day, unable to rise. When I learned about the incident the lamb was gone.

LAMB DIES IN CAPTIVITY

In April 1929, three weak ewes were rescued from starvation. Two lived and gave birth to lambs at Park Headquarters. One of the lambs did very well, but the other died on the second day after it was born. When it was discovered that the ewe had no milk it was too late to save the lamb. Possibly this type of tragedy accounts for the loss of some lambs at birth in the wild, especially after hard winters.

INSECTS SOMETIMES ANNOY SHEEP

On a few occasions flies were observed annoying the sheep considerably. On July 26, 1940, among the rock chimneys near Sable Pass all the sheep had sought the shade to avoid the large flies which were attacking them. Sheep out in the sun, where they had moved when I disturbed them, were much troubled by these pests. In desperation they would hurry to the shade of a rock. A ewe climbing a long slope opposite me was much bothered by flies, and stopped in the shade of the first cliffs she reached. An old ram lying in the shade was directly in the route I planned to follow to climb out of some rough cliffs into which I had descended. He moved off at my close approach, but when the flies attacked him in the sun he suddenly hurried back to the shade near me. As I approached him he faced me and looked as though he might hold the passage at all costs.

On July 19, 1939, I saw a ewe stamping her foot and watching an insect buzzing around her. She dashed rapidly away, then stood perfectly still, apparently waiting to see if the fly had followed. Three times I saw this performance, in which the sheep behaved much like a caribou when attacked by a botfly.

As a rule the sheep did not seem to be greatly bothered by flies. On the high ridges there is generally enough breeze to greatly minimize this annoyance.

Mosquitoes are said to have attacked some captive sheep at Park Headquarters, but it is not probable that they are of much significance in the sheep hills, where they usually are not plentiful.

Accidents

In 1939 a number of crippled animals were observed. Strangely, no cripples were seen the following two summers except one which had been snagged and was found dead. This difference was due in part to the greater time spent among the sheep in 1939, and possibly, in part, to lighter wolf pressure on the sheep in 1939. The animals injured will be enumerated in order to give an idea of some of the accidents to which sheep are subjected and to show that there is a certain percentage of obviously vulnerable animals, and some accidental casualties.

A lone yearling was found near the road on April 24, 1939, and it was so weak it could barely rise. When it did get to its feet it stumbled toward me (probably because I was between it and the rocks) and fell at my feet. The hoof of one forefoot was elongated, showing that it had not been used for a long time. One rib was broken and the area around it festered and bloodshot. Other spots showing serious suppuration were the injured foot and the knee, and two

Figure 29: A yearling sheep, whose right foreleg had been injured, apparently by a fall. The foot had been so little used that the hoof had grown long. [*Polychrome Pass, April 24, 1939.*]

spots along the spinal column. There was a sore on each side of the upper palate and sores around the lips. The bruises and broken rib suggested that the yearling had fallen in the rocks.

On May 13, 1939, a ram about 5 years old had a decided limp on a foreleg.

On June 18, 1939, a young ram on the east side of Cathedral Mountain was lame in a foreleg. When the animal fed, it either held this lame leg off the ground or rested on the knee.

A ram about 6 years old, observed at East Fork on June 27, 1939, had a horn which, instead of curving outward, curved toward the neck so that in time, as it grew longer, it might gouge into the top of the neck.

On July 26, 1939, a lamb was noted at the head of East Fork River which had a seriously lame foreleg.

On Big Creek on August 16, 1939, Emmett Edwards saw a lamb with a severe limp in a foreleg. On August 18 he saw a ewe with a large raw spot on the right ham which appeared to be the result of a severe bruise.

On September 11, 1939, a lamb was seen on Polychrome Pass with a long deep gash across the rear of one ham.

The hair around the wound was red from recent bleeding. The cut appeared to have been made by a rock. Possibly the lamb had fallen.

On September 12, 1939, on Igloo Creek, a lamb carried a crippled foreleg, not using it at all.

On September 20, 1939, I noted an occasional drop of blood in the tracks of some sheep which had been feeding in the snow. Nothing serious, but it indicates that the feet may become quite sore in crusted snow.

On September 29, 1939, a yearling was seen with a decided limp in a foreleg. A ewe in the same band was soiled from the tail to the ankle. In the distance it appeared to be dried blood, but of this I could not be certain. It may have been due to diarrhea.

On June 8, 1940, a 2-year-old ewe was found dead at Igloo Creek on a low slope. A snag had penetrated the abdominal cavity and the small intestine.

Some years ago a ranger found a sheep at Igloo Creek which had died from a fall incurred by slipping on a glacier.

At least two instances of sheep frozen in overflow on the rivers have come to my attention.

In September 1928, five young rams were found dead in Savage Canyon. They had died from eating dynamite.

In the Park Superintendent's report for 1927 it is stated that a ranger found the carcass of a sheep at Toklat River. When found, the carcass was fresh and there were no marks on it except where birds had picked a hole in the entrails. The tracks in the snow showed that the animal had walked off some glare ice a distance of 25 yards and had dropped dead. The suggestion is made that it may have slipped on the ice and hurt itself internally.

THE MENACE OF DEEP SNOW

The deep snows of the winters of 1928–29 and 1931–32 took a heavy toll of the sheep. Apparently in some cases entire bands, in crossing from one mountain to another, became exhausted in the valleys and died en masse. There is no detailed report on the situation but it is stated that bunches of sheep were found dead with no indication that they had been killed by wolves. Some of the sheep were no doubt later fed upon by wolves and foxes, making it impossible to know whether the animals had starved or been killed. Many of the sheep killed by wolves during these two hard winters were no doubt first weakened by snow conditions. Perhaps most of these sheep were doomed, but it is possible that some of those killed by wolves might have survived the severe weather.

In April 1927, one of the rangers found a ram and ewe in a weakened condition in the deep snow at Sable Pass. The ewe was brought to Headquarters but died a few days later. The ram was found dead when the spot was again visited.

In February 1929, when the snow was unusually deep, two rams were seen to jump on a drift of loose snow and sink completely out of sight. In such a circumstance they would be quite helpless if a predator were near.

In April 1929, three ewes and three rams were rescued at Igloo Creek in a weak condition due to deep snows. One of the ewes was too far gone and died in a few days. After the sheep had been kept a while at Igloo and regained some strength they were taken to Headquarters. They were later moved to the University of Alaska where they were kept for several years.

Ranger John Rumohr stated that in the spring of 1932 when the snows were deep he had seen 30 old rams on the low banks bordering East Fork River south of the road. Later he found five of them dead, untouched by any animal.

The deep snows have played an important role in the control of the sheep population. Probably the larger the population the more drastically are the sheep affected. A large population quickly devours the food available on ridge tops and they must all go down to the deeper snow in search of food. A smaller number might find sufficient food on the ridge tops to pull them through a severe winter. This is an example of one of the regulatory devices of Nature.

The Rut

Observations on the rutting of the mountain sheep were limited because during much of the rutting period I was checking on wolf movements along the north boundary, and snow made it difficult to cover much territory. The time of the beginning and ending of the rut was not learned. The rutting was probably early because the following spring the lambing period was early.

On November 15, 1940, I noted that the rut was in progress. On Polychrome Pass one old ram and 2 younger rams were with 5 ewes, and another old ram was very active rounding up a flock of 5 ewes. The following day considerable rutting activity was noted on East Fork River. A large ram herding 4 ewes walked a short distance to a large ram in possession of 4 other ewes. After standing around about 10 minutes he returned to his own harem just over the rise. One old ram had 7 ewes, and another was lying near a single ewe. Eleven large rams, 3 young rams, and 12 ewes were scattered over a small area observed. Some of the rams were not in possession of any ewes at the time.

Sheldon (1930) in 1907 found active rutting from about the middle of November to the middle of December. He noted several encounters between rams, and makes the following comments on the rut (p. 240): "Friendly rams remained among the ewes, serving them indifferently. The fights always occurred when stranger rams attempted to enter the bands. At times new rams intruded among the ewes and shared their privileges without apparent objection on the part of rams already with the band."

The rutting activities of the white

sheep are apparently very similar to those of the Rocky Mountain bighorn. One ram may serve a number of females and two or more rams may serve the same one. The ewes come in heat over a period of about a month, but judging from the lambing time it appears that most ewes come in heat during a two-week period.

Gestation Period

In 1907 Sheldon (1930) observed the sheep actively rutting in the latter half of November and early December. How late in December active rutting took place is not known because Sheldon's observation of the sheep was interrupted by trips after moose. The following spring he observed the first lamb on May 25. In 1940 I observed sheep rutting in mid-November but do not have data on the duration of the rut. The first lamb the following spring was seen on May 8. The gestation period seems to be between 5½ and 6 months.

Lambs

PRECOCITY

Lambs a day or two old, so small that they can walk erect under their mothers, clamber up cliffs so precipitous that even the mothers can scarcely find footing. Not only can the lambs climb but they possess unexpected endurance. Frequently very young lambs were seen hurrying after their mothers from near the base of a mountain to its very top without resting.

The travels of a captive lamb illustrate the endurance they possess. On May 13, 1928, a ranger brought to his cabin a lamb only a few hours old. It soon became a pet and amused itself by leaping about on the chairs and beds. It followed him and his cabin mate around all day and showed no desire to join the other sheep that were sometimes in view. It was raised with a bottle, on powdered milk. When only 2½ weeks old it followed the men for 30 miles over rough ground and through glacial streams. When a month old it became wet in a glacial stream when overheated and died of "pneumonia."

It surprised me when I first observed the speed of the lambs on relatively smooth slopes. On May 28, 1939, when most lambs were a little less than 2 weeks old, I came suddenly upon six or seven ewes and their lambs. My nearness gave them quite a fright, causing them to flee full speed down a gentle slope to the bottom of a draw and up the other side. Although the ewes galloped at full speed, the lambs kept up easily and at times two or three of them even forged out ahead. Upon reaching the bottom of the ravine and starting up the other side, the lambs seemed to have an advantage and "flowed" smoothly up the slope ahead of the ewes. When the group finally stopped to look around the lambs were as fresh as ever, and seemed anxious to make another run. This precocity of the lambs is, of course, of great value in avoiding wolves and other predators.

EWE-LAMB RELATIONSHIPS

During the first week or two, ewes that have lambs are especially wary. When approached, they hurry off with their lambs, often crossing over to another ridge so as to leave a draw between them and the intruder, or else climb high into rough cliffs. Before the lambs are born these same ewes might be rather tame, and as the lambs become older they again become tame.

Figure 30: Two ewes with their lambs which are only a few days old. As young lambs remain close to their mothers, eagles have little opportunity to attack them successfully. [*Polychrome Pass, June 3, 1939.*]

The lamb is not left lying alone as are the young of deer, elk, and antelope. It remains near its mother, pressing so close to her at times when traveling that it may be almost under her. When resting, the young lamb usually lies against the mother or only a few feet away. This habit of remaining close to the mother is of high protective value should eagles attack.

When the lambs are young, several mothers often congregate in rough cliffs. In such places a few of the ewes may remain with the lambs and the others go out 300 or 400 yards to feed on the gentler slopes. On May 26, 1939, 13 lambs were seen frisking about on some cliffs on a rocky dike on East Fork. With the lambs were 6 ewes—3 lying down just above the group, and 3 standing in their midst. While I watched, one of the ewes

moved off 150 yards and commenced to feed. A lamb followed her 10 yards, then dashed back to the others. One lamb ventured out alone 20 yards and a ewe at once became alert and moved four or five steps in its direction, whereupon the lamb hastened back to the group. Four ewes were feeding on a slope about 250 yards away from the cliffs. Occasionally one of them would look toward the lamb assemblage. From a point about a quarter of a mile away three ewes stopped feeding and came galloping across the face of a shale slope, calling loudly as they came. When they were still about 100 yards away two lambs

galloped forth, each joining its mother and nursing at once. The third ewe did not have such an alert or hungry lamb, for she smelled of five lambs in the top group, then walked briskly down to the rest of the lambs 15 yards below where she found her lamb, who belatedly came forth to nurse.

On June 5, 1939, there were 22 lambs on this outcrop of cliffs and an equal number of ewes were seen, but some of the ewes were feeding 200 or 300 yards away. One lamb on this

Figure 31: **Ewes with lambs frequently congregate on rugged cliffs when the lambs are young. When they go off to feed, some ewes leave their lambs in the care of other females.** [*Polychrome Pass, May 1939.*]

Figure 32: A ewe and her lamb in the fall of the year. [*Polychrome Pass, September 7, 1939.*]

occasion ran out about 60 yards to meet its mother and to nurse.

On July 12, 1939, a band of 52 ewes, lambs, and yearlings were feeding on some rather gentle slopes of Cathedral Mountain. The mothers frequently moved off 100 or 200 yards from their lambs which remained in a scattered group resting on the slide rock. Five or six ewes at different times stopped feeding and called loudly. Each time, a lamb would recognize the call of its mother and gallop down to nurse, usually for a minute or less. The sheep were quite noisy at times, the ewes "ba-a-ing" loudly, and the lambs answering more softly.

The tendency for ewes with lambs to bunch up is probably a natural outcome of their all having the same inclination to remain in the rougher terrain. Later there is more intermingling of the ewes with lambs and those without lambs.

Lost Lambs

When a ewe leaves her lamb in a group and goes off to feed she may lose her lamb temporarily. On June 7, 1940, I climbed to a small group of ewes and lambs which ran out of sight when I neared them. I was standing on the spot where they had been, when a ewe, which I had passed on the way up, approached me calling. There was not much

Figure 33: A band of ewes, lambs, and yearlings on Cathedral Mountain. Vegetation on the loose slide rock is dominantly dryas. A wide variety of herbs and some grass are also present. Note how some of the lambs remain close to their mothers. Others rested alone while their mothers fed lower on the slope. [*July 12, 1939.*]

room on the cliff where I stood so, when the ewe was seven or eight paces from me, I stepped to one side to let her pass. She was evidently perturbed at finding me where her lamb had been, for she called loudly and came toward me with lowered head which she jerked threateningly upward as though to hook me with her sharp horns. After I had warded her off with my tripod she stood for a few moments calling, then hurried in the general direction the others had taken and no doubt soon found her lamb, for the band had not gone far.

On June 13, 1941, I spent some time on Igloo Mountain observing about 50 ewes and 30 lambs. At first most of them were in a broad grassy basin. One ewe nursed her lamb, walked off 200 yards and fed with another ewe for an hour, never once looking toward the lamb. As I climbed, a small group of ewes and lambs, including the lamb of one of the two feeding ewes, moved upward, feeding higher and higher until they were out of my view. When the two ewes rejoined the main band, which in the meantime had moved 200 or 300 yards to some cliffs, one of them found her lamb at once but the other was not so fortunate. Calling continually, she searched through the entire band, duplicating her visits to some parts of it, but still with no success. She finally recrossed a gulch and climbed in the direction taken by the little group with which her lamb had gone. She showed good sense, and no doubt soon found her lamb. After the sheep had rested in the cliffs for some time another ewe suddenly commenced to call at short intervals from a prominent point. The ewe had called a long time when two lambs came forth from a large crevice in a rock a short distance away where they had been lying. The ewe saw them emerge and hurried to join them. One of them was her lamb and it immediately nursed.

PLAY

The lambs play a great deal, romping with speed and agility. Sometimes they butt each other, coming together after a 2- or 3-foot charge. Occasionally a ewe may play with the lambs. Once one played with three lambs, dashing after one, then another. A lamb would leave its mother, get chased, and rush back again to its parent. Apparently it was great fun.

Figure 34: Ewe, lamb, and yearling plow through a September snow. [*Igloo Creek, September 19, 1939.*]

WEANING

Lambs begin to nibble grass when they are a week or 10 days old, and as the summer progresses they feed more and more on green vegetation. Some of the lambs continue nursing well into the winter and I have seen them when they were yearlings trying to nurse. Sheldon (1930, p. 278) reports lambs nursing in February. Weaning is not an abrupt process. I expect that long before nursing is discontinued the lambs could get along very well without this nourishment. The lambs remain with the mother a year and sometimes in the case of female yearlings, another 6 months. It is not uncommon to see a ewe, yearling, and lamb together during the summer and fall. Often yearlings, 2-year-olds, and other youngish animals, along with barren ewes, may be found traveling together. In the spring male yearlings sometimes join the bands of rams.

Relation with Animals of Minor Importance

SNOW BUNTINGS COMPETE FOR FOOD

On October 11, 1939, a flock of about 100 snow buntings (*Plectrophenax n. nivalis*) in a high pass were feeding on the heads of *Calamagrostis*. A large patch had been quite thoroughly threshed by the snowbirds. Here was competition for food between animals which we would not expect to have much relation with one another. I had noticed that the sheep had been feeding extensively on these same grass heads which stuck up through the snow. *Calamagrostis* is a very common grass, so there is much of it available. But it so happened that the particular patch eaten by the snow buntings was up high where it would be available to the sheep when deep snows covered that growing lower down. However, this competition is no doubt extremely slight and is mentioned here only to show an unexpected relationship.

WOLVERINE AND SHEEP

The wolverine (*Gulo hylæus*) is widely distributed in the mountains in the park. In 1940 and 1941, after a period of low numbers, it was reported to be on the increase. It was reported as abundant in 1927 and 1928, but I do not know when the numbers became reduced. Wolverine abundance may have been correlated with the high sheep population when much carrion was undoubtedly available. Several times I found the scattered remnants of a sheep carcass which had been investigated by a wolverine, but I have no authentic data on the relationship of the wolverine to the sheep. One circumstance cited as evidence that wolverines prey on sheep is that the former are commonly found on mountains near timber line where mountain sheep range. However, it should be added that wolverines occupy a similar habitat in areas where there are no sheep. The number killed by wolverines under any circumstance is undoubtedly small.

LYNX AND SHEEP

During the period of this study the lynx (*Lynx canadensis canadensis*) was very scarce; not a single track was noted.

In the winter of 1907–8, Sheldon (1930) found two sheep which had been killed by lynxes. One of the victims was a 2-year-old ewe and the other a ram, about 2 years old. In each case, the predator had lain in ambush, leaped from above to the sheep's back, and had bitten the sheep around the eyes.

Ordinarily the lynx feeds on snowshoe hares, but when the hares become scarce during the ebb of their cycle, the lynxes are left without this usual food supply. Under these conditions, they are forced to seek other food. The fact that hares were scarce in 1907–8 probably accounts for the lynxes hunting sheep at that time. After the hares disappear the lynxes also go into a decline, so their predation on sheep is only for a short time and probably is never a serious factor.

In 1927 there was a big die-off in the hare population. It is reported that hares were unusually abundant in the fore part of the summer but that during August they became extremely scarce. It is interesting to note that in the Superintendent's reports for 1927 and 1928 the lynx was reported increasing. Possibly due to the hare die-off, lynxes began to wander about in search of food, especially in the sheep hills, and so were noticeable. After 1928 there is

no mention of lynx abundance, and they have been scarce since that time.

COYOTE AND SHEEP

The coyote, *Canis latrans incolatus* Hall, was so scarce in the sheep hills that there was no opportunity to study its possible effect on the mountain sheep population. I saw a coyote on three occasions at Sable Pass, and once near Teklanika Canyon. These were the only coyotes seen during the three summers and one winter which I spent in the field. In recent years they have been reported somewhat common near the northeast corner of the park where snowshoe hares have been present in moderate numbers; and in the low country north of the park a few are reported by trappers.

The coyote frequently has been listed as a destroyer of the Rocky Mountain bighorn in the States, but the few studies which have been made indicate that the coyote is not a serious enemy of these sheep. In Yellowstone National Park I found no evidence of coyote predation on the bighorn, not even in summer when lambs in some situations seemed to be vulnerable to coyote attack, and coyotes on these summer ranges were common (Murie, 1941). Other investigators in Yellowstone National Park have not found evidence that coyotes were a serious menace to the mountain sheep. In Jackson Hole, Wyo., coyotes were suspected of destroying many lambs, but investigations indicated that the lambs were dying of disease rather than coyote predation (Honess and Frost, 1942). In a study of a prospering bighorn herd in Colorado, where coyotes are common in the sheep area, known losses from coyotes were small (Spencer, 1943).

The scarcity of coyotes in the sheep hills in Mount McKinley National Park may indicate that they cannot find sufficient food there. Of course, in the absence of the wolf, there would be more weak sheep and carrion available to them, and more coyotes might then occupy the sheep hills. For this food supply they probably cannot compete with the wolf, since they are a weaker predator in respect to the sheep. It is possible that the wolf tends to drive out the coyote by attacking it, although both species once occupied the same general territory in the States. I am inclined to believe that the main reason that the coyotes are not in the sheep hills is that the staple rodent supply is more abundant in the lower country. Possibly coyote distribution is much influenced by the distribution of snowshoe hares also.

In 1932, when many sheep were succumbing to the unusually severe winter conditions and others were weakened by them, it is reported that some sheep were killed by coyotes. Such predation on weakened animals is not at all unlikely, but the information at hand does not indicate any consistent or serious predation by coyotes on the mountain sheep herds of Mount McKinley National Park.

GOLDEN EAGLE AND SHEEP

Lambs Well Protected When Young.—Charles Sheldon (1930, p. 33) writes as follows concerning his observations on relationships between the golden eagle (*Aquila chrysaëtos canadensis*) and white sheep: "While hunting sheep in the Yukon Territory during the two previous years, and also while in the Alaska Range that summer, I observed the relations between golden eagles and sheep, not once noticing any antagonism between them—but only complete indifference." On May 25, 1908, Sheldon saw an eagle swooping at some ewes and lambs and states that it was the first time that he had seen an eagle swoop at sheep or even notice them. The ewes stood over their lambs to protect them from the eagle. On June 7, 1908, Sheldon (1930, p. 382) reports seeing eagles swooping at lambs but states that no capture was made, and that the ewes were very watchful when the eagle was near. An eagle's nest was nearby and near it Sheldon found lamb remains. He shot the eagle on the nest and found the stomach filled with ground squirrel remains. He concluded that it was probably true that the eagles preyed heavily on young lambs but that they were seldom molested by them after they were a month old. The evidence to support his conclusions that "it is undoubtedly true that golden eagles take a heavy toll of the newly born lambs" was his observation of some eagles swooping at

ewes and lambs, and the lamb remains found at the one nest. His other experiences had caused him to conclude that eagles did not molest the sheep.

Joseph S. Dixon (1938) spent the summers of 1926 and 1932 making wildlife studies in Mount McKinley National Park. In 1932 he made observations on four eagle nests but found no fresh lamb remains in or below them. However, it should be taken into account that the lamb crop that year was very poor, so fewer lambs than usual were available to the eagles. Dixon (1938, p. 46) draws the following conclusion concerning eagle-sheep relationships: "Our experience in the region both in 1926 and in 1932 indicated that during these two seasons lambs were rarely taken by eagles, which were found to live chiefly upon ground squirrels and marmots."

Former Ranger Lee Swisher stated that he had visited several eagle nests but never found any lamb remains at them.

I have observed eagles dive at ewes and lambs, but such maneuvers do not necessarily gage the degree of eagle predation on lambs. Eagles have also been observed swooping low over grizzlies and wolves at times when there was no intent of predation. Once an eagle dove at an adult wolf which was standing near its den. About a dozen times the eagle swooped, barely avoiding the wolf which each time jumped into the air and snapped at it. The eagle turned upward at the right moment to avoid the leap, and apparently was enjoying the game.

During the first few weeks the lamb remains close to its mother. It usually lies down beside her when she is resting, follows her closely, or lies down only a few feet away while she feeds. In traveling, the young lamb often presses close to its mother's side, sometimes appearing to be partially under her. The lamb is near its mother except when left with other lambs, usually on a cliff, while she goes off a short distance to feed. But at such times the group of lambs is watched over by some of the ewes. So, at the time when the lamb would be most vulnerable to eagle attack, it is generally well protected, giving to the eagle little opportunity to prey on it.

Figure 35: "Come on!"

After a few weeks the lambs move about with more freedom and gambol over the meadows in little groups. Judging from their behavior, they are not greatly worried about eagles after 3 or 4 weeks. In late June and early July I have seen eagles fly low over lambs, separated from their mothers, without attempting to strike and without alarming them. Throughout the summer the eagle may occasionally dip downward at the sheep just as it does at other animals. On September 10 an eagle swooped low over two ewes and a lamb, giving them quite a start. It sailed close over them several times, calling as it passed. But after the first start the sheep seemed unafraid.

Few Lamb Remains Found at Nests.— Upon examining the vicinity of seven unoccupied eagle nests only one lamb was found. It was a skull which lay in slide rock some distance below the nest.

At the 13 occupied nests examined during the three summers, one old leg bone of a lamb was found below one nest and at another were the remains of two recently eaten lambs. The presence of two lambs at the one nest may have indicated that this particular pair of eagles was more inclined to attack lambs than were other eagles, or else were more fortunate in finding unprotected lambs, or possibly dead ones. One eagle was seen feeding upon a lamb which appeared to be about a week old. At 11 of the 13 nests occupied no lamb remains, old or recent, were found.

It should be pointed out that in some cases the eagle eggs do not hatch until the lambs are 3 or 4 weeks old and probably past the danger period. In these instances possibly lambs would not be taken to the nest. However, they might be brought to favorite perches near the nest where some of them would have been found if any significant number had been consumed.

During the period that the eaglets are at the nest the parent birds bring to it twigs of birch, heather, or willow, probably to cover debris accumulating in it. In one nest an eagle had brought several mats of shed sheep hair, the presence of which could easily have been misconstrued as evidence of predation.

Eagle Pellets Contain Few Lamb Remains.—During each of the three summers spent on the study, substantial numbers of eagle pellets were collected from perches and nests in the lambing area. The pellets give a fairly good index of the food habits of the eagle during these 3 years. Of 632 pellets analyzed, only 6 (2 each year) contained remains of lambs. This low incidence of lamb in the eagle pellets strongly corroborates the evidence from nest examinations and general observations. The considerable information available supports the conclusion that only occasionally does an eagle feed upon a lamb. Such lambs may have been carrion or may have been killed by the eagles. If killed, they may have been healthy, weak, or deserted. In any event, whatever eagle predation exists, it is apparent that it would have no appreciable effect on the mountain sheep population.

In two recent publications dealing with the Rocky Mountain bighorn, both of which have come to my attention since the above was written, no evidence was found that eagles preyed on bighorn. In a study of sheep in Wyoming (Honess and Frost, 1942, p. 56) the following statement on bighorn-golden eagle relationships is given: "To date no case of predation by eagles has been seen by a Survey member nor has one been reported for the Crystal Creek area." These eagles were living mainly on jack rabbits and ground squirrels. In a Colorado bighorn study (Spencer, 1943, p. 9) the following statement is made: "The hunting and food habits of the golden eagles in the Tarryall Mountains were observed and studied with a great deal of interest because many people consider these birds responsible for considerable predation on the bighorn sheep, especially the lambs. During the entire period of this study, not a single eagle was observed to attack or molest the bighorn sheep in any manner. The sheep were not disturbed when eagles came close to them, although the ewes were alert even when a raven came close to the lambing grounds." A study of the food habits of eagles nesting close to the lambing grounds showed that they were feeding mainly on prairie dogs. As many as seven prairie dogs were observed in the nest at one time.

Wolf and Sheep

Some of the information on the relationships between sheep and wolves that we should like to have would take several years to gather. Ideally, one should study the sheep in the absence of wolves for a few years, and in the presence of them for a similar length of time, and in several localities. What is not evident in one area is often readily revealed in another. But some data have been obtained which reveal their method of hunting mountain sheep, the sections of the sheep population suffering the heaviest mortality from them, and the lamb crop and its survival in the presence of wolves.

Significant observations on the actions of these animals in Mount McKinley National Park, and the wolf's hunting methods (with a number of hunting incidents) are enumerated below. This is followed by data regarding the portion of the white sheep population most subject to predation, based on examination of 829 sheep remains. Finally, consideration is given to the lamb crop and the question of its survival.

REACTION OF SHEEP TO WOLVES

A few incidents are here related which do not involve hunting but show how sheep and wolves sometimes behave when they meet.

On May 7, 1940, a scattered band of sheep moved slowly from one ridge to an adjoining one. The movement was so definite and consistent that I suspected the sheep were moving away from danger. A little later I peered into the draw below the ridge first occupied by the sheep and saw a black wolf investigating some cleanly picked sheep bones. The sheep had simply preferred to have a ridge between themselves and the wolf.

While eating breakfast at the Igloo cabin on May 3, 1940, a wolf was heard howling nearby. Stepping outside, we noticed three alert rams, each on a pinnacle, peering intently below them. They continued to watch for some time, evidently keeping an eye on the wolf we had heard. They apparently felt safe where they were even though the wolf was directly below them.

On August 3, 1940, Dr. Ira N. Gabrielson and I watched a black wolf trot leisurely down a short draw on the ridge opposite us and descend the narrow stream bed bordered by steep slopes. Two rams on the slope below us watched the wolf, and when it trotted out of their sight they moved to a point where they could again see it. Seven other rams grazing a short distance from the two paused but briefly to look. The wolf stopped a few times to look up at the rams, but continued on its way until finally hidden by a ridge. The rams and the wolf had shown a definite interest in one another, but that was all. The wolf probably examines all sheep in the hope of discovering an opportunity for a successful hunt, and the sheep keep alert to the movements of the wolf so as not to be taken by surprise or at a disadvantage.

On June 29, 1941, about 60 ewes and lambs on the south side of Sable Mountain all moved up the slope 100 yards or more and stood with their attention centered on the terrain between us. A search with the field glasses revealed a gray wolf loping westward between me and the sheep, about a half mile from them. Some of the sheep soon began to feed, others watched until the wolf had passed. The day was dark and rainy, so that the wolf, whose legs and lower sides had become wet from the brush, was unusually hard to see, yet the sheep had quickly discovered it.

Former Ranger Lee Swisher told me that he had seen six wolves suddenly come close to seven rams feeding out on some flats at Stony Creek. The rams bunched up and the wolves stopped 100 yards away. They made no move toward the rams, which, still bunched up, walked slowly and stiffly toward the cliffs. The slow gait was maintained until the cliffs were almost reached, then the rams broke into a gallop and quickly ascended the rocky slope. The incident seems to indicate that a wolf may to some extent recognize the ability of the rams to defend themselves. The wolves on this occasion may not have been hungry; possibly under other circumstances they at least would have made some attempt to single out one of the rams.

On one occasion Mr. Swisher said he let a sled dog chase some rams. They turned and faced the dog with lowered horns. After thus threatening the dog the rams started up the slope, and when the dog followed, they again turned on him. This incident is indicative of what the seven rams in the above incident would have done had they been attacked.

A dog belonging to Joe Quigley, a miner, is said to have escaped one night from his camp in the sheep hills. The dog returned 2 or 3 days later all battered. Sometime following this event when the team was driven up to some sheep carcasses this dog was not at all anxious to approach them. The inference drawn was that the bruises the dog had suffered during his absence had been administered by a sheep.

On June 19, 1939, 22 ewes and lambs were seen feeding among the cliffs a short distance above four resting wolves, one of which was lying only about 200 yards away. The sheep had already become accustomed to the presence of the wolves when I saw them for they grazed unconcernedly. Their confidence was probably due to the proximity of exceptionally rugged cliffs to which they could quickly retreat should the wolves attack.

On August 3, 1939, a band of 20 sheep ran up the slope of a ridge bordering East Fork River. A little later a wolf climbed the slope, making slow progress. Twelve sheep watched from a point up the ridge, three from some rocks not far from where the wolf went over the ridge top. Two eagles swooped at the wolf a number of times, continuing to do so after the wolf was out of my view so that its progress could be followed by watching the eagles. The sheep

quickly resumed grazing. They had not moved far from the wolf but had watched to see what it was up to.

HUNTING INCIDENTS

Five Wolves on a Hunt.—On the morning of September 15, 1939, five wolves (the East Fork band) trotted along the road to Igloo Mountain, then climbed half way up the slope which was covered with several inches of snow, and followed a contour level. I saw them a mile beyond Igloo cabin; three were traveling loosely together, a little ahead of the other two. Sometimes they were strung out, 50 yards or more apart. Generally they trotted, but occasionally broke into a spirited gallop as though overflowing with excess energy. Opposite me they descended to a low point, and the two gray wolves which had brought up the rear dropped to the creek bottom. A black one rounded a point and came upon three rams which it chased. The animals then went out of sight, but in a few minutes the wolf returned and I saw the rams descend another ridge and cross Igloo Creek. As they climbed a low ridge on Cathedral Mountain they kept looking back. When crossing the creek bottom they had not been far from the two gray ones which traveled a mile up the creek and then returned to join the others.

After chasing the three rams, the black wolf joined another black and the dark gray female and all moved up the slope. One of them stopped to howl, possibly a call to the two grays on the creek bottom. These two turned back about that time and later joined the others.

On a pinnacle of a high ridge stood a ewe peering down at the approaching wolves. She watched a long time but moved away while the hunters were still far off. The wolves went out of view on the other side of this same ridge. Later I saw some ewes farther along the ridge looking steadfastly to the west in the direction the wolves had last taken, and beyond these ewes there were three more gazing intently in the same direction. The sheep had fled to the highest points and were definitely cautious and concerned because of the presence of the wolves, which seemed to be coursing over the hills hoping to surprise a sheep at a disadvantage. The day before, I had seen a lamb in this vicinity with a front leg injured so severely it was not used. Such a cripple would not last long if found by these wolves. The habit of cruising far in his hunting gives the wolf opportunity to find weak sheep over a large range and to come upon undisturbed sheep, some of which he may find in a vulnerable location.

Sheldon Observes Wolves Hunting.— Charles Sheldon (1930, p. 315) tells of following trails of two separate wolves in March and finding that on nine occasions they had chased sheep unsuccessfully. On eight of the chases they had descended on the sheep from above. He said that the sheep in the region had become badly frightened and that "most of them kept very high." So many unsuccessful hunts suggests that these two wolves were testing out each band, hoping eventually to find a weakened animal or gain some advantage. It appears that wolves chase many sheep unsuccessfully and that their persistence weeds out the weaker ones.

Sheep Escape a Wolf.—On October 7, 1939, I saw the track of a single wolf that had crossed Igloo Creek and then had moved up the slope of Igloo Mountain. After following the creek about a mile, I saw two ewes and two lambs on a spur of Igloo Mountain watching a black wolf which was curled up on a prominent knoll on the next ridge about 200 yards to the west. The two ears of the wolf were turned in my direction, so in order not to alarm him I walked along as though I had not seen him until I was out of his view. Then I doubled back close to the bank and ascended the draw toward him. But when I came near the knoll he was gone and the sheep were lying down.

After back-tracking the wolf, I deduced that its actions were as follows: After crossing Igloo Creek, it climbed part way up the mountain. It followed a trail along a contour at the edge of some spruces, near the point where a wolf (perhaps the same one) had surprised a lamb among the spruces a few days before. The wolf crossed some draws and small spur ridges and arrived at a ridge on the other side of which the four sheep were feeding in a broad swale. The wolf climbed up the ridge, out of sight of the sheep, for 50 yards, so that he was slightly above them. He then advanced slowly until within 150 yards of the two ewes and two lambs and then galloped down the slope toward the sheep. The latter had escaped to the next ridge from which they were watching the wolf when I first saw them. The wolf chased up the slope after them but a short distance and then continued westward to the next ridge where he curled up in the snow. This time the sheep had the advantage and escaped It is significant that they did not run far beyond the wolf; apparently they were confident that they were safe since above them was much rugged country. The behavior of the sheep is definitely conditioned by the terrain they are in and their position in relation to the enemy. Approach a sheep from above and he feels insecure and hurries away. A sheep on a flat is much more wary and timid than one in rugged country.

A Lamb Surprised in Woods.—On October 4, 1939, by back-tracking a wolf I found a freshly killed male lamb. The tracks in the snow plainly told this story: The wolf was following a trail along the side of Igloo Mountain within the edge of the uppermost timber. Suddenly he came upon five or six sheep feeding among the trees. Those above the trail ran up the slope to safety, but a lamb which had been feeding farthest down found itself cut off from a possible escape to the top of the mountain and was forced to run on a con-

tour in the direction from which the wolf had just come. In chasing the lamb, the wolf was able to gallop back over the easy trail it had been traveling and thus keep above the lamb which was endeavoring to swing upward in front of it. The lamb traveled parallel to the trail over terrain broken up by the heads of numerous small draws. In one place he veered slightly upward until he came to the trail, but he must have been hard pressed for he again turned downward and now the wolf followed him directly. The chase led gradually down the slope, the lamb apparently keeping as much altitude as possible in the hope of gaining the rocks above. But he was too hard pressed to cut upward ahead of the wolf. Finally he descended a steep gravel bank to the creek bottom, crossed and recrossed the creek, started up the steep gravel bank at an angle, and returned to the creek where he was killed. He ran slightly more than a half mile before being overtaken. This time the wolf had the advantage not only of coming suddenly upon the lamb from above, but also in having a trail to follow while the victim was galloping over rough brushy country. If the sheep had been feeding in the open as they almost always do, the wolf probably would have been discovered before he was so close to them. This is an example of a situation where the predator gains an unexpected advantage.

Two Old Ewes Killed.—On October 5, 1939, there were fresh tracks of foxes, wolves, and a grizzly in the snow, all leading up a small cliff-bordered stream flowing into Igloo Creek. It was evident that there was some special attraction near at hand. My companion and I proceeded cautiously and soon saw a wolf run off. Farther on we saw a lone lamb in the rocks. An eagle flew away, and then we noticed a grizzly chewing on the skull of a ewe. I hoped the bear would leave the skull so I could get the age of the animal and examine the teeth, but when he finally moved off and climbed a low promontory the skull was in his jaws. He soon finished crunching the bones, then climbed to a rock a little higher where he lay down and after a few minutes went to sleep. The skull was a little close to the bear to retrieve, but that difficulty was solved by two magpies which, in fighting over it, knocked it off the cliff to a spot where we could safely get it. After considerable searching we found the skull of a second ewe on a grassy knoll a few feet above the gravel bed.

The two ewes had been killed 50 yards apart. Nothing now remained except a few large pieces of hide, some legs, entrails, stomach contents, and the two broken-up skulls. The assemblage of animals gathered at the kill may have consumed all the meat, or perhaps the wolves and foxes had cached what was not eaten.

The snow on the ground made it easy to back-track the chase. The story was simple. The two ewes and a lamb had been feeding on *Equisetum* on a broad moist swale not far above

Igloo Creek. (The stomach contents of the two victims were made up mainly of *Equisetum*.) The wolves had been following along the mountain slope at a level slightly higher than that where the sheep fed. Coming over a rise they spied the sheep feeding in the swale 150 yards below them. The tracks showed that the wolves did not start running until they were within 75 yards of the sheep. The latter galloped out of the swale and ran downward at an angle toward Igloo Creek which they crossed after descending a steep dirt bank about 100 feet high. The wolves followed directly after the sheep, but, instead of running among the large rocks in the canyon stream bed as the sheep had done, they ran alongside the rocks on the smoother ground covered with a sod of *Dryas*. A distance of 250 yards up this creek the two ewes were captured just before reaching some cliffs. The lamb escaped, and, as stated, we saw it alone a short distance above the carcasses. The ewes had run a half mile before the capture.

These two ewes had lived almost their full span of life, for one was 10 years old and the other was 11. The teeth had been used up, and they were no longer pushing out to compensate for wear on the surfaces. In one ewe the tooth surface was worn below the gum. In the other a molar had worn a "crease" in the palate. They were weak animals, less able to escape the wolves than a lamb, which itself is apparently in a vulnerable age class.

Old sheep killed by wolves.—Late in the winter of 1940, in the rugged draws on the north side of the Outside Range between Savage and Sanctuary Rivers, Harold Herning and Frank Glaser found much sheep hair, bloody pieces of hide, and wolf tracks, all indicating that the wolves had been killing sheep. No skull remains were found. The bones were no doubt hidden in the deep snow which filled the bottom of the draws. After the snow disappeared I hunted in these draws for skull remains. The skulls of four recently killed sheep and the hair remains of a fifth sheep were found. Two of the skulls were those of 11-year-old rams, one of a 12-year-old ram, and the other of a 12-year-old ewe. Here the wolves had apparently eliminated some animals doomed soon to die of old age.

Old Ram Chased Down Bluff.—On January 7, 1941, the tracks of five or six wolves were seen along the road toward Savage Canyon. A short distance above the canyon the wolves abruptly left the road and climbed a gentle slope to the top of an isolated rocky promontory. They chased a lone ram down its steep side to the creek bottom where I found remnants of hide, as well as the stomach contents and the skull. Apparently the wolves had seen the ram on this isolated bluff and had turned aside to circle behind him and cut off his retreat to high ground. He was 12 years old, past his prime, a weak animal. The method employed in capturing him—that of coming down from above and driving him down the slope—seems to be a typical hunting technique.

Ewe Captured.—On March 12, 1941, Ranger Raymond McIntyre found the carcass of a recently killed 6-year-old ewe at Toklat River. Tracks showed that two wolves had chased her down a steep slope and

Figure 36: **The lamb made it!**

captured her at its base. The usual manner of hunting, coming down on the sheep from above, had been practiced. There was no indication of necrosis on the skull. Of course the sheep may have had some other weakness not apparent in the skull.

Lamb Captured in Migration.—On September 28, 1939, Mrs. John Howard of Lignite, Alaska, saw three sheep, at least one of which was a lamb, crossing a valley a mile or more wide, between the "outside" mountain range and the mountains up Savage River. A little later she saw two of the sheep galloping up the long gentle slope leading to the "outside" range. The lamb ran down the slope and disappeared in a draw. The two sheep continued to the ridge, but she did not see the lamb again. Later in the morning she saw two black wolves near the spot where the lamb had disappeared. One of these crossed the flat to the south and returned, followed by two pups. Mr. John Howard investigated and found the lamb partly eaten and saw the wolves nearby. Sheep are especially vulnerable when crossing valleys, for wolves can outrun them on the flats.

Sheep easily avoid a Lone Wolf.— Some observations made in the sheep hills bordering East Fork River on the morning of May 26, 1939, show that, on a relatively steep smooth slope, sheep are easily able to avoid a single wolf. With a companion I had climbed to the top of a ridge from which I had a view of some snow-free ridges on the other side of a small creek below me. I noticed a band of sheep resting on a smooth slope, slanting at about a 40° angle or less. While I watched, the sheep bunched up and ran off to one side about 30 yards. Through the glasses I saw a gray wolf a short distance above. He loped toward them and the band split in two, some going upward around the wolf, the others circling below it. When the wolf stopped, so did the sheep, only 30 or 40 yards from him. He galloped after the lower band, which ran downward and then circled, easily eluding him. Compared to the sheep, the wolf appeared awkward. After a few more sallies the wolf lay down, with feet stretched out in front. One band lay down about 70 yards above him, the other about 50 yards below him. Only one sheep in the lower band faced him; the others as usual faced in various directions. One sheep fed a little before lying down. The lower group consisted of five ewes, one yearling, and three rams. In the upper group were four ewes, four yearlings, one 2-year-old, and two rams. All rested for 1 hour. Then the wolf again chased the lower band, which evaded him as before by running in a small circle around him. A flurry of snow then obscured my view. When it cleared a few minutes later, the wolf was disappearing in a draw and the sheep were grouped on the ridge above him.

In a short time he reappeared and slowly worked his way down the ridge to the creek bottom. Nine ewes, each with a lamb, appeared on the ridge near the draw which the wolf had just left. The lambs were at the time only a week or so old but still they apparently had been able to avoid the wolf. The utter lack of fear exhibited by these sheep is quite significant, indicating that a single wolf can easily be avoided on a slope.

Sheep avoids sled dog.—The behavior of a ram chased by Charles Sheldon's dog is somewhat similar to the behavior of the sheep attacked by the lone wolf. Sheldon (1930, pp. 368, 369) gives an excellent description of the event, as follows:

At that moment, a short distance ahead, I saw a three-year-old ram crossing the divide toward Intermediate Mountain. Here was a rare opportunity to observe the actions of a sheep when chased by a wolf. Quickly taking the pack off *Silas*, I led him ahead to within a hundred yards of the ram, which had not yet seen us. *Silas* dashed at him full speed. The ram rushed toward the slope a hundred yards ahead. For a hundred feet the dog did not gain, but during the next hundred he gained at least twenty-five feet, and during the next hundred he was gaining rapidly. Although the dog was clearly the speedier of the two, I thought that the ram deliberately slackened his speed as he neared the slope, which was sharply inclined. The dog was not forty feet behind when the ram reached it. Up he went bounding for forty feet; then turned and coolly stood a moment to watch the dog, which was running up at almost equal speed. Then the ram turned and rather leisurely ran upward a hundred feet, gaining somewhat on the dog, who by that time was going much more slowly. This time the ram stood and watched until the dog was within twenty feet, then easily ran up another hundred feet and again stood and looked at the dog. *Silas*, however, was now only trotting and his panting showed that he could not run upward any more. Yet he followed the ram, which kept repeating the same tactics, never losing sight of the progress of the dog, until within a hundred feet of the crest, where a sharp projecting rock rose almost perpendicularly from the slope. The ram quickly climbed to the top and looked down at the dog, which now was only walking. Nor did he move when *Silas* reached a point fifty feet below him. Then the two stood looking at each other. Finally the dog turned and trotted back to us.

Not once, after the first burst of speed on the level, did the ram show any fright. When he knew he could reach the slope he was deliberate in every movement, and after reaching it he coolly played with the eager dog. After each advance, however, he was careful to turn and watch his pursuer. He seemed to know that the dog would soon give up the chase, yet I believe he did not credit *Silas* with the persistence he had displayed. The actions of the ram led me to suspect that a wolf would not have followed more than a few feet up such a slope, its experience, which *Silas* lacked, having taught it that a sheep could easily escape when once headed upward on a steep slope."

Highway an Advantage to Wolf.—At several places, notably Igloo Creek, Polychrome Pass, Toklat, and a stretch opposite Mount Eielson, the automobile highway passes through winter sheep range. In some places it cuts into the heart of the more rugged cliffs utilized by sheep. The highway favors the wolves in three ways. First, it gives them an easy trail along the entire winter range so that they can move more readily from one part of it to another. Second, it gives the wolves easy access into the cliffs themselves; they need not make a laborious climb to get among the sheep but can follow a smooth easy grade. Finally, each blind corner in the road—and there are many of them—is a hazard, for the sudden appearance of a wolf may give the sheep no time to escape. This is especially true when the sheep are bedded down on the road.

A ewe, lamb, and yearling were killed on the road at Mile 67 on September 20, 1939. The victims had been bedded down near a sharp corner. Four or five wolves had come around the corner, made a dash at the sheep and captured them before they had run more than a few yards.

Several sheep killed by wolves were found on and beside the road at Polychrome Pass and at Igloo Creek.

While the road affects seriously only a small part of the winter range, it is a good illustration of disruption of natural wildlife relationships by an artificial intrusion.

Diseased Yearlings Captured.—In a high draw three yearlings were found which had been killed in early spring. Two of them showed necrotic lesions on the mandibles so probably were not in good health when captured by the wolves.

Lone Diseased Ewe Captured in Cliffs.— On the snow-covered mountain slope above our cabin at Igloo Creek on the morning of October 14, 1939, I saw a fox feeding, and on the same slope a raven and some magpies. Obviously there was a fresh kill. We climbed to the spot and found the remains of a 9-year-old ewe affected with severe necrosis of the jaws. The horns were short and stubby, perhaps indicative of a prolonged chronic ailment. The teeth were irregularly worn. Some were long and sharp, others were worn down to the gum. One tooth was shoved entirely out of line. A premolar was broken off. An upper premolar was bent outward. Cavities along the teeth were packed with vegetation. The animal had been alone on the cliff (sick animals are often solitary). Five wolves had killed the sheep on a steep slope below some cliffs. They had crushed the skull and eaten the brains. After feeding, the wolves had curled up in the snow on a rocky spur to one side of the remains, about a quarter of a mile from the cabin. There were seven beds, but only five of them were coated with ice. In the other two beds the wolves had not lain long. Although the ewe had been found in rough country under conditions favorable for escape, she was so weak that the wolves were able to make the capture.

DISCUSSION OF WOLF HUNTING HABITS

A few generalizations can be made concerning the methods of the wolves in hunting Dall sheep. It is my impression that the wolves course over the hills in search of vulnerable animals. Many bands seem to be chased, given a trial, and if no advantage is gained or weak animals discovered, the wolves travel on to chase other bands until an advantage can be seized. The sheep may be vulnerable because of their poor physical condition, due to old age, disease, or winter hardships. Sheep

Figure 37: The sheep feeding on this gentle terrain have access to nearby slide rock and cliffs for safety. [*Igloo Creek, June 13, 1939.*]

in their first year also seem to be specially susceptible to the rigors of winter. The animals may be vulnerable because of the situation in which they are surprised. If discovered out on the flats the sheep may be overtaken before gaining safety in the cliffs. If weak animals were in the band, their speed and endurance would be less than that of the strong and they would naturally be the first victims.

A wolf hunting alone apparently can be avoided easily by healthy sheep on a slope. The lone wolf must find his animals at a decided disadvantage to be successful. Two or more wolves can hunt with much more efficiency. The method is to get above a sheep and force it to run down, for a sheep running upward can quickly outdistance the wolves and escape. Sheep on somewhat isolated bluffs where space for maneuvering is limited are in danger of having their upward retreat cut off and of being forced to run down to the bottom. A number of carcasses were found in situations suggesting that the sheep had been chased down bluffs of limited extent. My general observations indicate that weak animals are the ones most likely to be found in such vulnerable situations. They often lack the energy to climb to more safe retreats to rest. Where the wolf population is relatively large its pressure on the sheep is probably proportionately great, eliminating a high percentage of weak animals and capturing more strong animals surprised at a disadvantage.

Do the Wolves Prey Mainly Upon the Weak Sheep?

THE PROBLEM

In any predation problem involving big game it becomes important to learn if the predation is indiscriminate or if it affects primarily certain classes of vulnerable animals such as those past their prime, those weakened by disease, or the young. The possibility is generally recognized that through predation the weak and diseased are eliminated, so that in the long run what seems so harmful may be beneficial to the species. Perhaps the evolution of the mountain sheep has progressed to a point where it is in equilibrium with its environment but still requires environmental stresses such as the wolf to maintain this equilibrium.

To learn what kind of predation is taking place and what effect it may be having on the population we must have information on the type of animals killed. There are difficulties in collecting quantitative data of this kind. First, it is hard to find a sufficient number of remains to give significant results. Furthermore, in the majority of cases, it cannot be

determined whether or not the animal was killed by the predator. There are some criteria that can be used, but usually the evidence is missing. Bloody pieces of hide are a strong indication of wolf predation, but this evidence in time disappears. The location of remains may be significant. If they are found beneath a bluff the chances are that wolves maneuvered the animal down to the bottom, but one cannot be certain of the cause of death in these cases. After knowing the immediate cause of death one must ascertain the condition of the animal when it died.

The number of deaths which may be assigned definitely to the predator are usually a small proportion of the total. Such being the case, one must often broaden the scope of the study from determining the type of animal being killed by predators to the type of animal dying from all causes. If the results are highly uniform, then significant conclusions on predation can still be secured. For instance, if it is found that most of the animals were weak at the time of death, then it may be concluded that whatever predation there was affected the weak part of the population.

Fortunately not all evidence is destroyed when the animal is eaten. The age of the animal can be closely determined from the horns and, in the absence of horns, the age group can be approximated from the teeth. The condition of the animal in a great many cases can also be determined from the condition of the teeth and skull bones.

Although I began to find an occasional sheep skull and other remains after arriving in the field, it did not seem possible that enough skulls could be gathered for any quantitative treatment of them. But as I continued my excursions among the sheep hills I began to learn where carcasses were most likely to be found. Small tributary streams having narrow bars bounded by steep cliffs were the most likely localities. Skulls were found in all sorts of situations, but the best places were along these narrow streams, especially beneath the steep rocky slopes. About this time I acquired the services of two boys from a Civilian Conservation Corps camp. With their help I made a methodical search along all the likely streams and draws. Of course those streams in the best winter ranges yielded the greatest returns. In going up the narrow streams and draws one of us would walk in the center, and the other two would follow the sides of the stream bed. In places where numerous small draws cut up a ridge we sometimes would each follow a draw. There was competition to find the most skulls and the "best" ones, which were those showing the most severe diseased conditions. In time we exhausted all the more likely places and discontinued the organized search. But whenever it did not interfere with my main objective I usually followed a course over the hills where chances were best for finding skulls. Thus I continued to pick up a few of them in all sorts of locations.

When a wolf or bear (or both, as often happens) has finished with a sheep carcass there usually is not much left. Sometimes there may be only a few patches of hair or some broken pieces of long bones. But usually the entire skull or parts of it are present in the vicinity. The skull may be considerably damaged, so that the vital parts, the tooth rows and horns, are broken apart and scattered. Wolves often eat away the entire face and most of the brain case of even an old ram, and, if the wolves fail to chew up the skull, a grizzly may come along and do so. When the skull, or parts of it, were not found at the location of the largest bunch of hair or hide, or at the stomach contents, hunting proceeded farther and farther away, and we were often repaid for our perseverance. Knolls above the kill, where it was likely a wolf or fox would go to chew on a bone, were examined, often with success. I was always anxious to find at least one horn for age determination and, if possible, all the tooth rows, because sometimes two or three tooth rows might look normal and the fourth show a severe condition of necrosis. Hence it was desirable to have as many of the tooth rows as possible. In many cases only a single mandible could be found. Although the bones last a long time, the horns soften up when they remain on the ground where it is damp and disintegrate relatively soon. Many large ram horns found lying in the grass were so soft where they were in contact with the ground that their surfaces could be scraped away with one's finger.

The mandibles and upper tooth rows of the ram skulls, and sometimes the entire skull and horns, were collected. Generally the skulls of the ewes were saved, since their horns and horn cores are not large and can be more easily carried.

A total of 829 sheep skulls were gathered. All but about 100 of them were picked up the first year in the field.

Some of the skulls were recent in origin; others were of animals which had died several years ago. Those designated as recent were, for the most part, those of animals that had died since 1938, though some probably dated back to 1937. The accumulation of old skulls would be considerably greater if there were not so much movement of gravel in the stream beds during the spring freshets and summer rainstorms. Skulls lying in the loose gravel bars are usually carried away or completely covered with gravel. Fortunately, those on the grassy benches or the sides of the stream beds remain findable for a much longer period of time.

DETERMINATION OF AGE

The Dall sheep is an exceptionally suitable species for a study of predation because the age of the animals can be established rather accurately from an examination of the horns, and, in the absence of the horns, from the teeth, although the teeth, except

Figure 38: These two horns show the variation in size in Dall sheep rams. The small horn is from a 7-year-old animal; the large horn is from a 4-year-old animal.

for the first 2 years, are less satisfactory as an index of age.

Each year the horn makes its main growth during the summer at a time when much nutritive food is available. During the winter there is scarcely any growth in the horn, probably due to the poorer quality of feed available. This season leaves its mark upon the horn which in the early years may be a slight swelling, and in later years a groove, more accentuated than other wrinkles on the horn. Thus the annual growths in the horn made in summer are divided by annual growth rings formed in winter.

The horns of a captive ram which I examined did not follow the development sequence found in the wild, probably because there was not such a marked seasonal change in its food. The ram was 5½ years old, yet had eight definite growth rings.

The base of the horn increases in circumference with age and the length of the annual growth increases the first 2 or 3 years, after which it tends to become shorter each year. The annual horn growths of a 12-year-old ram, measured on the outside of the curve, were as follows: First year, ½ inch; second year, 8⅞ inches; third year, 6¾ inches; fourth year, 4¼ inches; fifth year, 3 inches; sixth year, 3⅛ inches; seventh year, 2½ inches; eighth year, 2⅞ inches; ninth year, 2⅛ inches; tenth year, 1⅜ inches; eleventh year, 1 inch; twelfth year, ⅞ inch. The circumference of this horn was 9¾ inches at end of fourth year; 11 inches at end of fifth year; 11½ inches at end of seventh year; and 12⅝ inches at end of twelfth year.

The growth rings in ewes fall very close together in an old animal so that in the case of some horns it is difficult to get an accurate age determination. However, it is felt that the age can be rather accurately established in most cases.

In determining age one must carefully examine the tip of a horn to learn how much of the first year's growth remains. The first year's growth is often worn almost completely away so that the annual

Figure 39: **Two ewes, one showing diverging type of horns, the other, the more usual type, in which the horns diverge very little. [*Cathedral Mountain, July 12, 1939.*]**

growth ring at the end of the first year merges with the tip of the horn. Figure 40 shows the horns of a 6-year-old ewe in which the first year's growth is present in the upper horn and worn down to the annual ring in the lower horn. When the first year's growth of horn is worn away there is generally some indication of the annual growth ring at the tip. A clue to the amount of horn missing can be gained by examining the pattern of the annual growths present below the tip. Usually there is not much difficulty, however, in interpreting the tips of the horns.

When the horns are not found the age can be approximated by an examination of the teeth. The yearlings and 2-year-olds and probably the 3-year-olds can be definitely identified from the tooth formula.

A male lamb which died September 28 had horns an inch long. The premolars were fully erupted, and the first molars were just erupting. The lower molars were a trifle more advanced than the upper molars. There was scarcely any noticeable wear on the incisors.

In a yearling the first molars were fully functioning and showed some wear. There was no sign of the second and third molars.

In a 2-year-old female which died on June 8 the first and second molars were fully erupted, but the third molar was not. All the deciduous premolars except the third upper premolar on one side were shed. The first and second permanent incisors were functioning. The third and fourth deciduous incisors were still present.

In animals older than 2 or 3 years the approximate age can be determined by breaking away part of the jawbone and measuring the length of the molar teeth. In a young animal the roots of the molars reach to the base of the jawbone (Figure) 41. As the surface of the tooth wears away the tooth pushes upward, becoming shorter with age. The third molar in a 5-year-old measured 53 mm. in length; a 10-year-old, 17 mm.; and in a 13-year-old ram, 10 mm. There is considerable individual variation in the length of the molars so that one cannot allocate a skull to annual age classes without the possibility of some error. For instance, an 8-year-old sheep may have as long molars as a 7-year-old animal, or there may be an overlapping of 2 years. However, for deciding whether the animal should

Figure 40: Horns of a 6-year-old ewe. The upper one retains on the tip the entire first year's growth. Only an indication of the growth ring in the lower horn can be seen near the tip. The horns of many ewes and some rams have tips as in the lower specimen; this fact must be considered in determining age.

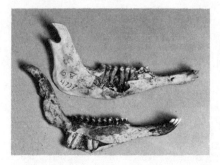

Figure 41: The lower mandible is that of a 4-year-old ram and the upper one that of a 10-year-old ram. The bone has been chipped away to expose the molars. The last two molars of the 4-year-old animal retain practically their full length, while those of the 10-year-old animal are almost worn away. As the surface wears down the tooth pushes upward until, after 10 or 11 years, little of it remains.

be placed in the old-age group or in the next younger group this method of age determination is very useful.

DETERMINATION OF SEX

The sex can be easily determined from the horns. The rams have large curved horns and heavy horn cores; the ewes have small, slightly curved horns and small horn cores. In the absence of horns, the sexes of sheep older than about 2 years can be determined by examining the mandibles. In the ewes, these bones, just anterior to the first premolars, are noticeably more slender than those of the rams.

SEGREGATION OF SHEEP REMAINS INTO CLASSES

Old Age Class.—An animal definitely past its prime becomes a member of the weaker part of the herd. Therefore, an old-age group can be segregated and placed in the category of weak animals which in this case are doomed to a relatively early death even in the absence of predation.

The oldest ram found was 14 years of age, and there were three of this age. Only one ram was found in the 13-year class. Many rams belonged to the 10-, 11-, and 12-year-old classes. It appears that few rams live beyond 12 years of age. When a ram is 11 or 12 years old, little remains of his teeth. Tooth wear indicates that an 11- or 12-year-old ram has about completed his life span, and animals a year or two younger are probably beginning to fail.

Four females were 12 years old; these were the oldest recorded. The growth rings on a female horn are close together when the animal is old so that a person could make a mistake of a year or so. Consequently what is recorded as a 12-year-old might possibly be a 13-year-old, but, even so, there were still only four in this class. While there are many rams in the 12-year age class, there are very few ewes reaching that age and there also are few ewes in the 11-year age class. These data on longevity strongly suggest that the ewes are shorter lived than the rams. Since few ewes pass the 10-year mark, it appears justifiable to place those 9 years or older in the old-age class. Possibly the old age group for rams should begin at 10 years, but in the interest of uniformity and simplicity they have been classified the same as the ewes. So far as these calculations are concerned, if old age for rams should be construed as beginning at 10 years, the change would not greatly alter the final figures.

Two- to 8-Year Class—Animals in Their Prime.—Animals from 2 to 8 years old are placed in one age group. It is thought that such animals are in their prime and are least vulnerable to predation and other factors of the environment.

Lambs and Yearlings.—The young are arbitrarily called lambs until about October, and after that until they are about 15 months old, they are called yearlings. Most yearling skulls are from animals less than a year old, from animals which have died during the winter.

It is difficult to evaluate the vulnerability of the young sheep. Everything indicates that it is probably correct to call them weaker than healthy animals in the 2- to 8-year class. But lambs a few weeks old are not easily captured by wolves, so one would expect that after a few months they would be able to avoid wolves almost as well as the sheep in their prime. Perhaps the young sheep, up until early winter, are not especially vulnerable, although they would be handicapped by inexperience. But as the winter advances and the quality of the food decreases they perhaps become progressively weaker just as the adult sheep become progressively thinner. Because they are still growing they may be more affected by hardship than older animals. Many

of course succumb to winter hardship, and apparently the strength of the healthier ones is somewhat reduced so they become less able to avoid the wolf. It is thought that on the average the term *weak* may be applicable to the yearlings so they have all been so classified in discussing the skull data.

Diseased and Injured Animals.—Actinomycosis: The ungulates in general seem to be subject to certain diseases which cause lesions in the mouth. These lesions may be caused by at least three diseases—actinomycosis, necrotic stomatitis, and actinobacillosis. The mortality in necrotic stomatitis is high, while in the other two diseases the infection is often chronic. There is some confusion as to the causative organisms, but actinomycosis and necrotic stomatitis appear to be caused by two species of a ray fungus, respectively known as *Actinomyces bovis* and *Actinomyces necrophorus*. Actinobacillosis is caused by another organism of similar appearance called *Actinobacillus lignierisi*. Tissues in the mouth cavity are invaded by these organisms through abrasions such as are sometimes caused by coarse vegetation or grass awns. The lesions may occur on the tongue, hard palate, cheeks, and near the teeth, especially around the molariform teeth. Actinomycosis is thought to generally affect the bone, and the other two diseases the soft tissues. But there is a possibility that necrotic stomatitis, when chronic, also affects the bones. Much more bacteriological research is needed, especially among game animals, to solve all aspects of the diseases. An affected bone may be eaten away or enlarged and made spongy. If the bone is necrosed near the teeth, which is frequently the case, the latter may drop out or grow at abnormal angles. When a tooth drops out, the one that opposed it usually becomes elongated and sometimes spikelike because it meets no surface or strikes only the side of another tooth. Mandibles affected are sometimes bent or so necrosed that they are almost severed. The mechanical difficulties in the teeth resulting from the disease are frequently considerable, and since mastication is so important to an ungulate, any injury to the teeth becomes a serious handicap.

In Jackson Hole, Wyo., where much work has been done on the diseases of elk, a large percentage of the elk deaths during the winter and spring months are due to necrotic stomatitis (O. J. Murie, 1930). The calves in their first winter are the principal victims, but older animals also succumb. In the acute form of the disease the animals do not last long and die while still in good flesh. In older animals the disease at times seems to take on a chronic form, causing severe necrosis of the bone. Whether more than one disease is present has not been completely worked out, but further bacteriological studies are in progress.

Evidence of what appears to be necrotic stomatitis has been found among wildlife in many localities, and in deer, antelope, moose, caribou, and Rocky Mountain bighorn, as well as in elk. W. Reid Blair (1907) reported finding actinomycosis in a severe stage in three of six skulls of *Ovis stonei* from the Stikine River country in northern British Columbia.

In the Jackson Hole elk herds the disease seems to take a regular toll. Some years it is a little more serious than others and it especially affects the calves. The young are especially susceptible, possibly because their mouths are tender and easily pierced by vegetation and the wounds in the mouth attending changes in the dentition afford a portal of entry. Although usually the incidence of the disease is not high and (according to paleontological evidence) has afflicted the animals for thousands of years, still it is important in the consideration of game losses and should be recognized in order that losses can be better analyzed.

The extensive necrosis and exostosis found in the skulls indicates that many sheep in Mount McKinley National Park are affected by either necrotic stomatitis or actinomycosis. Because of the bone conditions the disease has been referred to as actinomycosis although bacteriological studies would be necessary to determine the organism. Evidence of the disease was found in animals of all ages. Many had undoubtedly recovered but had been left handicapped with misshapen jaws and loose and missing teeth. Some yearling skulls were found which showed strong evidence of the disease. But since it appears that yearlings often die before the bone is affected, especially from necrotic stomatitis, many yearlings afflicted with it would not show evidence of its presence.

In the present study, animals whose skulls showed *severe* conditions of necrosis or exostosis were considered weakened by disease. Those with but slight necrosis were considered healthy. Figures 42 to 45 show malformations resulting from necrosis and exostosis.

Some animals affected by these bone changes would be unable to masticate the food well enough or fast enough. Others would have chronic infections in the mouth when the food kept the sores open and irritated. Still others would be ailing with the disease itself. All but six of the diseased sheep listed in Tables 4 to 7 inclusive (pp. 122 and 123) are those showing severe cases of what has been referred to as actinomycosis.

Some notes on domestic sheep are suggestive of the effect of old age and missing teeth, or what is termed a "broken mouth" by sheepmen. O. J. Murie recently discussed the matter with some experienced, successful sheepmen. One of them said that after ewes are 6 years old they do not survive well on the desert in winter even though they have all their teeth. Teeth generally "spread" and fall out after the sixth year and the losses then become heavier. After the ewes are 6 years old they are disposed of or put on a ranch. It was also stated that the sheep probably never exceed 14 years of age. Another sheepman thought that ewes win-

tered fairly well at 7 years and stated that sometimes he had wintered them on the desert even as old as 9 years. But all of the sheepmen agreed that as soon as a ewe had missing teeth her chances for wintering successfully on the desert dropped considerably.

C. L. Forsling (1924, pp. 20–21), in his studies, has come to similar conclusions concerning the effect of age and tooth deterioration on domestic sheep. He writes: "Ewes should not be kept in the range bands after they are 5 or 6 years of age. Animals that have reached that age are less able to rustle forage than are younger sheep. Furthermore, if such animals are held over, they may not be in condition to mother lambs or survive a critical period. The condition of the teeth usually determines whether or not ewes will do well on range feed. Gummers, or animals with few or irregular teeth, are of doubtful value on the range and should be dis-

Figure 42: The upper specimen shows one side of the palate of an 8-year-old ewe partially destroyed by necrosis. The lower specimen shows necrosis and exostosis near the angle of the mandible of an old ewe.

Figure 43: Mandibles of a 9-year-old ram. The one on the left, greatly enlarged and porous, shows an extreme diseased condition.

Tables 4 to 7 (pp. 122 and 123). Diseases other than actinomycosis cannot be determined from the remains, so that some sheep designated as non-diseased might possibly have been diseased.

Malformed Teeth: Four animals were found in which there was severe malocclusion of the molariform teeth which seemed not to have been caused by disease. The teeth did not occlude normally, on a flat surface, but slid past each other wearing off the sides of the teeth and forming sharp-edged chisel-shaped tooth rows. As an example, in one case the lower molars were worn on the outer side, and the upper molars on the inner side, resulting in beveled teeth. On one specimen the lower molars slid past the uppers and gouged into the upper gum. Since these animals were undoubtedly greatly handicapped they are listed as diseased.

posed of." These conclusions correlate tooth deterioration with loss in stamina, suggesting that a similar correlation may exist in mountain sheep.

Severe necrosis may only be present in one mandible or along one tooth row, and the remainder of the tooth rows may appear quite normal. On a few occasions two or three of the tooth rows were picked up, none showing at the most more than slight necrosis, and the presence of severe necrosis was not known until the last tooth row was found. Since a number of skulls are represented by only one or two tooth rows, some cases of severe necrosis were no doubt missed so that the incidence of the disease was probably higher than recorded in

Figure 44: Lower jaw bones of Dall sheep. The mandible at top shows necrosis on the side of the molars. The mandible below is bent due to necrosis, and a tooth is missing. The side of the molar behind the cavity has become worn, thus making a sharp-pointed tooth.

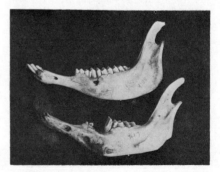

Lungworm: The lungs of one yearling were examined and were found to contain many adults, larvae, and eggs of a nematode which probably belonged to *Protostrongylus* or a related form (Goble and Murie, 1942). Further information is not available as to the incidence of lungworm or its effect on the sheep. No animals are listed as being weakened by heavy lungworm infestation.

Injuries: A yearling was found weakened by internal infections apparently resulting from a fall. A 2-year-old died as the result of a snag puncturing the abdominal cavity. These are listed as diseased.

DISCUSSION OF SKULL DATA

The wolf preys mainly on the weak sheep.—For an analysis of the data, the skulls have been placed in two groups according to the years in which the sheep died. One group is composed of skulls from animals which died between 1937 and 1941. The skulls in this group, at the time I found them, showed that the sheep had died in the last year or two. They had died during winters which were not severe, perhaps a little more favorable to them than the average winter. A crust on the snow in 1940 compensated somewhat for the otherwise favorable nature of these winters. This recent material portrays the current picture and is thought to present more accurate information of sheep mortality in the presence of wolves than does the old material.

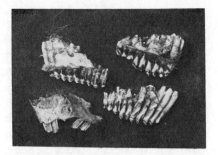

Figure 45: Teeth of Dall sheep. The specimen at lower left shows crooked teeth resulting from necrosis and missing molars. The other three tooth rows show an abnormal condition in a 6-year-old ewe. The upper and lower molars should have met on the flat surface. Instead they slid past each other, wearing the sides so that sharp chisel-edges resulted. The white areas on the sides of the teeth indicate wear.

The second group of skulls includes those from sheep which died previous to about 1937. These skulls are segregated because the winter conditions when the animals died are not so well known. A few of these skulls may date back to the days before the wolf became abundant, and an unknown number of them, no doubt, date back to the severe winters of 1929 and 1932 when apparently in many cases the strong and the weak alike succumbed in the deep snows. Skulls of sheep which died in 1929 and 1932 would probably show a lower proportion of old age and diseased animals and a greater number of healthy animals in their prime years. More of these old skulls are incomplete, several being represented by single mandibles. The incomplete skulls would be less likely to show presence of disease.

The data for each group are presented in Tables 4 to 7 (pp. 122 and 123). In Tables 4 and 6 the number of sheep in yearly age classes is given, and in Tables 5 and 7 the yearly age classes are combined into the 2- to 8-year and old-age classes. The lamb and yearling data are the same in both sets of tables. Besides being segregated according to ages, the skulls are segregated according to sex and the presence or absence of severely diseased skull bones.

In the recent material there are 221 skulls. Of these, 153, or 69 percent, are in the old-age class; 21, or 9 percent, are in the 2- to 8-year class but are severely diseased; 10, or 4 per-

TABLE 4.—*Skulls of 221 sheep which died between about 1937 and 1941, showing number of diseased and nondiseased animals in annual age classes. Sexes of lambs and yearlings are combined.*

Sex, age, and condition	Lambs	Year-lings	Age in years														Total
			2	3	4	5	6	7	8	9	10	11	12	13	14	Mis-cella-neous [1]	
Both sexes, no disease noted [2]	8	22	---	---	---	---	---	---	---	---	---	---	---	---	---	-------	30
Both sexes, diseased [2]	---	7	---	---	---	---	---	---	---	---	---	---	---	---	---	-------	7
Ewe, no disease noted [3]	---	---	1	1	---	1	3	---	2	16	10	6	2	---	---	22	64
Ewe, diseased [3]	---	---	1	---	1	2	3	3	2	6	2	2	---	---	---	5	27
Ram, no disease noted [3]	---	---	1	---	---	---	---	---	1	4	11	20	28	---	1	2	68
Ram, diseased [3]	---	---	---	---	1	2	---	5	1	6	2	4	2	---	1	1	25
Total	---	---	---	---	---	---	---	---	---	---	---	---	---	---	---	-------	221

[1] Exact age not known because of absence of horns, but teeth showed that the animals were 9 years of age or older.
[2] Lambs and yearlings.
[3] Adults.

TABLE 5.—*Skulls of 221 sheep which died between about 1937 and 1941, segregated into four age groups. Skulls showing serious diseased conditions are segregated from the normal ones.*

Sex, age, and condition	Lambs	Year-lings	2 to 8 years	9 years or older	Total
Both sexes, not diseased [1]	8	22	-------	-------	30
Both sexes, diseased [1]	---	7	-------	-------	7
Ewe, no disease noted [2]	---	---	8	56	64
Ewe, diseased [2]	---	---	12	15	27
Ram, no disease noted [2]	---	---	2	66	68
Ram, diseased [2]	---	---	9	16	25
Total	---	---	-------	-------	221

[1] Lambs and yearlings.
[2] Adults.

TABLE 6.—*Skulls of 608 sheep which died before about 1937, showing number of diseased and nondiseased animals in annual age classes. Sexes of lambs and yearlings are combined since usually they are not known.*

Sex, age, and condition	Lambs	Year-lings	2	3	4	5	6	7	8	9	10	11	12	13	14	Miscellaneous[1]	Total
Both sexes, not diseased[2]	33	85															118
Both sexes diseased[2]		3															3
Ewe, no disease noted[3]			1	2	2	8	6	9	11	14	20	4	2			56	135
Ewe, diseased[3]			2		2	4	14	8	7	6	8	1				26	78
Ram, no disease noted[3]			4	5	3	2	3	4	15	11	33	42	28	1	1	49	201
Ram, diseased[3]				1		4	5	8	9	16	6	9	2			13	73
Total																	608

[1] Exact age not known because of absence of horns, but teeth showed that the animals were 9 years of age or older.
[2] Lambs and yearlings.
[3] Adults.

TABLE 7.—*The skulls of 608 sheep which died previous to about 1937 are here segregated into four age groups. Skulls showing serious diseased conditions are segregated from the normal ones.*

Sex, age, and condition	Lambs	Year-lings	2 to 8 years	9 years and older	Total
Both sexes, no disease noted[1]	33	85			118
Both sexes, diseased[1]		3			3
Ewe, no disease noted[2]			39	96	135
Ewe, diseased[2]			37	41	78
Ram, no disease noted[2]			36	165	201
Ram, diseased[2]			27	46	73
Total					608

[1] Lambs and yearlings.
[2] Adults.

cent, are in the 2- to 8-year class and show no sign of disease; 7, or 3 percent, are from yearlings showing signs of disease; 22, or 10 percent, are yearlings with no evidence of disease; and 8, or 3 percent, are lambs.

In the old material there are 608 skulls. Of these, 348, or 57 percent, are in the old-age group; 64, or 10 percent, are in the 2- to 8-year class but are severely diseased; 75, or 12 percent, are in the 2- to 8-year class, without evidence of disease; 3, or .5 percent, are from yearlings and show signs of disease; 85, or 14 percent, are from yearlings with no indication of disease; 33, or 5 percent, are lambs.

These figures are remarkable because they show that most of the sheep dying belonged to the weak classes. In the absence of predation we would expect the mortality to be distributed among the weak, namely the old, diseased, and the young, but in the presence of a strong predator like the wolf, known to be preying extensively on the sheep, it is interesting that so few animals in their prime are represented. In the recent material 211 skulls, or 95 percent, were from the weak classes in the population and only 10 skulls, or 5 percent, were from sheep in their prime which were healthy. In the old material 533, or 88 percent, of the skulls were from weak animals and only 12 percent from sheep in their prime which were healthy so far as known. The figures for both groups are roughly similar, considering the fact that in many cases disease or weakness would not be shown in bony remains.

It is significant that the incidence of disease is much higher in the skulls of the 2- to 8-year class than in the old-age class. In the recent material, 68 percent of the skulls in the 2- to 8-year class show evidence of serious disease, as compared with only 20 percent in the old-age class. In the old material 46 percent of the skulls in the 2- to 8-year class show a serious diseased condition, while diseased animals comprised only 25 percent in the old-age group. From these figures it becomes apparent that disease is an important factor in the predation among sheep in the 2- to 8-year group and not so important in the old-age group. In the old-age group the effects of age in weakening the animal are, as we would expect, more important than disease.

It is of interest to note that in the old-age group the youngest animals (those 9 years old) are the part of the group showing the highest incidence of disease. This is logical, for the older the animals become the more their weakness would be due to old age rather than disease. In the old material the incidence of disease is significantly higher among the ewes than among the rams. Possibly more of the ram skulls date back to the hard winters of 1929 and 1932 when conditions were so severe that disease was not an important factor. This is suggested as an explanation, since ram skulls would be expected to last longer than ewe skulls. In the recent material there is no appreciable sexual difference in disease incidence.

It is not known how many of the dead sheep the wolves killed but it is certain that they killed many of them. The figures on mortality are so uniform in showing that the weak are the ones dying that for our purpose we do not need to know how many of the sheep the wolf killed. Because of the high percentage of vulnerable sheep (95 percent in recent material) among the dead, whatever predation was done by the wolf would necessarily mainly affect the weak sheep. Perhaps we should expect the wolf predation to operate in this way, for prey-predator relationships between large animals, where numbers are limited, must be rather finely adjusted from the standpoint of species preservation. The wolf and the mountain sheep have existed together under conditions largely as at present for a long time, so that an adjustment between them, whereby both can survive, should be expected. If the wolf were powerful enough to capture the sheep indiscriminately it would long ago have exterminated them, for the law of diminishing returns in the case of mountain sheep hunting would not begin to function very early in the process of decrease. The adjustment seems to be such that, in mountain habitat having a considerable degree of ruggedness and extent, the wolf catches a few of the strong animals but preys mainly on the weak members of the population. This conclusion is supported by the skull data, by field observations of animals killed, and by the hunting methods whereby successive bands of sheep are chased by the wolf as he courses over the hills.

Some related big game-predator findings.—Many persons have taken for granted that the large predators prey upon the weak. It seemed to them that such a relationship was necessary and logical. Others have been skeptical of any such relationship, feeling that the predators preyed indiscriminately on all classes. Actual data have been scarce because quantitative information bearing on this type of problem is difficult to accumulate. I have not reviewed the literature thoroughly, but two reports of studies bearing on the subject have come to my attention. Some observations which I made on the coyote and mule deer in Yellow-

stone National Park are pertinent. Because these three studies are closely related to the wolf-sheep problem, the conclusions will be given briefly.

Some such relationship as exists among the wolves and Dall sheep also appeared to exist between the mule deer and the coyote in Yellowstone National Park (Murie, 1941). On the better ranges, where the fawns were strong, there was little predation, but on a poor range, where the fawns weakened as the winter progressed, they were preyed upon by coyotes. The prey-predator adjustment seemed to be one in which, as a rule, the prey was not taken until somewhat weakened. Here the predation affected mainly the weak and tended to quicken the adjustment of the deer population to the condition of the range.

Sigurd F. Olson (1938, p. 335) in a paper on the wolves of northern Minnesota, stated: "Long investigation indicates that the great majority of the killings are of old, diseased, or crippled animals. Such purely salvage killings are assuredly not detrimental to either deer or moose, for without the constant elimination of the unfit the breeding stock would suffer."

In an interesting study of the cougar, Hibben (1937), reported on 11 deer which had been killed by c o u g a r s. He wrote as follows concerning these deer: "The fact that, of the 11 deer, all showed abnormal or subnormal characteristics is almost too complete to be mere coincidence, and yet coincidence it may be. It is certainly logical that not every deer which a lion kills is subnormal. It is claimed by many hunters that the lion kills at will and takes the best as he chooses. The evidence does not seem to support this theory. Often in the course of this survey lions have been followed which were hunting. These were obviously trying to catch any deer they could. One lion made at least three attempts before he secured a meal. When he did get one, it was * * * the one with the abscessed neck. * * * All the evidence seems to show that the lion catches what he can, and that may very well be the less ablebodied prey." Here again is a large predator whose ability to catch its prey seems to be closely adjusted to the ability of the prey to escape.

Effect of Wolf Predation on the Sheep as a Species

It is with a definite hesitancy that I venture to discuss the effects of the wolf on the sheep as a species because of the limitation of knowledge in this general field. The ways in which Nature operates to bring about or retain transformations are still rather mysterious. There is much that we do not know about fundamental premises, such as the causes of variations, which may alter our evaluation of other phases of the problem such as the elimination of the weak. The mathematics involve figures which we do not have, and a time element which

we cannot evaluate. A slight trend which may to us seem insignificant could perhaps be of major importance if given a long enough period in which to operate. But because the elimination of the weak at once suggests a racial benefit, it seems apropos to consider briefly predation on the different categories of weak sheep as it may have a bearing on natural selection.

The predation on the old-age group would seem to have little bearing on evolution since the old animals are the successful ones, and their characteristics have already been lodged in many offspring. But some sheep may become infirm at an earlier age than others and be the first of their age group to be eliminated by the wolf. The stronger would continue breeding another year or two and impart their characteristics to a few additional offspring. So even in this group predation may result in a greater number of offspring from the stronger sheep. Characters such as tooth durability related to longevity would be favorably affected. The influence of the wolf might be less than appears, however, for some of the early infirm sheep taken by the wolves probably would have been ineffective breeders. But at least a tendency for selection of favorable characters may be conceded.

Predation on sheep weak from disease may operate in more than one way. Disease itself may be a selective agency, eliminating the weak; or it may affect the strong and weak alike. Actinomycosis is perhaps generally acquired by both the weak and the strong, depending somewhat upon the character of the food and accidental presence of abrasions in the mouth. If the wolf should prey on a sheep which has recovered from this disease but has become weakened because of resulting malformed dentition, the wolf may be eliminating an animal with inherent resistance and thus neutralize the selective influence of the disease. If a sheep acquired the disease because of faulty tooth succession and recovered, then the wolf, in destroying it, would be a selective agent. Thus the wolf's predation on the diseased sheep might operate to neutralize selection due to disease or at times might be eradicating some unfit animals. On the whole, it seems that predation on the diseased animals is not an important factor in natural selection or survival.

Because losses are so heavy among sheep in their first year, it is among these animals that selection would have to operate to be most effective. But unfortunately it is in this group that the information regarding natural selection is least complete, because the condition of the yearlings at the time of death is usually not known. The most important information not obtainable from an examination of the skulls is the general physical vigor and strength of the yearlings that are taken by wolves. No doubt the crippled yearlings and those diseased are eliminated early. In the fall most of the lambs are probably strong enough to avoid the wolf under favorable circumstances.

As winter progresses all the sheep become thinner and some of the growing yearlings succumb, regardless of predation. Other yearlings weaken but would probably recover in the absence of the wolf. It is in the predation on these yearlings that the wolf would have an important bearing on selection.

The percentages involved in these theoretical calculations are not known. Some day we may find a situation which will give us this information on yearlings. The escape ability of the yearlings is so high that we would expect eventually to find the wolves largely eliminating the less able individuals in this group.

It is difficult to arrive at a definite conclusion. Many of the deaths among the sheep have no bearing on selection so far as wolf activities are concerned; others seem to be significant in this respect. What effect predation on the weak has on a species is hard for any of us to say in the present state of our knowledge. It may be much greater than many believe; it may be important along with other forces in Nature. If the sheep has reached a point, at least for the time being, in equilibrium with its environment, then perhaps the wolf is important in maintaining the type.

We have been discussing the elimination of the weak and the part this activity may play in the maintenance or improvement of the species. There is another angle that could be considered. As an evolutionary force the wolf may function most effectively by causing the sheep to dwell in a rocky habitat.

I have tried in this brief review to point out that much of the wolf predation, although affecting the weak sheep, may have a limited selective value, but that there is a tendency toward some selection which may be of great importance to the sheep as a species.

Classified Counts of the Mountain Sheep

Basic for our understanding of mountain sheep ecology is a knowledge of lamb and yearling numbers. Knowing the size of the lamb crop, we can then determine by later counts what time of the year losses among them occurred. The counts in the spring give the size of the new lamb crop, and also the number of yearlings which have survived the winter, a critical period in the sheep's life. The counts in late summer and fall show the lamb survival during the summer.

The lamb and yearling ratios are obtained by comparing the lamb and yearling counts with the ewe counts, rather than with the combined counts of ewes and rams. The basic relationship desired is the ratio of young to the ewes. Knowing the number of rams, the ratio can then be given in terms of the entire population if desired. The figures would be more precise if the 2-year-old ewes could be consistently segregated. Small errors in yearling ratios in the fall counts may be present because

at this time some yearlings are with the rams and the proportion of rams counted may vary. During the winter a certain number of ewes would die which brings in a variable that tends to raise the yearling-ewe ratio. But the errors introduced by the roughness of the data in these particulars are apparently slight and unimportant. In comparing spring and fall counts, specific localities are not compared, for unless total counts are available for the locality one would expect enough variation in the sampling to make comparisons unprofitable.

In counting the mountain sheep, they were generally classified as ewe, lamb, yearling, and ram. When the 2-year-old animals were tabulated the sexes were lumped. Young rams—those up to 3 or 4 years old—were tabulated separately on a few occasions. These partial tabulations of 2-year-olds and young rams are retained in Table 8 and the 2-year-olds also in Tables 9 and 10 (pp. 130 and 131), but it should be understood that this differentiation is far from complete.

When only a part of a band was classified the record was not placed in the tabulations. Since ewes with lambs tend to segregate when the lambs are young, special effort was frequently made to classify the whole ewe population in an area in order to include the bands with many lambs and those with few lambs and thus attain a representative figure. Classifications were begun in early spring before the lambs were born and were continued through the summer and early fall, except in 1941 when the work was terminated in early August.

Sheep from practically all parts of the range were classified during each of the three summers that counts were made. The opportune time to obtain classifications by locality is early June before the sheep have begun their summer migrations and late enough to include most of the lambs. In the fall the sheep return to the spring haunts, so the populations can again be classified by locality and the summer losses can be determined.

No dependence should be placed on the sex ratios shown in the classified counts, because rams and ewes segregate for most of the year, and

unless one is certain that a complete count in an area has been made one does not know what proportion of the ewes or the rams in the area has been included.

The greater number of ewes in most of the tables is largely due to the special efforts made to classify the ewe bands. The data from the skull collections indicate that the sex ratio among the sheep is about 50–50. In the recent skull material there were 91 females and 93 males above the yearling age. In the old material there were 213 females and

Figure 46: A ewe with two lambs which appeared to be her twins. No other twins were identified as such. [*Polychrome Pass, September 25, 1939.*]

274 males, but here the number of male skulls may be greater only because they are found more readily. Ewe skulls are more easily covered by gravel and hidden by vegetation. In the recent material, however, the skulls of ewes are found almost as easily as those of rams because hair remains are often present to direct one to the skull, and few skulls have as yet been covered by debris.

The lambing period may vary considerably in different years. In 1908 Sheldon (1930, p. 366) saw the first lamb of the season on May 25. Dixon (1938, p. 216) states that in 1926 he encountered the first lamb on May 5, and in 1932 on May 31. In 1939 I saw two lambs on May 14, and one was reported on May 11. Soon after May 14 many lambs appeared, and by June 1 most of them had been born. In 1940 the lambing was late. None was seen until June 4. By the middle of June the lambing was largely finished. In 1941 two lambs were seen in Nenana Canyon on May 8. Most of the 1941 lambs were born about the middle of May.

The majority of the lambs seem to be born within the first 2 weeks of the lambing period. During the third and fourth weeks there are additional arrivals, and sometimes births occur quite late in the season. On July 19, 1939, a lamb was seen which was about half the size of the

TABLE 8.—*Classified Spring Counts—1939* [1]

Locality [2]	Date	Ewe	Lamb	Year-ling	2-year-old	Old ram	Young ram	Total
Savage River Canyon	July 18	36	22	11	2	23		94
Sanctuary Mountain	May 31	32	12	15	8	30		97
Big Creek	June 23	22	11	11	8	31		83
Big Creek, head of	June 30	30	26	10			14	80
Do	do	19		7	5	10	7	48
Big Creek	July 3	10	7	1	1	30		49
Igloo Mountain	June 6	29	9	15	8	4		65
Do	June 8	20	8	4	3	10	8	53
Cathedral Mountain	June 20	16	11				1	28
West of Cathedral Mountain	do	26	17	6	3		2	54
Lower East Fork River	June 5	22	20	4	3	11		60
East Fork River	May 26	105	63	20	9	84		281
Polychrome Pass	June 3	15	8	7	9	6		45
Toklat River	do	9	5	3	5			22
Intermediate Mountain	June 12	23	7	11		8		49
Stony Creek	May 30	11	3	5	3	5		27
Mile 66	June 10	4		2				6
Total		429	229	132	67	252	32	1, 141

[1] The best counts are included, following as nearly as possible the close of the lambing period. There is very little duplication, and figures give lamb crop and yearling survival for majority of mountain sheep in Mount McKinley National Park.
[2] Arranged from east to west.

others. It appeared to be about 2 weeks old which would place its birth early in July. Twins are a rarity. Only one pair was noted. Often a ewe is followed by two lambs (or more), but if a person watches long enough he generally will see a second ewe appear and claim one of the lambs.

Sheep classified totaled 4,985 in 1939, 1,157 in 1940, and 2,732 in 1941. There were many duplications since the total number of sheep in the park is not more than 1,500.

TABLE 9.—*Classified Fall Counts—1939* [1]

Locality [2]	Date	Ewe	Lamb	Year-ling	2-year-old	Old ram	Young ram	Total
Savage River Canyon	Sept. 29	29	13	12		11		65
Sanctuary Mountain	Sept. 27	31	17	16	2	15		81
Big Creek	Oct. 11	29	12	5		13		59
Igloo Creek	Oct. 15	10	3	1	3	3		20
Cathedral Mountain	Oct. 2	12	2	4				18
West of Cathedral Mountain	Sept. 9	24	16	8		7		55
Sable Pass	Sept. 30	15	5	2				22
East Fork River	Oct. 2	52	33	10		33		128
Polychrome Pass	Oct. 22	20	10	7	2	8		47
Toklat Bridge	Sept. 11	35	19	16	3			73
Lower Toklat River	Sept. 4	4	1	4		4		13
Total		261	131	85	10	94		581

[1] Includes the most complete fall counts available for different localities. Lamb survival through the summer and proportion of yearlings are shown.

[2] Arranged from east to west.

TABLE 10.—*Classified Spring Counts—1940* [1]

Locality [2]	Date	Ewe	Lamb	Year-ling	2-year-old	Ram	Total
Cathedral Mountain	June 18	25	3	3	1		32
Tattler Creek	June 8	16	1	3			20
Sable Pass	June 20	21		6	1		28
East Fork River	July 22	15	4	1		139	159
Polychrome Pass	June 14					8	8
Toklat River	June 11	20	3	6	4	11	44
Total		97	11	19	6	158	291

[1] The sample is small but representative. The lamb crop is extremely small and the yearling survival low.

[2] Arranged from east to west.

Table 11.—*Classified Fall Counts—1940* [1]

Locality [2]	Date	Ewe	Lamb	Yearling	Ram	Total
North of Headquarters	Sept. 27	26	7	7	14	54
Savage River	Oct. 4	34	7	5	9	55
Sanctuary Canyon	Oct. 9	20	5	3	2	30
Igloo Mountain	Sept. 15	30	3	6	14	53
Cathedral Mountain	Sept. 7	17	3			20
Tattler Creek	Sept. 5	9	2		1	12
East Fork River	Sept. 16	43	2	5	98	148
Polychrome Pass	Oct. 4				6	6
Toklat River	Sept. 10	13	5	4	3	25
East Branch Range	do	9		1		10
Mile 57	Aug. 25	7	1			8
Total		208	35	31	147	421

[1] The small lamb crop revealed in spring count is again evident here.
[2] Arranged from east to west.

Table 12.—*Classified Spring Counts—1941* [1]

Locality [2]	Date	Ewe	Lamb	Yearling	Ram	Total
Savage Canyon	June 3	19	9		3	31
Sanctuary Canyon	June 2	51	25	4	53	133
West of Teklanika Bridge	May 27	4	4		8	16
Do	May 29				19	19
West of Igloo Mountain	June 6	20	10		8	38
Igloo Mountain	June 12	50	36		8	94
Cathedral Mountain	June 5	11	9	1		21
Tattler Creek	do	21	6			27
Do	June 11	17	9			26
Double Mountain	do				6	6
Sable Mountain	June 7	21	15	2		38
East Fork River	May 26	40	23	3	50	116
Lower East Fork River	do	17	8		11	36
Tributary Creek	do	7	7		13	27
Polychrome Pass	May 27	5		1	9	15
Mile 50	June 4	8	3	1		12
Toklat River	June 8	49	24	4	14	91
Stony Creek	June 4				3	3
Do	June 14	1	1			2
Mile 66	June 4				3	3
Do	June 10	19	10			29
Intermediate Mountain	June 23	26	10			36
Lower Toklat River	do				25	25
Total		386	209	16	233	844

[1] Shows 1941 lamb crop and survival of 1940 lambs to yearling age.   There is a minimum of duplication.
[2] Arranged from east to west.

TABLE 13.—*Classified Summer Counts—1941* [1]

Locality [2]	Date	Ewe	Lamb	Yearling	Ram	Total
Savage River	June 12	21	12			33
Sanctuary Mountain	June 18	14	7		20	41
Igloo Mountain	Aug. 4	6	3			9
Cathedral Mountain	do	13	9	1		23
Tattler Creek	do	25	10		1	36
Double Mountain	do	13	7			20
Teklanika Range	do	24	16			40
Sable Mountain	do	2	1		11	14
Do	do	19	10		1	30
Tributary Creek	July 28				90	90
Head of East Fork River	July 9				9	9
Toklat River	Aug. 4	16	12			28
Do	do	14	11			25
Do	do				13	13
East Branch Range	do	19	5			24
Mile 66	July 25	9	8			17
Total		195	111	1	145	452

[1] Field work was terminated in early August, so these counts were made earlier than the late-season counts for 1939 and 1940.

[2] Arranged from east to west.

TABLE 14.—*Comparison of lamb-ewe and yearling-ewe ratios for the years 1939, 1940, 1941*

	Lamb-ewe ratios			Yearling-ewe ratios		
	1939 percent	1940 percent	1941 percent	1939 percent	1940 percent	1941 percent
Spring count [1]	49	11	54	28	19	4
Fall count [1]	49	16	57	32	15	.5
Total count [2]	50	19	54	25	16	3

[1] The "spring count" and "fall count" consist of the most complete counts in each locality over the range rather than a total of all counts during the spring or fall season. Thus duplication was avoided.

[2] "Total count" consists of all the classified counts made during the year.

CLASSIFICATIONS FOR 1939

Total count.—Between the latter part of May, when practically all lambs had been born, and late October 4,985 sheep were classified. There were many duplications, but the count probably included 90 percent or more of the sheep. Some sheep were undoubtedly counted oftener than others, so that in the total count there is some danger of the averages being unduly influenced by some of the duplications. However, the results are about the same as the selected counts where there was very little, if any, duplication. The figures for the total classification are as follows: Ewes, 2,055; lambs, 1,064; yearlings, 549; 2-year-olds, 163; rams 1,154. The lamb-ewe ratio is 51 percent, that is 51 percent of the ewes had lambs. The yearling-ewe ratio is 26 percent. If the lamb crop in 1938 was about the same as in 1939, then one-half of the lambs had succumbed during the first year. This I would presume to be a normal, good survival. The 2-year-olds were not counted consistently, so the count of them is smaller than it should be. In most other counts 2-year-olds were not segregated, so it may be best here to place half of them with the ewes and half with the rams, so as to make all the figures comparable. This would reduce the figure for the lamb-ewe ratio from 51 percent to 50 percent and the yearling-ewe ratio from 26 percent to 25 percent.

Spring Count.—In the total count there were more duplications in some parts of the range than in others and if they happened to fall in localities where the lamb and yearling numbers were especially high or low, the final figures for the lamb and yearling ratios would be too high or too low. One representative count has therefore been selected from the field record in each locality. These were made as soon after lambing as a good count could be obtained, in order to have a classification of most of the population with a minimum of duplications. Although the counts were not made on the same date (there is

more than a month separating some of them) I am confident there is little duplication. Where there could have been duplication, judging from the localities and dates appearing in Table 8, the movements of the bands were well enough known during the critical period to eliminate largely any probability of it. A range-wide count closely following the completion of the lambing gives a lamb-ewe ratio before potential summer losses have occurred.

The selected early 1939 counts, totaling 1,141 animals, are given in Table 8. The lamb-ewe ratio is 53 percent and the yearling-ewe ratio is 30 percent. If one-half of the 2-year-olds are placed with the ewes, the lamb-ewe ratio becomes 49 percent, and the yearling-ewe ratio 28 percent. These ratios do not differ greatly from those derived from the total count.

In this particular early count a fairly accurate count of 2-year-olds was obtained, although it is perhaps a little lower than it should be, since it was not always possible to count this age group. However, the figure gives some indication of the survival of sheep to that age. Sixty-seven 2-year-olds were counted, giving a ratio of 2-year-olds to ewes of 15 percent. The size of the lamb crop from which these 2-year-olds came and the number of these lambs surviving to the yearling stage is not known, but if similar to the 1939 lamb and yearling ratios, one might guess that a little more than one-half the yearlings had survived to the 2-year-old class.

However, there is too much conjecture involved to accept this figure for the yearling loss with any assurance.

Fall count.—In order to check the survival of lambs during the summer, I have listed the most comprehensive fall counts for 1939 in such a way as to avoid duplication. Counts are available from fewer localities than in the spring, but the figures seem large enough to be significant. This late 1939 count is given in Table 9. One-half (5) of the 2-year-olds listed are added to the ewe figures. The lamb-ewe ratio is 49 percent, the same as in the spring, and the yearling-ewe ratio is 32 percent, four points higher than in the spring. The figures indicate that there were few losses of lambs and yearlings during the summer months. This was also the impression I gained from general field observations, for no indications of disease were noted, and wolves, after the appearance of the caribou, did not molest the sheep.

CLASSIFICATIONS FOR 1940

Total Count.—In 1940 the total count—1,157—was small, but the various counts were well distributed according to locality. The results of the total classification are as follows: Ewes, 479; lambs, 93; yearlings, 78; 2-year-olds, 20; rams, 487. The lamb-ewe ratio is 19 percent, and the yearling-ewe ratio is 16 percent.

Spring Count.—The best early classified counts are given in Table 10. They do not include two important localities—Savage River Canyon and Sanctuary and Teklanika Canyons—

which were classified a little too early to get the lamb counts. The count is as follows: Total, 291; ewes, 97; lambs, 11; yearlings, 19; 2-year-olds, 6; rams, 158. The lamb-ewe ratio is 11 percent; the yearling-ewe ratio is 19 percent.

Fall Count.—The fall count given in Table 11 is a good sample. It is as follows: Total, 421; ewes, 208; lambs, 35; yearlings, 31; rams, 147. The lamb-ewe ratio is 16 percent, and the yearling-ewe ratio is 15 percent.

It will be noted that the lamb-ewe ratio in the spring was 11 percent, while in the fall, when it would be expected to be the same or smaller, it was 16 percent. If three bands, which were classified in the fall, had been classified in the spring, the lamb-ewe ratio for the spring would be raised to about 17 percent. It just happened that the lamb-ewe ratio was higher than average in these particular bands. There were apparently few lamb losses during the summer.

The losses in the 1939 lamb crop were too large to maintain the herd. The 49 percent lamb-ewe ratio of the fall of 1939 had been reduced by the following spring to a yearling-ewe ratio of 19 percent or less.

CLASSIFICATIONS FOR 1941

Total Count.—In 1941 the total count was as follows: Total, 2,732; ewes, 1,331; lambs, 722; yearlings, 38; rams, 641. The lamb-ewe ratio is 54 percent; the yearling-ewe ratio is about 3 percent.

Spring Count.—In the spring of 1941 large counts from many localities are available as shown in Table 12. Some of the counts were made as early as May 26, but by this date most lambs had been born. The count is as follows: Total, 844; ewes, 386; lambs, 209; yearlings, 16; rams, 233. The lamb-ewe ratio is 54 percent; the yearling-ewe ratio is 4 percent.

Summer Count.—In 1941 I left the park in early August so could not make counts in the fall. Most of the counts included in Table 13 were made in July and early August. Counts made about the middle of June at Savage and Sanctuary River Canyons are used in order that these localities can be included to make this count more comparable with the spring count. The count is as follows: Total, 452; ewes, 195; lambs, 111; yearlings, 1; rams, 145. The lamb-ewe ratio is about 57 percent, slightly higher than the 54 percent obtained in the "total" and "spring" tabulations (Table 14). Indications are that few lambs were lost during the summer.

The yearling-ewe ratio is about 0.5 percent, only one yearling being recorded in this late count. If the yearling-ewe ratio in the fall had been the same as in the spring there would have been eight yearlings in the fall count. The number of yearlings involved is so small that one hesitates to conclude that there was a yearling loss during the summer. A band or two harboring a few odd yearlings would bring the fall yearling ratio up to the spring ratio.

All the counts in 1941 show a high lamb crop (more than 50 percent)

and an extremely low number of yearlings. Very few of the 1940 lambs survived the winter.

DISCUSSION

Variations in lamb crop.—The lamb crop in 1939 was about 49 percent; in 1940 about 16 percent; and in 1941 about 54 percent. The 1939 and 1941 lamb crops were probably slightly better than average, with relatively small losses occurring during lambing time. The analyses of wolf droppings indicated some predation on the 1939 lambs before the caribou moved into the region with their calves. Possibly this wolf predation was just sufficient in 1939 to lower the 1939 lamb crop below that of 1941. However, we are dealing with rather small differences, and the slight wolf predation on lambs probably had little effect on the ratio.

The 1940 lamb crop was abnormal in two respects; the season was very late and the number of lambs unusually small. In 1940 the first lamb was found on June 4. On this date the lambing had been practically completed in the 1939 and 1941 seasons. The lamb crop in 1940 was one-third or less than that of 1939 or 1941.

It is not easy to account for the small lamb crop. According to some of the trappers there is occasionally an exceptionally poor lambing year. It is possible that the small 1940 lamb crop is correlated with crusted snow conditions reported for January of that year. The ewes may have been affected in some manner, causing a lowering in the lamb numbers. Since the lambing was so late, possibly the early bred ewes were affected most by the snow conditions. It may be significant that in 1932, after the severe winter, the lambing was also late and the lamb crop very small. On the other hand, the winters preceding the high 1939 and 1941 lamb crops were favorable for the sheep. The crop, in part, may be dependent on winter conditions.

Ewe-lamb ratio normally about 50 percent.—A good average lamb-ewe ratio appears to be about 50 percent, although this is based on the classification of only three lamb crops, one of which was almost a complete failure. But a 50 percent lamb crop is about what one would expect in a good year judging from the reproduction rates of big game in general. The 2-year-old ewes are included in the ewe counts even though ewes probably do not produce lambs until they are 3 years old. However, their inclusion does not change the figures more than a few points, still leaving the ratio near 50 percent.

In 1941 L. J. Palmer (1941) classified a number of sheep in the Mount Hayes region of the Alaska Range east of Mount McKinley National Park. He did not segregate the yearlings so the figures are not strictly comparable. He counted 501 ewes and 214 lambs, and estimated that one-half of the 2-year-olds and yearlings survived. If one-half the yearlings survived, we would have about 100 to subtract from the ewe count, to make his ewe count comparable with mine. This would give us about 400 ewes. After making this adjustment, which still includes the 2-year-olds as in my figures, we get a lamb-ewe ratio of 53 percent. This percentage is surprisingly close to my "total" and "spring" counts the same year (Table 14). This close agreement between the figures for the Mount Hayes area, where wolf predation is probably less than at Mount McKinley National Park, and those in the park, strengthens the conclusion that a lamb-ewe ratio of about 50 percent is a good normal lamb crop.

Lamb and yearling ratios in different parts of range.—The lamb-ewe ratios tended to be uniform over the range during the 3 years that these ratios were determined.

In considering yearling survival, however, there does seem to be some real difference between localities. The yearling survival in the general East Fork area was below average, while at Savage and Sanctuary River Canyons and at Toklat River the yearling survival was consistently above average. In the areas where there is a slightly higher than average yearling ratio it appears that the country is rougher and of such a nature as to give greater protection to the yearlings from wolves. Sanctuary and Teklanika River Canyons with a mountain between them seem to be especially favorable localities for yearling survival. Although there apparently are local differences, the general average in different localities each year does not vary greatly.

Summer losses.—In comparing the spring and fall counts in each of the 3 years it is obvious that the losses of both lambs and yearlings during the summer were slight. There was relatively little wolf predation on lambs in 1939, and practically none in 1940 and 1941 so far as I could ascertain. The only sick animal noted was a young lamb observed in June by rangers.

Lamb survival first winter.—We do not know what the lamb-ewe ratio was in 1938, but judging from the number of yearlings present in 1939 it apparently was high. If it were somewhere near 50 percent, which seems likely, then more than half of the lambs survived the winter. Such a survival is probably sufficient to cause a definite upward trend in the population. The number of 2-year-olds in 1939 was also quite high, so that the sheep seemed to have done well for two successive years.

The excellent 1939 lamb crop suffered heavy casualties during the winter and a number of these casualties may have resulted from the crusted snow conditions prevailing for part of the winter or heavy wolf pressure due to scarcity of caribou in the sheep hills. The yearling-ewe ratio in 1940 varies from 15 to 19 percent (the lamb crop in 1939 was about 50 percent). About two-thirds of the lambs failed to come through the winter. Such a heavy loss no doubt means no increase, or a possible decrease in the population, for the yearling survivals would hardly compensate for the winter losses among the older animals.

As has been pointed out, the lamb crop in 1940 was only about a third the size of the crop in 1939 and 1941. Of this small crop, 20 percent or less survived the winter as yearlings, so that there were scarcely any yearlings in the population in the summer of 1941.

Thus for two successive years the survival of yearlings was so small that it is probable that the sheep population suffered a decline in numbers each year. So far as known, there was no disease among the yearlings except actinomycosis which generally affects only a nominal number of the animals. The cause of heavy losses appeared to be due to wolf predation.

Some Wolf-Sheep Relationships

Effect of Artificial Intrusions on Wolf Predation

In a national park the objective is to preserve a piece of primitive nature where natural interrelationships may prevail. The more complete the biotic unit and the larger the area the greater is the opportunity to achieve that ideal. But unfortunately few national parks are large enough to be uninfluenced by artificial activities taking place both within and outside their boundaries.

In Mount McKinley National Park the automobile highway passes along the sheep hills for some 70 miles. This road gives the wolves a

Figure 47: **At Polychrome Pass the highway traverses the heart of excellent winter range for mountain sheep. This affords wolves ready access to the range, and an opportunity to surprise sheep at sharp curves on the road. [*October 22, 1939.*]**

special advantage in that they have an easy trail to different parts of the sheep range. In several places the road winds among the cliffs used by sheep in winter, saving wolves a laborious climb. Because of the many sharp turns in the road the wolves have an opportunity to surprise the sheep at close range. These advantages to the wolves are not especially great because the road affects vitally only a small part of the sheep range. This illustrates the need for carefully examining all proposals for park developments.

Another activity which intrudes on the natural conditions within the park is the trapping of wolves on lands outside the park. Trapping adjacent to the park boundaries,

and a certain amount of control within the park, annually has eliminated some of the park wolves. The effect on the wolf-sheep relationships is not well known, but probably such trapping does not take the annual increase during most years or greatly alter the wolf population. The status of the wolf within the park probably is, at the present time, similar to the status of the wolf in Alaska as a whole.

Still another artificial intrusion is the shooting of caribou adjacent to the park. Although this hunting does not now appear to be important it apparently has been extensive in the past. The reduction or curbing of the caribou herds by shooting might increase the wolf predation on the sheep by leaving a smaller caribou population.

The effect of the artificial intrusions will have to be carefully evaluated in considering the conservation of the wildlife in the park.

Do Caribou Divert Predation From Sheep?

Frequently there is serious direct competition for food between ungulates. Although the food habits of sheep and caribou overlap broadly, their ranges, especially in winter, overlap very little. Generally the caribou feed on the lower hills and rolling terrain where lichens are more abundant, and the sheep are up on the wind-swept ridges.

The caribou is an exceptionally good example of a buffer species. This is especially noticeable in the spring. When the caribou calves make their appearance they furnish to the wolves a large and easily obtainable food supply. At this time wolf predation on sheep practically ceases.

The caribou also serve as a buffer in winter. There are some suggestive correlations between wolf predation on sheep and the presence or absence of caribou in the vicinity of the sheep hills in winter. In a year that caribou wintered among the sheep hills the predation on sheep appeared to be less than when caribou were absent.

In the winter of 1938–39 between 1,500 and 2,000 caribou wintered between Teklanika and Savage Rivers and others wintered along the north border of the park. That year there was a high survival of yearlings among the sheep. In the winter of 1939–40 there were practically no caribou in the sheep areas. The survival of sheep yearlings that winter was about half of what it had been the preceding winter (assuming that lamb crops were about equal). In the absence of the caribou the wolves turned to the sheep. However, crusted snow conditions also favored the wolf in his sheep hunting in the winter cf 1939–40, so the two winters are not strictly comparable. The 1940 lamb crop was so small that one cannot draw many conclusions from the figures. There was a heavy winter mortality among the few lambs present even though caribou were present to act as a buffer. Wolf pressure on individual lambs may have been higher than usual because there were so few lambs.

Although the caribou are very definitely a buffer species at times, there is still a question whether or not they increase or decrease the wolf predation on the sheep over a period of years. It is likely that because of the presence of the caribou, the sheep range supports a larger wolf population. True, when caribou are present they probably bear the brunt of the predation. But when caribou winter elsewhere, the wolf population, whose size is probably adjusted to their presence, is, so to speak, left stranded, and dependent on sheep for sustenance. The majority of the wolves in the park do not move off with the caribou as some persons have assumed. Wolves are accustomed to obtaining their food in the one territory. Thus it appears that the caribou herds, because of their periodic absences from the sheep ranges, may influence predation in such a way as, in the long run, to lower the size of the sheep population. But because of the small amount of information on this point our conclusions must be tentative. There is no doubt, however, that the caribou at times is a highly important buffer species for the sheep.

HISTORICAL EVIDENCE THAT WOLVES ARE CURBING SHEEP NUMBERS

During the period of wolf scarcity beginning sometime between 1908 and 1916 the sheep prospered, in fact built up to what apparently was an overpopulation about 1928. Unusually severe snow conditions in 1932 reduced the population which already had been depleted by the hard winter of 1929. According to one observer, not more than 1,500 sheep remained. This population was not far from that present on the range in 1941, 9 years later. We do not know definitely the number of sheep in 1932 after the die-off but it probably was not less than at present. During this 9-year period, so far as we know, a rather uniform wolf population existed and it is known that wolves preyed extensively on sheep. The fact that sheep increased

rapidly in the absence of wolves and have not increased during their presence strongly indicates that the wolves have been the factor preventing the sheep from increasing. I am fully aware how frequently "obvious conclusions" are wrong, especially in prey-predator relationships. However, I found no other factor which seemed sufficiently operative to hold the sheep numbers in check. It seems, therefore, that the wolves are the controlling influence. Granting that the wolves have held the sheep in check for several years, that does not necessarily mean that the sheep will not increase or decrease in the future in the presence of the same wolf population. The presence and numbers of the caribou is an uncertain factor which influences wolf predation on sheep so the yearly movements of the caribou and their status must be considered. Furthermore, the abundance or scarcity of snowshoe hares may have an important bearing on relationships. Other factors, of course, may change to alter the relationship, so one cannot predict with certainty the future relationships and population trends.

The historical data corroborate the evidence obtained in the field study that wolves are the chief factor limiting the sheep population at the present time.

EFFECT OF THE WOLF ON SHEEP NUMBERS

At the time that the sheep population was at its maximum many of the sheep lived away from the traditional rocky habitat and occupied low hills and even high banks along the rivers. The use of this gentle terrain was probably necessary because of food shortages in the rugged hills. In the absence of the wolf they were able to survive in the areas lacking protective cliffs. But when the wolf appeared and became plentiful the sheep in these places became so vulnerable that no doubt the strong as well as the weak could be captured. In the presence of the wolf, therefore, the range of the sheep was gradually constricted, and they were confined to more rugged habitats where they could cope with the wolf on better terms. In confining the sheep to the cliffs, the wolf is an important factor in molding their habits, and through the past ages probably has done much to develop and preserve the sheep as we know them today.

The relationship between wolves and sheep probably differs according to the types of terrain. Where the cliffs are exceptionally rugged and extensive a sheep population might be largely immune from wolf attack until it becomes so large that it overflows into less rugged surrounding country. Where cliffs are only moderately rugged or not very extensive, the sheep might remain rather low in numbers, perhaps at a point where the law of diminishing returns makes it unprofitable for the wolf to hunt them; in some unfavorable cliffs perhaps all the sheep would be destroyed. Therefore we would expect to find considerable variation in the abundance of sheep, in the presence

of wolves, in different sheep areas, due primarily to the character of the country.

Since the wolves appear to hold the sheep in check it is of interest to discuss how predation, which apparently is mainly upon the weak, operates to control the population.

The predation on the old-age animals and those weakened by disease curbs the numbers to some extent. A few of the old ewes, although weaker than the average and doomed to die in a year or two from old age, might still bring forth a healthy lamb if not eliminated by the wolf. The same is probably true for some of the sheep suffering from malformed dentition as a result of disease. Predation on the healthy sheep, captured by chance or otherwise, eliminates a few members of the population and their potential offspring. But this predation does not appear to be as important as that on the yearlings.

From the skull study it could not be determined how much the wolves increased the death rate among the yearlings. Comparative studies in periods of wolf scarcity would be enlightening in this regard. But it was evident that the losses among the yearlings in the winters of 1939–40 and 1940–41 were so great that, combined with all other losses, they resulted in a reduction in the total sheep population. It appears to me that the large losses were due mainly to heavy wolf predation. The lamb and yearling losses in mountain sheep herds in Wyoming, in the absence of any serious predator, are sometimes fully as great as in Mount McKinley National Park. But in Wyoming it was evident that the young were diseased for they coughed considerably in late summer, and many died during the summer and fall. This disease is probably correlated with poor range conditions. In Mount McKinley National Park the young sheep appeared healthy at the beginning of winter. No coughing or other evidence of disease was noted excepting actinomycosis which would probably affect only a nominal number of animals. On the other hand, the wolf was known to prey upon the sheep extensively at times. From the total observations made, the conclusion seemed evident that large losses among the yearlings are caused by wolf predation at times, and that these losses are probably most important in holding the sheep numbers in check.

The Sheep and the Wolves May Now Be in Equilibrium

It is unfortunate that we do not have accurate information on sheep numbers since the die-off of 1932 so that we would know more about the trend of the population. One ranger thought that the low was reached about 1936, and that in 1939 there was a definite increase over the past few years. These thoughts were based on general observations. In 1940 and again in 1941 there were decreases. My impression is that the sheep numbers have not varied greatly since 1932. If this is actually the case then it is probable that the sheep and the wolves have reached an equilibrium, with, of course, some ups and downs. If we were assured that there would not now be any striking reduction in sheep numbers, the wolf-sheep relationship might be considered a satisfactory one, especially to anyone who has seen the ungulate over-populations and the over-grazed big game ranges in the States. Artificial intrusions may give the wolf an undue advantage over the sheep, hence it is desirable to continue observations in order that the status of the sheep may at all times be known and proper steps taken when needed to assure their perpetuation under as natural conditions as possible.

CHAPTER FOUR

ᏍᏍᏍ-ᏍᏍᏍ-ᏍᏍᏍ-ᏍᏍᏍ-ᏍᏍᏍ-ᏍᏍᏍ-ᏍᏍᏍ-ᏍᏍᏍ-ᏍᏍᏍ-ᏍᏍᏍ-ᏍᏍᏍ-ᏍᏍᏍ-ᏍᏍᏍ-ᏍᏍᏍ-ᏍᏍᏍ-ᏍᏍᏍ-ᏍᏍᏍ-ᏍᏍᏍ-ᏍᏍᏍ

Caribou

ᏍᏍᏍ-ᏍᏍᏍ-ᏍᏍᏍ-ᏍᏍᏍ-ᏍᏍᏍ-ᏍᏍᏍ-ᏍᏍᏍ-ᏍᏍᏍ-ᏍᏍᏍ-ᏍᏍᏍ-ᏍᏍᏍ-ᏍᏍᏍ-ᏍᏍᏍ-ᏍᏍᏍ-ᏍᏍᏍ-ᏍᏍᏍ-ᏍᏍᏍ-ᏍᏍᏍ-ᏍᏍᏍ

Description

THE CARIBOU is a circumpolar deer adapted to life in the Arctic. Both sexes carry antlers. The cow's antlers are small and branching, those of the bull large and picturesque with a well-developed brow tine extending over the nose from the base of one or both antlers. The blunt, curved hoofs provide a broad support for walking on the tundra or in snow. The long, thick coat of the bulls is dark brown, contrasting conspicuously with the pure white neck and mane and white stripe along the flank. The cows are similarly colored but the white is duller and the coat in general paler.

The shoulder height varies from 46 to 55 inches. The average dressed weight of 18 bulls, according to O. J. Murie (1935, p. 13), was 247 pounds, the heaviest 305 pounds. Of 6 adult bulls the average live weight was 366 pounds. The dressed weight of 12 adult cows averaged 148 pounds, and the average live weight of 5 adult cows was 213 pounds. A male calf taken by O. J. Murie in September weighed 75 pounds dressed, another 121 pounds live weight.

The caribou is a gregarious animal usually found in large herds. Sometimes the herds contain seven thousand or more animals, but a few hundred is the usual number. On the move much of the time, the caribou make extensive migrations which involve hundreds of miles of travel. The migrations follow general route patterns over a period of years, but have many variations and sometimes there are drastic changes. After passing over certain areas for a number of years, the animals may shift their ranges to entirely new areas. This migratory habit and the shifting of ranges are highly beneficial to the vegetation in that they tend to lighten use and give the forage plants opportunity for recovery. This is especially beneficial to the lichens (favorite caribou food) which recover slowly after being overgrazed.

According to O. J. Murie (1935), there are five principal caribou herds in Alaska, each of which is segregated sufficiently to be considered as a unit. There is, no doubt, some intermingling of animals from different herds. The animals in Mount McKinley National Park form a well-defined group, occupying a range which centers in the park and vicinity. They range over a region at least 300 or 400 miles in diameter; the exact limits are not known. At times this herd probably has some contact with the Yukon-Tanana herd which is the largest group. The total number of caribou in Alaska 20 years ago was estimated at more than a million. So far as known the status of the herds has not changed greatly since that time. However, there has been considerable hunting in recent years and the wolf population has been greater so that there may have been some decrease in late years. The park herd, numbering 20,000 to 30,000, constitutes only a small part of Alaska's caribou population.

Classification

The Alaska caribou have all been placed in the "Barren Ground group." Two subspecies have been recognized—*Rangifer arcticus granti*, to which the caribou on the Alaska Peninsula have been referred, and *Rangifer arcticus stonei* which includes all the other caribou in Alaska (O. J. Murie, 1935). There is great individual variation in antler form which has often given the impression that the woodland and Barren Ground caribou are both found in interior Alaska.

Numbers

During the 5 days between June 28 and July 2, 1941, about 14,685 adults and 6,900 calves were seen within the park, or a total of more than 21,000 caribou. There was not much possibility of duplication but no doubt some nocturnal migrants were missed. It is not known what part of the herd this count represents. The main bands of bulls, which had already moved west of Wonder Lake, were missed, and there no doubt were others which were scattered about to the west and elsewhere. It is safe to say that the Mount McKinley National Park herd numbers between 20,000 and 30,000.

Movements of Mount McKinley National Park Caribou

BRIEF SURVEY OF MOVEMENTS FROM 1925 TO 1941

Detailed information on the movements of the Mount McKinley National Park caribou herds is lacking, but there is enough information in the Park Superintendents' monthly reports to give an approximate idea of the annual movements. There are, of course, many gaps in our knowledge since much of the territory used by caribou is not easily accessible and is infrequently visited by man. I have reviewed the monthly reports of the Superintendents and summarized the information contained therein. An understanding of the movements of the caribou is important from the standpoint of the park visitors because so often they are disappointed at failing to see the animals, which at the time of their visit may have moved beyond the region accessible by road. For the benefit of future workers in this area, and to place on record facts that may prove of value in further studies of caribou wanderings, the data are given here in some detail.

1926.—In the winter of 1925–26, 2,000 or more caribou wintered in the region around Toklat River and McKinley Fork, but there were few in the eastern section, including the area between Teklanika River and Park Headquarters. Apparently they had been wintering to some extent along the north boundary. Many at this time had been wintering in the Broad Pass region along the railroad, but there is no mention of any migration to this area. In 1922 and 1923 O. J. Murie and I observed an eastern migration in the fall between Savage River and Park Headquarters.

In July 1926, six or seven thousand caribou were found in the Toklat River region, and hundreds were found at the head of Savage River. In August they were reported to have gone westward.

In October 1926, there was a general migration from the western part of the park, over Sanctuary Pass to Windy and points east in the Broad Pass area. But there was also a large herd in the general area west of Stony Creek and a few stragglers wintered at Savage. Apparently the main herd had split in two, some wintering east

of the park and some in the western part. There is no report of the return of the caribou from the Broad Pass region. They probably dribbled westward inconspicuously.

1927.—In July 1927, several thousand were reported in the East Fork and Toklat River sections. In October 1927, six or seven thousand caribou again moved out of the park through the Windy region to Broad Pass. This migration was not noticed on the north side of the main range but it was thought that these caribou did come from the north side. In December 1927, 1,500 were reported in the Kantishna region and there were other signs of large herds moving east along the northern boundary. Large numbers seen on both sides of the Tanana River were thought to have come from the park herd.

1928.—In February 1928, a herd of 1,000 caribou entered the park near Cantwell, moving west, and in March other herds followed. They were seen over much of the park in March. In June large herds were reported in the Clearwater Creek region south of McKinley Fork. The report stated that tourists were obliged to travel beyond Copper Mountain if they wished to see the large herds in summer. In August bands near Wonder Lake were starting eastward, and in September several small herds were seen in the eastern section of the park. In October several thousand caribou traveled eastward across the Teklanika River and over to Windy and into the

Broad Pass area. About 1,000 were reported wintering near Windy. It was reported that most of the caribou went 40 miles down the Kantishna River to winter. About 200 wintered near Savage River.

1929.—In May and June caribou were reported plentiful in the park, especially in the western section south of McKinley Fork. In September thousands headed south past Windy.

1930.—In October a scarcity of caribou in the park occurred but thousands were reported in the Valdez Creek area east of Windy. The migration to this area escaped observation. In December about 5,000 were reported passing through the central part of the park.

1931.—In April the caribou returned to the park, traveling west, and many were reported present in summer. In the winter of 1931–32 there was apparently no migration to the Broad Pass region. Thousands were reported wintering in the Lake Minchumina region to the northwest.

1932.—In May caribou were reported returning to the park from the west and they were common in June. In November there were few caribou in the park but they moved in from the west in December, and 3,000 were estimated to be wintering in the eastern section.

1933.—The caribou were abundant in the eastern part of the park from December to August, when they moved westward. In November there were few caribou in the park. At this time they were reported abundant near Lignite, 25 miles north of the park and along the railroad. Some wintered along the north boundary.

1934.—In June, 10,000 caribou were estimated in the eastern part of the park. A few animals wintered near Savage River in 1934–35.

1935.—In April large bands returned to the Wonder Lake section, presumably from the west or north and by May were ranging as far east as Savage River. In July approximately 5,000 caribou were seen in Sable Pass. In August they were scarce from Toklat to Park Headquarters. Notes are meager, but apparently few caribou were in the park in the winter of 1935–36.

1936.—No caribou were seen in May but in June it was estimated that there were 25,000 between Igloo Creek and Mile 72. In July only a few were seen.

1937.—In the winter of 1936–37 few caribou were found in the park. None was reported in May, but in June 2,000 were seen between Igloo Creek and Toklat River. In July it was estimated that there were 25,000 within the park boundaries. In August the migration had passed and only a few scattered ones were seen. During the fall caribou were scarce in the park.

1938.—During the winter of 1937–38 a few caribou wintered at Savage River. Large herds were reported in the Kantishna area. Former Chief Ranger Corbley saw 500 on McKinley Fork bar in March. Many caribou were seen in the Wonder

Lake area in April. In May, Ranger Rumohr reported 20,000 in the Kantishna region. During June bands of 20 to 200 were seen along the highway. In early July many migrated westward from Sable Pass. By August the caribou had gone to the west, and during the fall few were seen from the highway. It was estimated that from 1,500 to 2,000 wintered in the Savage and Sanctuary River regions, and that 10,000 wintered between McKinley Fork and Herron Creek.

1939.—In the summer caribou were abundant in the park in May, June, and early July, and then they moved westward. Presumably they wintered west of Wonder Lake.

1940.—In May caribou returned to the eastern section of the park and were plentiful in June and early July. In September there were many near Wonder Lake and along the north boundary.

1941.—Many caribou spent the winter along the north boundary and west of Wonder Lake. They were abundant in the park in May and June.

WINTER MOVEMENTS

From 1922 to 1931 a large part of the caribou herd moved over the Alaska Range in the fall and wintered in the Broad Pass region. Since 1933 the records indicate that the main herds have wintered in the Lake Minchumina area northwest of Wonder Lake and along the north boundary of the park. I am told that prior to 1935 about 1,000 caribou

wintered on lower Savage River along the north boundary but that for a few years thereafter they were scarce. The number wintering within the park between Savage and Sanctuary Rivers has varied considerably. During the winters of 1935–36, 1936–37, and 1937–38 very few stayed here. In 1938–39 two or three thousand wintered in this region; in 1939–40 there were scarcely any, but in 1940–41 caribou were again wintering here. Although the main herds may winter in relatively small areas, smaller groups sometimes are rather widely distributed. Thus each year certain minor and major variations may occur.

SUMMER MOVEMENTS

For short periods in spring and summer large herds of caribou may be seen passing through the park, but within a few days the scene may change from one of abundance to scarcity. In the years that the caribou were wintering in the Broad Pass area there was a spring and fall period of abundance between Wonder Lake and Savage River. In the spring the caribou passed through the park going westward; in the fall they passed through it going eastward.

In recent years many of the caribou have come from the west in May and June and apparently crossed the Alaska Range at the head of Sanctuary River. Some caribou may cross the Range from Muldrow Glacier and eastward. In 1939, for instance, tracks were noted at Muldrow Glacier and as far west as McGonnagal

Pass. In a few weeks they have re-crossed the range and again traveled to the west.

Data gathered from the monthly reports of the Park Superintendents show that caribou have been abundant in the park east of Wonder Lake during the following months:

1926—July, October
1927—July, October
1928—March, October
1929—May, June, September
1930—No data
1931—April, May, June, July
1932—May, June
1933—January to August
1934—June
1935—April, May, June, July
1936—June
1937—June, July
1938—April, May, June, July
1939—May, June, early July
1940—May, June, early July
1941—May, June, early July

1939 MOVEMENTS

I observed the caribou movements in 1939, 1940, and 1941 so can describe them in more detail than was possible for the earlier years. In 1939 the estimated 2,000 caribou wintering between Savage and Sanctuary Rivers had moved north early in April. South of Wonder Lake many caribou were calving in May. Small bunches moved eastward so that in late May and early June a few scattered animals were encountered as far east as Sanctuary and Teklanika Rivers. The main bands remained in the vicinity of the calving grounds for a few weeks The first large bands moving east-ward were seen in Sable Pass on June 12. A thousand caribou, mainly cows and calves, were observed. They were moving along steadily. On June 13 one band in Sable Pass contained 800 adults and about 400 calves. Between the north side of Cathedral Mountain and Teklanika River about 800 cows and calves were seen moving south. They had come through passes north of Sable Pass. On June 14 about 1,500 of them were seen in Sable Pass and north of the road along the Toklat River. On June 16 about 3,500 were seen at the Teklanika Forks. These were traveling in bands of from 100 to 250 which consisted mainly of cows and calves with a few bulls. Another 700 were seen traveling along the base of Double Mountain, making a total of 4,200 caribou for the day.

On June 17 about 2,000 were seen at Teklanika Forks; on the 18th about 500; and on the 19th about 400. These caribou were traveling steadily. All the bands seemed to go 6 or 7 miles up the west branch of Teklanika River to the glaciers, back to the Forks and up the east branch and back to Double Mountain, where they crossed to Sanctuary River. On June 20, 200 were seen on Cathedral Mountain, 100 on Teklanika River, and 400 on Toklat River above the road. By June 22 the main herds of cows and calves and some bulls had passed eastward to Sanctuary River, up which they traveled, presumably crossing to the south slope of the Alaska Range. A trapper told me that for several seasons large bands of caribou had come in June to the Chulitna River on the south side of the Alaska Range and disappeared after spending about 2 weeks there. That information is in harmony with the data on migration as observed in the park, for after the caribou have gone east they soon are seen returning and going west.

Apparently the herds made up mainly of bulls, and a few herds of cows, did not make the long migration up Sanctuary River. On June 24 more than 1,000 caribou, mainly old and young bulls, were reported on McKinley Fork bar going west. On June 25 a band of 48, mainly bulls, was noted at Copper River bar, and at Stony Creek 45, mainly bulls, were traveling west. On June 27, on Sable Pass, a band of 50 bulls and another of 60 cows and calves were moving west. On June 30 about 500, mainly bulls, came up Teklanika River. It appeared that some bands consisting largely of bulls had moved eastward near the north boundary, most of them going only to Teklanika River, then had circled south toward Sable Pass and upper East Fork River, and then had turned west again. On July 2 about 2,700 caribou, including many calves, were seen on Copper River bar. I do not know where these caribou came from but it seemed likely that they had gone up Sanctuary River and recrossed the Alaska Range on the upper Toklat River or at some other place along the Range, possibly Anderson Pass. Most of these seemed to have recrossed the Range between Toklat River and Anderson Pass since few were seen east of Toklat River in the westward migration.

A few small bands were seen dribbling westward in early July, and on July 13 a band of 800 was seen at Toklat River going west. On July 16 a band of 149 and another of 125 were on Sable Pass moving west. A large band was seen on Stony Creek. After this date only a few odd animals were seen. The caribou remained scarce east of Wonder Lake up to the middle of October, when I made my last observations that year.

1940 MOVEMENTS

In the winter of 1939–40 caribou were scarce in the park, at least between Park Headquarters and Wonder Lake. No data are available on where they wintered but presumably it was to the west, possibly in the Lake Minchumina region.

On May 6 at McKinley Fork near the highway about 100 caribou were seen and many tracks showed that some had come down on McKinley Fork bar from the west. On May 9 a number of caribou were noted on the bar just south of Teklanika River Canyon. They were coming over the mountain from the Sushana watershed to the northwest. From the top of the mountain to the bar there was a line of caribou coming down the steep slope. When I was forced to leave, the caribou were still streaming over the top of the mountain. In the afternoon when I returned they were spread out over the tundra between Teklanika and Sanctuary Rivers and moving south. I do not know how many there were in the herd. They apparently continued to pass this point for several days.

On May 11 a band of 100 was moving east on Sable Pass. Between May 9 and the last of the month there were several hundred between Teklanika and Savage Rivers. They kept moving southward. Large bands moved up the Teklanika River and Igloo Creek and went west over Sable Pass. Many of these animals seemed to have come from the north boundary in the general region of the Sushana and Teklanika Rivers and moved south to Sable Pass, then traveled westward. Others went up Sanctuary River and perhaps crossed the Alaska Range before traveling westward.

From May 29 to July 2 about 12,000 adult caribou were seen traveling west between Sable Pass and Toklat River. Some which came from upper Sanctuary River no doubt included those that had come into the Teklanika River region on May 9 and later. Others came up the Teklanika from the north and turned west at Sable Pass and at passes to the north of Sable. Some came up East Fork River from the north and turned west just south of the highway. During July and August very few caribou were seen. In September the caribou reappeared in the Wonder Lake region. On September 6, I saw about 500 near Wonder Lake and about 500 on McKinley River bars. There were large herds north of Wonder Lake in the Kantishna region at this time. In October many of them worked east along the north boundary, almost to the railroad.

During the winter of 1940–41, beginning in October, many caribou were found on both sides of the north boundary of the park. One trapper said the caribou had come to Lignite and to Dry Creek near the railroad on the north boundary. Lee Swisher, trapping on the Teklanika and Sushana Rivers, estimated four or five thousand caribou wintering in that region. In traveling along the north boundary from Savage River to Wonder Lake in January I saw many caribou tracks on both sides of the boundary. On the return trip, no caribou sign was noted between Mile 70 and Mile 27 on the highway. A few were found between Savage and Sanctuary Rivers along the highway.

1941 MOVEMENTS

During March and April bands totaling two and three hundred caribou were seen near the road at Savage River, but early in May few remained.

On May 14 large bands of caribou came into Sanctuary River Valley from the northwest. A ranger reported seeing 2,000 that day. The following day I saw but 600 in the same locality, indicating that they were moving southward. On May 18 there were about 1,000 animals east of Savage River and south of the road. On May 28, on the rolling hills between Savage and Sanctuary Rivers south of the road, there were about 6,000 adult caribou and 3,000 calves. During the next 2 or 3 days they kept moving southward up Sanctuary River Valley. On June 3 about 350 were seen, mainly far up Sanctuary. After that only scattered ones were seen between Savage and Sanctuary Rivers.

On June 4 about 250 caribou in small bands of a dozen or less traveled to Copper River bar from the north. These caribou were mainly old and young bulls and yearlings; no calves were among them. On June 5 a band of 150 cows with calves was traveling south along Igloo Creek, coming up from Teklanika River. Between June 6 and June 9, small bands of bulls were seen between Sable Pass and Mile 74. They seemed to be dribbling in from the north, probably coming from the region along the north boundary. On June 9 a band of 60 cows and 10 calves was seen on Stony Creek traveling east and two other bands of cows at Mile 69 and Mile 40 were going east. At this time all bulls were traveling west.

Between June 10 and June 26 few caribou were seen. But on the evening of June 27 a party reported seeing a band of 4,000 on Stony Creek traveling west. The following day I saw about 4,000 adult caribou at Mile 70, about 1,000 on Copper River bar, 600 at Stony Creek, 700 at Toklat River, and 200 others along the way. The adults were largely cows. Usually the calves were not counted because when the caribou are traveling in big bands or lying down in the distance it is difficult to count the calves. Samples were counted which indicated that about half the cows were followed by calves. There were approximately 6,500 adult caribou and perhaps about 3,000 calves. These animals were traveling hurriedly. On June 29 I counted about 3,000 adults. In these bands there were probably from 1,000 to 1,500 calves. On June 30 I saw a band of about 2,000 adults and perhaps 1,000 calves, and other bands totaling 1,750 adults and 800 calves. On July 1, I saw a total of 875 adults and 400 calves. On July 2 about 560 adults and 200 calves were counted. I was unable to count caribou from July 3 to 5 because of floods washing out and blocking the roads. Only a few were seen on the 6th; 70 were seen on the 7th. Apparently the main run had lasted about 5 days. Between July 3 and July 22 very few were seen. Then on July 24 about 1,500 were seen going north from McKinley Bar toward the north boundary. Those that had gone west were now moving back east a short distance, thence northward. My observations were discontinued August 4.

Trails

Wherever the caribou migrate they leave many parallel trails, for the large herds often travel on a broad front. In some places there may be a hundred or more trails only 2 or 3 feet apart. Not nearly all the trails are used each year and they may be in disuse for a period of years. Most trails in Mount Mc-Kinley National Park lead east and west along the migration route but many also follow the rivers in a north-and-south direction. The trails tend to follow the contours, but in many places they ascend and descend steep slopes, and may go over mountains.

Food Habits of Caribou

The caribou is a grazing and browsing animal with a special fondness for lichens. The more important foods eaten in the Mount McKinley region consist of lichens, grasses, willows, and dwarf Arctic birch.

WINTER FOOD

Although lichens, and to a lesser extent mosses, are relished at all times of the year, they are especially sought during the period when the abundance of green foods of summer are not available. My summer observations in Mount McKinley National Park indicate that relatively few lichens are eaten. Perhaps more are eaten at this season farther westward where such food is in greater abundance. In September, when the green vegetation has largely disappeared, caribou seek out and feed extensively on lichens. Species of the genus *Cladonia* seem to be the favorite ones. Throughout the winter, the caribou paw through the snow for lichens as well as grasses. One of the requirements of a wintering ground seems to be the presence of lichens, even though they by no means form the exclusive diet.

Grasses, sedges, and willows are also eaten extensively in winter. Even patches of coarse sedge were closely grazed in some places. So far as I could tell, practically all species of grasses and sedges were utilized. The willow twigs are eaten and some of the dry leaves are picked off the ground. Willow was much utilized during the winter months.

SUMMER FOOD

The important summer foods are grasses and sedges, willows, and dwarf birch, supplemented by an assortment of herbs. In early spring the caribou near Wonder Lake were seeking the new green shoots of sedge and grass. Grasses and sedges form a large part of the summer food. When the willows and the dwarf birch leaf out in May they are eaten in large quantities. For a period in May and early June willow and dwarf birch seem to make up the bulk of the food. The leaves are stripped from the twigs, and some of the fine twigs are also eaten at this time of the year, perhaps more or less accidentally. Where large bands of caribou have fed, many of the willow twigs which have had the leaves removed are withered. Several kinds of willows are eaten, including two or three species of dwarf willow that are highly palatable. More than half the stomach contents of a cow which died July 15 consisted of two species of dwarf willow. Willows and dwarf Arctic birch are widely distributed and abundant in the park.

Various herbs such as *Boykinia*,

Hedysarum, and *Dryas* are eaten in summer. *Hedysarum*, growing abundantly on the gravel bars, is eagerly sought, so that where herds of caribou have passed, hardly a plant has escaped a close grazing. *Equisetum* was especially sought on several occasions. (For a large list of food plants see O. J. Murie, 1935.)

When migrating a caribou may settle down for a period to feed, but much of the time it eats hurriedly as it travels. Often, before a willow twig is stripped of leaves, the caribou has moved forward and is reaching far back to complete the action. Even when the caribou has settled down to feed more leisurely, it faces in the direction it is going. This is so consistently true that one can almost always know the direction of the general migration of a herd by watching the movements of a single animal. When the animals are on the wintering grounds or on the calving grounds they feed more leisurely, although even then they are usually moving about a great deal.

Stomach contents of some dead caribou found on the range were as follows:

Calf—June 14, 1939. Toklat River:
  Green grass 99 percent.
  Dwarf Willow, *Salix* sp., trace.
  Lichen, trace.
  Vaccinium vitis-idaea, trace.

Cow—July 15, 1940. Igloo Creek:
  Green grass, 40 percent.
  "Smooth" dwarf willow, *Salix* sp., 30 percent.
  Reticulated dwarf willow, *Salix reticulata*, 29 percent.
  Other plants, 1 percent.

Cow—July 2, 1941. East Fork:
  Green grass, 99 percent.
  Willow, *Salix* sp., trace.
  Hedysarum sp., trace.
  Dwarf Arctic birch, *Betula* sp., trace.

Rutting Period

The rutting period begins some time after the middle of September and continues to the latter part of October. On September 14, 1940, two bulls were seen paying attention to cows, but most of the bulls seen were not yet with the females. On October 7, 1940, four small bands were seen, each with a bull in charge. Three of the bands consisted of 11, 4, and 13 cows, and in each band there were two calves. The fourth band was larger than the others but no count was obtained. During the rutting period the old bulls lose the large amount of fat accumulated during the summer period and face the winter in a gaunt condition. The fact that bulls have used up so much reserve energy during the rutting period may have a bearing on their survival through the winter months.

Caribou Calves

DESCRIPTION

The newborn caribou calf is reddish-brown, with a strip of black sometimes 3 or 4 inches wide running down the middle of the back. Some calves are more red than others. They lack the spots found in deer and elk. The blunt, squared-off muzzle is black. A few days after birth the pelage becomes a faded brown. The bulk of the calves are rather uniformly colored, but variations are fairly common. One calf was a bright orange color. Another was exceptionally whitish, and it was significant that the mother of this one was also unusually light colored. The first coat is lost in July, the change taking place first on the face. On July 13 several calves were noted which had lost most of the first coat and had acquired the new pelage which at first appeared almost black. This pelage soon becomes similar to that of the adult, but the white on the necks and sides is absent the first year.

A female calf born on May 18, 1940, had the following measurements: total length, 32 inches; tail length, 3¾ inches; hind leg, 14 inches; ear, 3 inches; shoulder height (from tip of hoof), 24 inches. Another newborn calf was 22 inches high at the shoulders.

The calves have a deep guttural, short call, reminding one of the quality in the bullfrog's note or the deep grunt of a pig. The calves are often quite noisy, especially in a moving herd or in a herd that has been disturbed. A single calf is the rule, no twins having been observed.

CALVING

The calving period is roughly from the middle of May to the middle of June. In 1940 the first calf was seen on May 12, and in 1941 on May 14. Most of the calves were born during the following 2 weeks. The latest record I have is for June 22 when a calf only a day or two old was seen.

Figure 48: **A calf caribou less than a day old. Note the black, square muzzle.** [*May 24, 1939.*]

To give birth to their calves, cows generally wander off varying distances from the main herds. At this time a lone cow is almost sure to be near a newborn calf. Generally these lone cows still carry one or both antlers. Within a few days the cows with their calves join the main herds. Sometimes the mothers band together in groups of a dozen or so, and move about together for a short period.

The open rolling tundra in the region about McKinley, Cache, and Clearwater Rivers is often referred to as a favorite calving ground. The caribou calved in that region in 1939, but in 1940 and 1941 most of the calving took place on the gently rolling tundra between Savage and Sanctuary Rivers. Possibly the location of the principal calving grounds depends largely on where the caribou happen to be at the time. The fact that the same areas are used several years for calving may simply mean that the general movements of the herds are similar for those years.

In 1940 large herds of caribou first moved into the calving area between Teklanika and Savage Rivers on May 9. Large bands were last seen in this region on May 29. Most of the caribou had left before the 29th and had moved southward toward the head of Sanctuary River. In 1941 large bands moved into this same region on May 14. Some calved on the north side of the outside range and moved into the area later. On May 28, bands totaling 6,000 animals, not including calves, were seen moving southward between Sanctuary and Savage Rivers. On May 29 about 2,000 adult caribou with calves were seen in the region, and on May 30 only about 100 adults with calves were noted. There is some movement of the herds before all the calves are born, but for the most part during this period there seems to be an interval when the herds wander about locally.

The calves are unusually precocious. On May 17, 1940, I found a calf in a spot which I had passed about 3 hours before, so that it was known to be not more than 3 hours old. There was a packed-down area in the snow about 12 feet across, and a little blood was noted in two places. The calf's legs were still moist. It managed to stand up with considerable effort and after walking a few steps in the snow it fell down. It tried walking several times, seeming to gain additional strength with each effort until finally it was able to follow me around, which it insisted on doing. It gave the typical guttural grunt. While I was with the calf the mother circled about 200 yards away.

The behavior of this calf was similar to that of a number of other newly born calves which were observed. I was unable to check closely on a calf's development, but in a day or two they can follow the mother, and I would guess that in about a week or 10 days they are able to run almost as fast a their mothers. On June 1, I saw calves, chased by a wolf, keeping up with the cows. Most of these calves were not more than 2 weeks old.

RELATION OF CALVES TO COWS

I found no indication of cows leaving their calves while going off to feed, as do antelope, deer, and moose. From the time the calf is born it remains close to the mother. When able to follow readily, the calf as a rule remains close beside or behind the mother like a shadow. This close attachment is important from the standpoint of survival in a herd animal, for a great many calves would otherwise lose their mothers. Some observers have stated that the calves seem to have little attachment for their mothers and wander off at random. After watching thousands of calves my impression is that the calves do remarkably well in remaining close to their mothers. It is true that when a large herd has been disturbed a few calves become separated, but with several hundred animals milling around it is surprising that more of them are not left astray. On several occasions I have seen cows and calves searching for one another.

On May 29, 1941, I observed an interesting incident in this connection. On the rolling tundra between Savage and Sanctuary Rivers I saw a band of about 700 adult caribou with calves moving westward and then circling northward. They had moved away from two grizzly bears. After the caribou had moved a little less than a mile, I noticed that two calves were lost, a half mile from the main herds. One calf joined up with a cow and calf and followed in their wake for some distance, and then moved off in another direction, obviously searching for its mother, which in the meantime had returned from the main herd and soon found her calf. When the mother came the youngster at once commenced to nurse vigorously. It had been lost at least a half hour. The other calf wandered toward the herd, started for several cows, then circled back toward the place it had left. It then disappeared in a swale and was not seen again. This calf was searching for its mother, and after following the herd had returned to where it apparently had last seen her. A cow, probably the mother of the second calf, was searching but while

I watched she did not go back far enough to find the calf.

On July 1, 1940, a lone calf came running in my direction and stopped within 15 yards of me. It apparently was looking for its mother and came to investigate me. It later crossed some broad gravel bars and found her.

The cows are reasonably solicitous when their young are in apparent or real danger. On May 24, 1939, I approached a cow with a calf that was less than a day old. When the cow ran off the calf followed slowly. Part of the time the mother trotted slowly enough for the calf to keep up, even though I was hurrying after them about 75 yards behind. Each time the mother found herself a short distance ahead, as happened four or five times, she returned and nuzzled the calf. When it finally lay down, the cow stopped about 50 yards away and did not run off until I captured the calf. Then she ran over a nearby rise and circled above me, keeping watch from a distance of about a half mile until I left. This mother seemed more solicitous than a mother elk would be.

On May 24 two rangers and I chased a calf which was following a cow slowly. When one of the rangers overtook the youngster, the mother, a short distance ahead, turned and showed her defiance by pawing the air. After they ran off we caught up to another cow and calf and both calves dropped in the brush when they were unable to keep going. The mothers peered anxiously at us from the steep slope opposite. After

Figure 49: A mother caribou trots slowly so her newborn calf can keep up with her. [*McKinley River, May 24, 1939.*]

going over the hill one of the cows returned and came within 75 yards as we were departing. Some cows run off more readily than others, often disappearing after a brief show of solicitude. Quite often they return to peer over a hilltop to see if the intruder has gone.

On occasions when wolves have killed a calf I have seen the mother searching the area for it. Once I observed a cow smelling of her calf at least several hours after it had been killed. On one occasion a cow with a calf too young to follow, ran off with the herd, but returned to the calf in 10 minutes.

The calves soon begin to feed on green food so that by the time they are a month old their main food is vegetation. On June 12 the calves were feeding extensively on vegetation. The stomach contents of a calf found dead on June 14, 1939, was well filled with green food including the twig of a willow. Since the bulk of the food of very young calves is vegetation, the weaning would not seem to have much effect on the physiology of the calves. By fall the bodies have become accustomed to being nourished almost entirely by vegetation which, we can assume, furnishes a balanced ration. I do not know how late the calves continue to nurse. A cow killed by O. J.

Murie on October 18, 1922, had considerable milk in the udder so that the calves were apparently getting some milk at that time.

Parasites

Two parasites—the warble fly (*Oedemagena tarandi*) and the nostril fly (*Cephanomyia nasalis*)—annoy the caribou considerably and at times, perhaps, are a serious drain on their vitality. O. J. Murie (1935, p. 10) writes as follows about these parasites:

The warble fly deposits its eggs on the hair of caribou; the larvae hatch, bore through the skin, and migrate to the back region, where they develop just under the skin, until they finally work out and drop to the ground, producing the familiar perforated skin condition. In July and August, the active egg-laying time, these flies cause the caribou much uneasiness. Although the fly does not sting, the animals fear them and stand in a strained, alert attitude, stamping a foot or shaking the head when one hovers about. It would be interesting to know to what extent the animal is able to avoid these attacks by such vigilance. The writer has seen a caribou suddenly run for more than a quarter of a mile, then abruptly drop on a sand bar, in the shelter of a steep bank, and remain there quietly for a long time. Such flight is probably effective, if long enough and in the right quarter of the wind, for the flies probably hunt by scent.

On one occasion, while traveling overland with a companion, using several dogs as pack animals, the writer noticed a warble fly buzzing along behind the dogs, flying along until it caught up with the rear dog, but not alighting. Presently the fly seemed to become fatigued and lit on the ground. When the dogs were some distance ahead the fly again took up the chase and soon was hovering about the dog once more. This procedure continued for some time, leaving the impression that the fly was fatigued each time it dropped to the ground, and that after a period of rest it again followed the scent of the animals. In the absence of caribou, the fly probably was somewhat attracted by the scent of the dogs but not to the extent of laying eggs.

The nostril fly deposits its larvae in the nostrils of the caribou, and they finally lodge in the soft palate, in the posterior part of the mouth cavity. In spring they become very noticeable and appear as a tightly packed wad of larvae, the writer in one case having counted 125 in the throat of one animal. In April caribou were seen coughing repeatedly for some time, apparently as a result of such irritation. The larvae drop out probably in May.

On July 30, 1939, I watched a yearling for half an hour, alternately holding its head in a clump of willows and biting at flies. At times it cocked its ears and appeared to be watching a fly in front of it. It frequently licked its hind leg near the ankle, and several times a front foot and a hind foot. Occasionally it shook itself. Sometimes the nose was held almost touching the ground. This caribou seemed to be endeavoring to avoid warble flies and possibly nostril flies too. Such behavior was seen several times.

The animals would sometimes bunch up on the river bars. After reading what Sdobnikov (1935 p. 64) says about this habit in reindeer, it appears that the caribou may avoid warble flies by standing close together. He states that "in order to lessen the injury to the reindeer, caused by the gadfly [warble fly], the experienced herder puts the herd on 'tandara'." The term "tandara" means a place where the herd is kept closely together during the flight of the warble fly. There the herd stands sometimes for from 8 to 10 hours. The animals in the center of the band are scarcely molested.

If the caribou should become too abundant in a region these two parasites might become so numerous and infest the caribou to an extent that would greatly reduce their vitality. The shifting of the ranges and movement of the caribou probably reduces the degree to which they are affected by the parasites. Exceptionally heavily infested animals would presumably become weakened and more subject to predation and disease. Sdobnikov (1935) states that in Russia the warble fly may utterly exhaust the reindeer when the infestation is heavy. More than 1,000 larvae have been found on one animal.

The bladderworm (*Taenia hydatigena*) is found in the liver. Another tapeworm (*T. echinococcus*), becomes encysted in the lungs, and a hair lungworm has been found in the lung. The protozoan *Sarcosporidia* was found in one caribou by Hadwen and Palmer (1922). It produced a "pitted" appearance on the surface of various bones and tendons. The incidence of these parasites in caribou is not yet well known.

Disease

The Park Superintendent's report for January 1926 speaks of the presence of a disease among the caribou the previous year as follows: "No indications of disease have manifested themselves of late, and much to the relief of all concerned, there does not seem to be any further advancement of the ailment which killed a number of caribou last year." I have found no other mention of this "disease" so do not know its nature or how large the losses were.

Several skulls that were picked up showed severe necrosis and exostosis of the jawbones, especially around the teeth. Very likely the caribou are subject to a disease similar to necrotic stomatitis common among the elk in the States.

A cow found dead July 15, 1940, had probably succumbed from some kind of internal infection. Pus completely filled one lung and part of the other. On the tissue adjacent to one lung was a nodule of pus 2 inches in diameter.

Concerning disease of caribou, O. J. Murie (1935, p. 9) writes as follows:

No opportunity during this investigation was had to make a careful study of caribou diseases, but none of the observations made indicated that these animals are subject to disease to a serious degree. Seymour Hadwen and L. J. Palmer (1922) discuss various diseases and parasites found among the domestic reindeer, and some of these may occur in caribou. They found, however, that in a number of cases conditions were aggravated by close herding, and it is therefore probable that the caribou— scattered over a wide territory—are much less susceptible to disease than are the reindeer.

The caribou move about so much that losses would not be easy to discover, but so far as we know the losses from disease are not great.

Some Predator-Caribou Relationships

LYNX, WOLVERINE, AND CARIBOU

No signs of lynx were noted; the wolverine was relatively scarce and so secretive that no observations on this animal in relation to the caribou were made. During calving time both of these species might prey on calves, but ordinarily the predation would be unimportant.

COYOTE AND CARIBOU

So few coyotes are present in the park that no data were secured on their relationship to the caribou. If numerous they might kill a few calves, but it seems probable that a cow could generally ward off a coyote attempting to get her offspring. A young bull kept in captivity by my brother and me in 1923 showed much dexterity in the use of its hoofs. When we tried to force him to one side of a corral with a rope he struck the rope on the ground fiercely and accurately with fore hoofs and then with hind hoofs. This bull was full of spirit and often chased us when we came near. Only the heavy toggle to which he was tied stopped his rushes. This exhibition in the use of the hoofs indicates that they could be used effectively on a coyote.

GRIZZLY AND CARIBOU

On May 28, 1941, a lone grizzly and a pair of grizzlies were seen between Teklanika and Savage Rivers where many caribou calves were being born. The lone grizzly was surprised feeding on the carcass of a very young calf, and a little later it was seen feeding on another calf carcass. The pair of grizzlies was also feeding on calf carcasses.

On May 29 a large herd of caribou was noticed moving away from two approaching grizzlies. The bears did not follow the herd, but the general movement of the caribou indicated that they considered the grizzly an enemy.

After the first few days the calves are probably fairly safe from grizzly attack unless taken by surprise. But before the calves gain strength and speed the bears evidently are able to get some of them. The total effect of grizzly predation is not large, however, for there seems to be no special movement of grizzlies to the calving grounds, and the few bears preying on calves would not take a heavy toll. Some of the calves eaten probably represent carrion, and there would be many afterbirths which might also attract bears. No information indicating bear predation on adults was secured. The best time for predation on weak adults would be in the winter, and at this period the bears are not active. Six adult caribou were found eaten by bears. Two of these carcasses were greatly decayed when eaten. Some of the caribou eaten were known to be carrion and the probability is that they were all dead when found by the bears.

GOLDEN EAGLE AND CARIBOU

Eagles are known to prey on caribou calves but the number they kill is insignificant. Not only is the number of eagles extremely small in proportion to the number of calves, but also, so far as I could determine, the eagles seldom prey on young caribou, which are vulnerable to eagle attack for only a short period.

A Mr. Brown, an Alaska Road Commission foreman, told me of an interesting incident which occurred about June 13, 1938. He saw a calf left behind by a startled cow. Soon an eagle appeared and commenced to swoop at the calf, which warded the eagle off by rearing up on its hind legs and striking at it with front hoofs. The calf finally took refuge in some willows. When it came forth, two eagles began swooping at it. Once it struck one of the eagles with its forelegs and caused it to cry out. For a few seconds there was a mingling of calf and eagle. The besieged calf again took refuge in the willows, where it lay down. When it emerged, two more eagles had arrived and four eagles were swooping at it. After fighting them off for a time, it again hid in the willows. The eagles were perched on the ground in the general vicinity of the calf when Mr. Brown left the scene. It was surprising that the calf was able to put up such a spirited defense. If the cow behaved normally, she would in time have returned to her offspring. Lone calves evidently sometimes fall prey

to eagles but probably a calf with its mother is seldom attacked.

On June 14, 1939, I found the carcass of a recently killed calf east of Toklat River. While I was examining it, an eagle soared overhead. It had been feeding on the dead animal, and wounds indicated that the bird had killed it. The talons had punctured the hide and penetrated the muscle on both sides of the neck. The skull was cracked from one eye to the antler bur on the opposite side. At this point there were no punctures in the skin, so it appeared that the skull had been cracked by a blow from the eagle. The wounded areas were all bloodshot. Only the eagle had fed on the carcass.

Later in the day another eagle was seen perched on a dead willow 2 feet from the ground. Twenty-five yards from the perch was a freshly killed calf. Part of the brisket, lungs, and tongue had been eaten and a part of one jaw had been torn loose. There were talon marks surrounded by bloodshot areas on the left shoulder and just behind it. The rear part of the skull was cracked open, apparently by a blow, as the skin was not punctured. The evidence indicated that an eagle had killed this calf, too.

Both calves were probably less than 2 weeks old. They were found where large herds had recently passed, so it is possible that they had strayed and had been left behind. As mentioned elsewhere, calves are occasionally lost, especially when large herds are suddenly disturbed. The above observations are the only ones which showed calves being molested by eagles.

Relation of Reindeer to Caribou

The domestic reindeer is a smaller animal than the fine, large Alaska caribou. Unfortunately the two animals readily cross, so that when reindeer are brought into caribou country there is grave danger of the caribou herds deteriorating because of crossbreeding. In view of this danger the reindeer herds should be kept away from the region inhabited by the caribou.

In 1922 a large herd of reindeer was brought through Mount McKinley National Park and for a few years was kept in the Broad Pass region. During the drive many reindeer strayed and joined the caribou. Since the caribou migrated to the Broad Pass region at the time the reindeer were kept there, some reindeer had opportunity to join the caribou herds. The reindeer at Broad Pass were permitted to stray and now are entirely gone. Many crossings no doubt were made with the caribou and, although they may have had some effect on the herd, it is not now noticeable. It is fortunate that the reindeer in that region were exterminated. Perhaps the wolves were an important factor in ridding the caribou country of these reindeer.

Wolf Predation

PREDATION ON ADULT CARIBOU

Despite the fact that there is much wolf predation on adult caribou one must be cautious and examine all accounts of such predation critically. A suprising number of reports, both written and spoken, do not bear scrutiny. One evening in 1939 some boys told us that they had just witnessed two wolves pull down a cow caribou. They gave a vivid account of the incident and told us where the hunt had occurred. After supper three of us set out to examine the carcass. We found it, but the animal had been dead at least a week. The hair slipped all over the back and even on the legs. The boys had probably seen one or two wolves at the carcass and had made a good story of it.

Another similar incident is also interesting. A man had come into Fairbanks from the direction of Circle with a report that wolves were killing great numbers of caribou, and described how a pack of wolves had killed a number of them. The story passed many lips. A man interested in wolves hunted up the observer to get particulars. The observer said he saw tracks of a band of wolves and one caribou they had killed. For the sake of accuracy, he was asked if one wolf could not make many tracks. The observer admitted that one wolf might make as many tracks as he had seen. He was asked how he knew the wolves had killed the caribou and if it wasn't possible that hunters had killed it since it was near the road. The observer did not know about that. In this instance, although the wolves may well have been killing many caribou, the observer had little evidence on which to base his assertions. It illustrates how an erroneous evaluation of a situation from the quantitative standpoint may be built up in the public mind.

Most of the predation on adult caribou seems to occur during the fall and winter months. During the calving period and throughout the summer the calves, when available, are preyed upon and apparently only a few adults are then killed. But sometimes there are stray adults and no calves and then probably adults are hunted. It seems that wolves run the adult caribou until they are exhausted, for in a short chase the grown animals can run away from the wolves. At times perhaps wolves may maneuver so as to bring a caribou down more quickly. Weak and lame animals would not be expected to run very far.

On October 14, 1940, tracks were seen which showed that at least four or five wolves had been chasing a large bull caribou which had galloped in a straight course through a patch of spruce. Along the trail there was some blood which may have come from bruised feet rather than from wounds inflicted by the wolves. The chase emerged from the spruces and went out on the gravel bar where tracking became difficult. But it was obvious that a large caribou had been chased by the wolves. A carcass was found later in the general area, but there was no way of knowing whether or not it was that of the animal that had been chased by wolves.

On March 19, 1941, on the rolling hills between Savage and Sanctuary Rivers I came upon the trails of four galloping caribou. Trails of two wolves showed that they were running after them. The chase had swung over to the north side of a broad basin, through a fringe of spruce, across to the south side, and up a rather steep ridge. Two caribou continued climbing the ridge to the top, but the other two, when near the top, cut down the ridge, galloping through a heavy growth of willows which filled the bottom of the basin. All the way the snow had been about 18 inches deep, but here it was even deeper, and the caribou broke through to their bellies. When the wolves came to the place where the four caribou had split, it may be significant that they gave chase to those which had failed to climb the ridge and had run down hill. After running down hill the two caribou floundered through the deep drifts among the willows in the hollow, then gained a slope on the other side largely free of snow. Here they followed some low ridges where the travel was easy and then started to climb the long slopes of the Outside Range of mountains. It was too late to follow the tracks far up the mountain so I never learned if the wolves overtook the two caribou. I had followed the chase for 3 or 4 miles.

On the morning of July 2, 1941, I saw three wolves on the middle of East Fork bar. They were from the East Fork den and consisted of the gray female, the black-mantled male, and the light-faced male. They watched me for a few minutes, then the black-mantled male trotted slowly to the east slope. The light-faced male trotted a few yards to the carcass of a caribou but in a moment followed the other male. The female trotted up the bar toward the den. Four hours later I examined the carcass which proved to be that of a young cow. It was still warm, hence the wolves must have killed it that morning. There were several bloodshot tooth marks on the neck. The animal had not been hamstrung. At this time the caribou herds were far to the west so that the only caribou available were stragglers.

Otto Geist of Fairbanks told me that he once saw a caribou run past him with tongue out, obviously weary. A little later a wolf appeared on the trail and it also seemed weary. The next morning Geist followed the trail down river to the end of the chase. The wolf had killed the caribou, had eaten his fill, and was sleeping on the river bank opposite the carcass.

It is well known that wolves kill adult caribou but it is difficult to learn what proportion of the caribou killed are below standard in strength. It is hard to know how "nip and tuck" the relationships are between the two species; how many healthy caribou chased by wolves escape, and how many succumb.

PREDATION ON CARIBOU CALVES

In the spring the wolves prey extensively on the calves. The first day or two after birth they cannot run fast enough to give the wolves a chase, but in a few days they can almost keep up with the cows and then they force the wolves to do their best. In no instance was the wolf seen stalking caribou. Such maneuvers are unnecessary, for the wolf has no difficulty in approaching within a few hundred yards of them. Generally the caribou seem not to be worried much by wolves unless chased. Bands were frequently noted watching the wolves when they could have been moving away to a more secure position.

The wolf's method of hunting calves seems to give an opportunity for the elimination of the weaker animals. Usually the wolf chases a band of cows containing several calves. The speed of the calves is only slightly less than that of the wolves, at least on level terrain, so they make the wolf do his best, and the chase continues long enough for a test of the calves. The weakest, the one with the least endurance, falters after a time and drops behind the others, and this is the one the wolf captures. In some instances I suppose a calf falls behind because it is younger than the others, but after these animals are a few weeks old the differences in time of birth probably are unimportant, and the one actually weaker than the others is the one that succumbs. Thus the wolf appears to be a factor in maintaining quality in the herds.

There may be more weak animals in populations than has been generally realized. In this connection some observations of the elk in Jackson

Hole, Wyo., are pertinent. In the spring of the year there is much variation in the strength of the yearlings. If a large herd is started running, some of the yearlings may be seen to collapse, exhausted by their efforts. Most of these animals at this time are able to rise again after a rest, being weak only from the winter hardships. Others are apparently diseased for they die soon after tumbling. In the presence of a predator probably these weaker animals would be eliminated as the winter progressed.

HUNTING INCIDENTS

For a better understanding of the hunting habits of wolves and the behavior of the hunted caribou, a number of illustrative incidents are here described.

Typical Wolf Hunt.—On June 16, 1939, I had my first full view of a wolf capturing a caribou calf. My assistant, Emmett Edwards, and I were sitting on a ridge high enough above the river bars to give us a good view of the prospect before us. We were classifying according to sex and age the bands of caribou passing up the river. All day, band after band passed us, going up the west fork of the Teklanika River to the glaciers of the high Alaska Range; others were coming down this fork and going up the east fork. About noon we noticed in the distance a band of about 250 caribou, mainly cows and calves, coming downstream. Soon they were near enough so that we

could make out that they were galloping. Suspecting that they were being disturbed, I looked through the field glasses and saw a black wolf galloping after them. When the caribou reached the triangular flat between the forks of the river in front of us, the wolf was close upon their heels. The caribou in the rear fanned out so that they were deployed on three sides of the wolf. He continued straight ahead, continuously causing those nearest him to fan out to either side, making an open lane through the herd. Those on the sides stopped and watched the wolf go past. Soon most of the caribou were on either side of the wolf's course.

On the flat the wolf stopped for a moment and so did all the caribou. Then he continued straight ahead after a band of about 30, and these again fanned out, whereupon he swerved to his left after 15 of them, which then started back in the direction from which they had come. The wolf chased these for about 50 yards and stopped. Small bands of caribou, some of them only 100 yards away, almost surrounded him. It seemed strange that they did not run away from the vicinity of danger. Then the wolf seemed to have come to a decision, for he started after 25 cows and calves farther from him than those he had just been chasing. Before they got under way he gained rapidly. For a time the race seemed to be going quite evenly, and I felt sure the band would outdistance their enemy. But this was my first view of such hunting activity and I was mistaken.

The gap commenced to close, at first almost imperceptibly. The wolf was stretched out, long and sinewy, doing his best. Then I noticed a calf dropping behind the fleeing band. It could not keep the pace. The space between the band and the calf increased while that between the calf and the wolf decreased. The calf began to lose ground more rapidly. The wolf seemed to increase his speed a notch and rapidly gained on the calf. When about 10 yards ahead of the wolf the calf began to veer from one side to the other to dodge him. Quickly the wolf closed in and at the moment of contact the calf went down. I could not be sure where the wolf seized it, but it appeared to be about at the shoulder. The chase had covered about 500 yards and the victim was about 50 yards behind the herd when overtaken.

In a few minutes the black wolf trotted a short distance to meet a silvery-maned gray wolf which was limping badly on a front foot. Together they returned to the dead calf, sniffed it, then moved off, and circled to the left side of the ridge at the forks and climbed it slowly. Halfway up the slope they rested for a half hour, and then they continued to the top of a promontory about 1,000 feet above the river bars. On the way they flushed an eagle which circled and twice swooped low over them. The wolves lay down on the point of the ridge until 7 p. m. At this time we decided to examine the calf carcass and descended from our ridge, taking advantage of a high bank along the river to keep out of sight of the wolves.

When we reached a point on the bar opposite the kill we saw the limping gray wolf coming down the slope. Then we saw the black one feeding on its prey about 300 yards up the slope from where the kill had been made. He had no doubt carried the carcass while we were walking along the bar. Several runs were made at six or seven magpies which were feeding with him. Soon the wolf left, returning once to chase the magpies from the meat. The gray animal which had been lying a short distance above the black one then approached the meat and carried off a large piece. When we reached the spot there were only a few ribs and some entrails left. As we walked towards camp the gray female was again seen resting on top of the ridge.

Unsuccessful Hunt.—On June 17 we returned to the forks of the Teklanika to watch the wolves. A band of 15 caribou, without calves, trotted along the bar followed by a trotting gray wolf. When the wolf stopped to sniff at a fox den the caribou stood watching him from a distance of only 75 yards. The caribou moved off and the wolf disappeared, perhaps to rest.

Later in the morning (about 10 o'clock) eight or nine cows and four calves were seen galloping across the river bar followed by a gray wolf loping easily. They all crossed the east fork of the Teklanika River and came out on the flat where the day before a calf had been killed. The wolf galloped rapidly across the flat after the fleeing caribou, which with a long lead reached the rough country at the base of the ridge. The wolf gained on the caribou while they ran up and down the slopes and it ran on the level, but when the wolf also reached the rough country it was quickly left behind. On top of the first slope it gave up the chase after running somewhat over a half mile.

An Afternoon Hunt.—On June 1, 1940, from a lookout near the East Fork den I saw an interesting hunt. At this time there were many bands of cows with calves, some feeding only a quarter of a mile from the den. One group walked within 50 yards of it. From the lookout I counted 1,500 caribou. At 4:40 p. m. the black-mantled male looked into the den and then walked down to the bar. He was followed closely by Grandpa, and shortly the black male came out of the den and also followed. It looked as though the black-mantled male had looked into the den to let the black male know he was going hunting. The three disappeared in a ravine leading up the long slope. Grandpa was limping badly on a hind leg, not using it at all when he galloped. The gray female started late, after the others were in the ravine. The black female was left to watch the den, resting near the entrance.

Far up the ravine the black-mantled male, followed closely by the black male, appeared on a large snowdrift. The black-mantled male

waited for the black male and when it came up, jumped and romped with him. The wolves seem to enjoy romping on these late spring snowdrifts, and I have seen mountain sheep also jump about and play on them. The female wolf was following a couple of hundred yards behind. The black-mantled male turned southward at right angles and followed a bench. The others turned also, about 100 yards lower down the slope. Far in the rear appeared Grandpa, still limping badly. He turned about a third of a mile below the others, being out of their sight on the slope below the bench on which they were traveling. They moved southward, the black-mantled male loping in a rocking-horse fashion, apparently from excessive spirits. Several bands of caribou in front of the advancing wolves galloped rapidly up the steep slope. A mile or more to the south I lost sight of all except Grandpa, who had stopped and howled.

Soon the others had swung around Grandpa, who acted as a pivot, and they all moved northward again toward the den. The black-mantled male was just below Grandpa and far down the slope came the black male and the gray female. By the time these three came abreast of Grandpa, about 200 caribou in one band, and some smaller bands, were galloping northward ahead of them. Some of the caribou ran up the slope. The larger band was followed by a grizzly galloping below and parallel with it. The bear seemed to be hurrying to get away from the general commotion. He veered off to the river bar and there stood up on his hind legs and looked up the slope in the direction from which he had come. Then he dropped to all fours and continued across the bar.

The wolves stopped soon after they had started northward, and the black male howled. When the black-mantled male answered him from up the slope, all the wolves assembled on the high point where he stood. They lay down for a few minutes, then the black male moved down the slope at an angle and chased some caribou. For a time the caribou did not run, so the black male was well within 250 yards before they began to flee. He galloped hard up a low ridge and down into a shallow ravine where he captured a calf after following it in a small half circle. In about 10 minutes the black male came out in the open and howled, whereupon the three wolves on the point started toward him. The black male trotted toward the den, turning aside on the way to follow the fresh tracks of a cow and calf for several yards. The black male arrived at the den at 6:20 p. m., 1 hour and 40 minutes after leaving it. He disappeared in the den for a few minutes. Soon the other three wolves returned and the gray female immediately went into the den, while the two gray males walked up above to lie down. The last three wolves arriving had not gone to the kill but had come directly to the den.

The first part of the hunt seemed to follow a system of herding the caribou, but after the wolves assembled on the point three of them took no further part in the hunt.

Three Male Wolves Seek Calves.— Preceding the departure for this hunt there had been much tail wagging and some howling, which has been described in the wolf chapter beginning on p. 32. After the ceremonies, at 7:30 p. m., the three males trotted across the bar westward parallel to the highway. The two females remained behind, lying a few feet apart near the den and watching the departing hunters. The males were out for the regular night hunt. All day caribou had been in the vicinity of the den, but the resting wolves did not molest them.

Soon after their departure, caribou on the flats ran off in various directions, showing that they had seen the hunters. The wolves kept trotting southwestward. The black male, ahead and to the right, soon passed out of my sight behind a ridge. The black-mantled male was far out on the bar, and Grandpa was out of sight near the black male. The wolves crossed the neck of tundra between two forks of the East Fork River. In the meantime I hurriedly returned to the road and drove westward in my car, stopping on Polychrome Pass high above the rolling tundra over which the wolves were traveling.

Small bands of caribou were scattered over the tundra below me. Now the black male was far ahead of his two companions. As usual he seemed to be doing most of the hunting. He approached two or three bands in his course and watched them while they ran away. In these bands there happened to be no calves so I wondered if the wolf was looking over each band to see if calves were present. The two grays caught up with the black male, and part of the time the large black-mantled one was in the lead, trotting gaily and briskly with tail waving. Once he dashed at a band, then stopped to watch. The scattered caribou came together in a bunch and ran off. There were no calves. Once the black male galloped hard after a herd but stopped to watch when he was near to it. As the wolves continued traveling the mantled male lingered far behind and from a knoll in the tundra raised his muzzle and howled. He was answered by the deep, hoarse howl of one of the wolves in the lead. After traveling 5 miles they again were together and as yet had made no serious effort to kill caribou. There were many calves in the country, but the small bands containing 15 or 20 caribou which the wolves had encountered along the way happened not to have any. It appeared that the wolves were searching for calves. At 10 p. m. the wolves crossed the road and went out of sight behind a ridge.

Some of the bands that ran from the wolves went off to one side only a few hundred yards. Others which went straight ahead in the course taken by the wolves ran as much as a mile. Some bands fled because they saw others run, and on a few occasions took a course nearer the wolves.

The Black-Mantled Male Feeds Alone.—On June 4, 1940, at 5:45 p. m., I saw the black-mantled male howling as I was going to the den. He was lying on a knoll a mile from the den. In order not to disturb the wolves I retraced my steps. For 5 minutes after I reached the road the wolf continued howling at short intervals and then he trotted briskly toward Sable Mountain. When I arrived at a point where I could get a view of the slope, I saw about 250 caribou, including calves, running hard. Then I noticed the wolf feeding on something, probably a calf caribou. Whether he had just made a kill or had returned to an old kill I do not know but I suspect that it was an old kill. He fed about 10 minutes, then lay down beside the carcass and stretched out on his side. At intervals of 10 or 15 minutes he raised his head for a look around. While the wolf was lying there, small bands of caribou passed near him. One band of 10 adults and 3 calves passed within 50 yards of him. After these had passed he looked up, then galloped easily after them for a hundred yards, stopped, and after watching them a few moments, slowly returned to his resting spot. The cows and calves fled full speed along the base of the mountain, a calf leading the flight. At 9 o'clock the wolf trotted slowly westward.

The Two Gray Males Chase Caribou.—In the dim twilight of June 13, 1940, south of Polychrome Pass, two wolves which appeared to be the black-mantled male and Grandpa were harassing some bears which probably had raided their kill. After a half hour the two wolves trotted westward and from above approached a herd of about 200 caribou which included many calves. Both wolves galloped hard toward the caribou, which angled up a slope. After a few hundred yards of running, the rear wolf stopped, and then chased a lone adult caribou which was standing nearby. This caribou was chased for 200 yards and then the wolf started up the long slope toward the herd its companion was chasing. Near the main Alaska Range where the chase led, the shadows were so deep I could not see all that happened. But after the herd had gone almost up to the rugged slopes it had turned westward to a broad flat between two ridges. A little later the wolves were chasing the herd up this relatively level flat to near the head of the valley but then the animals were again lost in the deep shadows and I could not see if a kill was made. A half hour later the two wolves were back harassing the bears. The early return of the wolves suggested that they had not been successful, but in any event the caribou had given the wolves a long chase.

A Cow and Calf Hurry Away From the Wolves.—Usually the caribou did not run far from a wolf unless pursued, but on June 16, 1940, a cow and calf were seen galloping across the east side of Sable Pass. Evidently they had winded four wolves which were approaching. The caribou traveled a mile and a half or more while we watched and, still hurrying, disappeared behind some hills. Later the four wolves appeared but were not on the trail of the cow and calf.

To hunt, the wolves had gone to Teklanika Forks, 10 miles or more from the den, and yet during the day at least 400 caribou had been feeding a mile or two west of the wolves, and at least two bands with calves had passed within a quarter of a mile of them. Wolves seem to enjoy traveling and probably have favorite hunting grounds.

Black Female Goes on a Short Lone Hunt.—On June 17, 1940, only the two females were seen at the den. Grandpa was seen at Teklanika Forks 10 miles away and perhaps the other two males were also spending the day there. The black female seemed restless all day; perhaps she was hungry. At 5:30 p. m., as it commenced to rain, she trotted to the den, then over to the gray female lying 50 yards away, and, after stopping with her a moment, trotted across the river bar. In about 5 minutes she appeared south of me, about a mile from the den, chasing a large band of caribou containing many calves. Some of the caribou ran off to one side and soon began to feed. A calf brought up the rear of a group she was chasing. When it appeared that the wolf might overtake the calf, most of the band and the rear calf veered upward to the left and seemed to increase their speed. The wolf singled out another calf which was running straight ahead with four or five adults, but in a moment the chase went over the ridge. Then it commenced to rain so hard that the visibility became too low to see anything. It seemed to me that the wolf might be successful.

Caribou Escape After Short Run.— On June 19, 1940, the five adult wolves were observed near the den from 8:30 a. m. until 6:10 p. m. A half mile north of the den at 11 a. m. one of the black wolves chased a band of 35 cows and calves for about 400 yards and then gave up without catching any calves. During the day five bands of cows with calves, averaging about 100 animals in a band, passed within a third of a mile of the den without being molested.

A Maneuver by Two Wolves.—On June 22, 1940, at 8:35 p. m., the black-mantled male and the black male followed the river bar southward from the den. About 3 miles away 200 or 300 caribou were feeding on a grass-covered flat. For about a mile the two wolves trotted together; then the gray one fell far behind. He moved along the east bank while the black one trotted briskly diagonally across the river bar toward the caribou. When about 200 yards from them he watched for about a minute as though to size up the situation, then started galloping forward. He ran in such a way as to drive all the caribou off the grass-covered flat toward the gravel bar. He did not try to catch any of them but was definitely herding the scattered animals. When he had run the length of the scattered herd and had the

caribou all galloping out on the bar he swung around the front end of the herd and then came back chasing them all before him. As the wolf caught up with a band it would veer off to one side. Then he continued straight ahead to the next little band which in turn would veer off to one side. Finally he stopped, sauntered over to the bank, wandered around as though investigating the area, then trotted across the bar in the general direction of the den. He went into some willows where he probably lay down for I saw him no more. The caribou moved on westward along their migration route, feeding as they went, behaving as though they had completely forgotten the chase.

The black-mantled male wolf in this hunt lingered on the other side of the bar. Some of the caribou which had been driven out on the bar had drifted over near him and he had chased a band up in the tundra. They ran far to the east, but the shadows were so deep that I could not follow the hunt closely enough to learn whether any calves were killed. I was able to see the running caribou, but caught only an occasional fleeting glimpse of the wolf.

I do not know whether the hunt had followed a general pattern of cooperative maneuvering but it might be so interpreted. In this case there was no great advantage gained by the wolves but under different conditions the maneuvers could be advantageous to them. If the black wolf had chased the caribou toward the gray wolf far enough to tire the caribou somewhat then the gray wolf could have taken up the chase fresh.

A Long Chase.—On June 23, 1940, at 9:30 a. m. I saw 250 or more cows and calves running hard, a mile or more east of Toklat River. A wolf, apparently the black male of the band, was chasing them. The wolf chased one group after another, so that he finally had the various groups running in different directions. Although galloping hard he did not bear down on any herd. It looked as though he were testing the groups, looking for a specially vulnerable calf. After considerable chasing, the wolf ran after four adults and one calf, driving them off by themselves. The calf broke off to one side and kept veering as though trying to return to the herd, and in so doing lost ground, for the wolf could then cut corners. When the wolf was apparently about 20 yards behind the calf, it was unable to reduce the gap for some time, but when the calf began to zigzag it lost ground. The wolf gradually reduced the distance to a few yards, but still the chase continued for another 200 yards or so. For a time I thought the calf might escape, so well was it holding up. But the wolf finally closed in, and the calf went down. While the wolf stood over the calf, apparently biting it, it jumped up suddenly and ran for 75 yards before it was again overtaken. A few minutes after disposing of the calf the wolf trotted a short distance toward the herd, then returned to his prey. The caribou herd continued on its way westward.

Caribou Undisturbed By Wolf Howling.—On June 25, 1940, at about 5 p. m., more than 200 cows and calves came out on the bars above the East Fork wolf den. They were strung out in a long straggly line, feeding as they moved. A wolf howled from a short distance above the caribou and soon its howls were answered by two or three wolves at the den. Although the caribou were between the lone wolf and those at the den, they continued feeding. I could not see that any of them heeded the howling. About this time a heavy rain obliterated the view, and it continued raining all evening so no further observations could be made.

Three Calves Killed By Wolves.—When the calves are only a few days old the wolves can kill them with little effort. On May 29, 1941, two calves, probably 2 or 3 days old, were found dead, 25 yards apart, between Sanctuary and Savage Rivers, where hundreds of calves were being born. Birds had fed a little on each. Bloodshot wounds on neck and back were such as to make it plain that the calves had been killed by wolves. Some neck vertebrae of one were crushed. Very likely the two calves had been killed about the same time. Less than a half mile from these two carcasses I saw a lone cow smelling of a calf. She walked away a few steps and then returned to smell again. Then she moved off 200 yards to feed. I walked to the calf and found that it was dead. On skinning it, I found tooth marks around the head and back, which apparently had been made by a wolf. The calf was only a day or two old. The three calves had been killed within the preceding 24 hours.

The Black Male Easily Captures a Calf.—On June 29, 1941, at about 3 p. m., my attention was attracted by a band of about 400 caribou running over the rolling tundra a mile west of the wolf den. The black male wolf first ran toward one end of the band so as to chase the caribou forward. The herd broke up into groups of 50 or 60, and the wolf dashed along in the middle, and I could not be sure of the status of the chase. Then the wolf started after 50 cows and calves. There was a chase of about a half mile, and the wolf kept closing in upon the herd. Once he stumbled as he galloped, and rolled completely over. But he was quickly on his feet, and little time was lost. Then a calf dropped behind the others. This seemed to encourage the wolf to put on added speed, and in less than a quarter of a mile he overtook the calf, knocking it over as he closed in. The wolf was hungry and fed for about half an hour. This calf was captured more readily than usual.

Crippled Wolf Hunting Caribou Calves. —Foreman Brown of the Alaska Road Commission camp told me that on June 29, 1941, at Stony Creek, he had seen a gray wolf with a crippled hind leg chasing calves with no success. After chasing some bands without catching any calves the wolf moved off and waited for the herds to approach. But while the caribou were still some distance away it jumped up and gave chase. It had good speed for a short distance but quickly tired and fell behind. It caught no calves while Mr. Brown was watching.

A Lone Calf Captured.—About 10 a. m., July 19, I saw the black female wolf on the East Fork bar circling back and forth with her nose to the gravel. She made a sweep of 100 yards downstream, then returned upstream, and finally waded the river. After crossing the stream her ears were cocked forward and she started on an easy lope up the creek, apparently focused on a definite point. I looked ahead of her and saw a caribou calf lying on the bar beside the creek, watching the wolf. When the wolf was about 150 yards away the calf jumped up and galloped upstream. It crossed and recrossed the creek a dozen times, and every time the wolf followed. The calf did not seem to be as speedy as much younger ones had been, for the wolf was running rather easily and gaining. A full half mile from the start the calf, now hard pressed, wallowed in a deep part of the stream and on the next leap stumbled and fell. In a jump or two the wolf caught up and pulled the struggling calf, which once gained its feet for a moment, across the deep part of the stream to the shore where it was quickly killed. The main herds had passed westward some time before, so this calf was a straggler and may therefore have been a weakling. Upon examining the gravel where the wolf had been sniffing around in circles, I found fresh calf tracks. I believe the wolf had not seen the calf before I arrived because a short while before she had been observed 3 miles up the road.

Animals Found Dead From Causes Other Than Predation

One encounters enough carcasses on the range to indicate that quite a number of caribou die from natural causes other than wolf predation. Sometimes upon examining these carcasses no cause for death can be found; at other times diseased conditions are evident. Below is information regarding some of the carcasses found on the range which were sufficiently fresh that I could at least eliminate predation as a cause of death, and in some cases determine the cause.

May 1939.—Ranger Edward Ogston reported that some caribou calves lost their lives in crossing McKinley Fork. During May 1939, the stream was open in places but was bordered by perpendicular walls of overflow ice several feet in thickness. He saw calves go into the streams and fail to get out. Since hundreds of cows with calves crossed the stream at that time, he thought that several of the calves probably were trapped by the overflow ice. The number of calves lost in this way is probably small.

July 21, 1939.—The carcass of a cow which was found on a tributary of East Fork was being eaten by eagles and magpies. There was not a bear or wolf track leading to it so it probably was not a victim of predation. No cause for death could be determined.

August 8, 1939.—A cow which had recently died had severe necrosis around the lower molars. It appeared that the necrosis was sufficiently severe to have weakened the cow and possibly killed her.

May 19, 1940.—A newborn calf was found dead. Apparently it had died at birth. No doubt a certain percentage of the calves die at birth. No food was found in the alimentary canal.

June 2, 1940.—Near T e k l a n i k a River a yearling was examined which had been reported hamstrung by wolves. The hide had been bruised on one tendon but the tendon was intact. The joint below the tendon was swollen to about twice its normal size and was bursting with pus. There were no tooth marks on the joint. Apparently the infection had killed the yearling.

June 7, 1940.—The carcass of an old cow was found which had not been fed upon. There was no indication of what might have caused her death except that she was very old.

July 15, 1940.—Late one evening a Road Commission employee arrived with a message from photographer Al Millotte stating that there was a dead caribou in a tributary of Igloo Creek. I drove there that night to examine the carcass while it was still intact. The caribou had died within the last day or so. Two legs had been carried away and birds had eaten the meat from the backbone. The animal was an adult cow. Upon examining the organs I found one lung completely filled with pus, the other partially filled. The tissue adjacent to the lung was in one spot swollen with pus, forming a round ball 2 inches in diameter. This infection was, no doubt, the primary cause of the animal's death. I dragged the carcass out of the water and in a few days wolves and bears had consumed the flesh and dragged away the bones. The main caribou herds had moved westward so this one was a straggler which had been left behind.

June 2, 1941.—On the flat on top of Sanctuary Mountain I found a cow with one antler shed. The animal had been dead for about 2 weeks. There was an unborn calf, normal in appearance and as large as one already born. The only indication of disease was blood in the nostrils. The animal had not been killed by wolves. Later it was eaten by bears.

Crippled Caribou

Crippled animals were noted on several occasions. Often they brought

Figure 50: A caribou calf bruised beyond recovery by a fall in the rocks. [*McKinley River, June 25, 1939.*]

up the rear of a band. Most of the crippling was probably due to natural accidents since the herd is not hunted heavily by man. These crippled animals would be highly vulnerable, and probably are the first to succumb to the wolf. Those seen are listed to give an indication of their prevalence. Perhaps if the wolf were absent more cripples would have been evident. One trapper told me that since the wolves became common he has seen far fewer crippled caribou.

June 10, 1939.—The front leg of a cow was bent as though it had been broken and had later healed. She had a decided limp.

June 14, 1939.—A cow was noted limping on a front foot.

June 16, 1939.—Two cows limped decidedly. Both were lame on a front foot.

June 19, 1939.—A cow, limping badly on a foreleg, brought up the rear of a band.

June 25, 1939.—Near the base of some steep cliffs and talus slopes I found a calf which was breathing with difficulty, unable to stand. Upon examining it, I found a femur and mandible broken, and ribs and shoulder bruised. It apparently had fallen in the rocks. There was no cow in the vicinity.

July 7, 1939.—I saw a calf with a severe limp on a front foot. I also saw a very thin yearling with one horn about 6 inches long and the other horn 2 inches long, a stunted condition which indicated that the animal was not normal.

July 9, 1939.—I found an old ulna

and radius of an adult caribou which had been broken and later healed. The healing had been accompanied by considerable exostosis. This animal no doubt had been handicapped in traveling.

July 13, 1939.—Bringing up the rear of a band of about 800 caribou I saw a calf limping on a front foot, a thin cow limping on a front foot so that her head went up and down violently with each step, and another cow with a hind leg which most of the time was not used.

July 16, 1939.—A calf, bringing up the rear of a band of about 200, limped badly on a foreleg, hardly using it. In another band there was a cow with a pronounced limp.

July 27, 1939.—Near Teklanika River I saw a lone caribou with a definite limp in a foreleg.

June 7, 1940.—In the rear of a band I saw a cow not using one of its hind legs.

January 8, 1941.—In a band of six, a cow brought up the rear, limping badly.

July 8, 1941.—A lone bull on Igloo Creek was lame.

Calf Crop

At times it is difficult to get a good calf count. Large herds often travel so compactly that many of the calves remain hidden behind the cows. When the herd is lying down the calves are hard to see. Therefore satisfactory counts of resting herds were usually not obtained. In 1939, when I had an assistant, I used field glasses and called off the classification of each animal as it passed and my assistant kept the tally. In this way we classified a number of herds. But in 1940 and 1941 I was alone practically all the time and usually found it extremely difficult to classify the animals accurately. In 1941 when the herds moved westward after the calving period the animals were so massed that there was little opportunity to count calves. During the latter year one herd numbered roughly 4,000 adults, another 1,000, and another 2,000, and the animals traveled in compact groups.

1939 CALF CROP

The counts obtained in 1939 give a fairly accurate figure for the calf crop. On several occasions conditions were ideal for classifying the herds. On June 16, 17, and 18, from a ridge, we observed the caribou moving along slowly on the river bars, often in single file. All of the caribou passing were not counted because of the interruptions caused by other events such as a wolf chasing a caribou calf. In addition, many bands bunched to an extent that the individuals could not be counted. On July 13 another excellent count was secured of a single herd of 827 animals. I was able to classify this herd twice.

To show how the bands vary in calf percentages I have tabulated the classified bands for 1939. See Table 15 (p. 178).

Although the calf percentage in many herds does not vary far from the average, some herds do show

TABLE 15.—*Classified Caribou Counts, 1939*

Date	Cow [1]	Calf	Year-ling	Adult bull [2]	Young bull [3]	Date	Cow	Calf	Year-ling	Adult bull	Young bull
May 24	201	3	49	0	0	June 18	0	0	1	4	2
May 29	2	0	0	10	0		0	0	1	15	5
June 12	122	43	(4)	0	0		0	0	6	12	7
	105	36	(4)	0	0		5	1	14	20	18
	10	8	0	0	0		9	1	4	0	0
	42	9	(4)	0	0	June 19	12	4	1	1	0
	30	10	6	0	0		18	15	0	0	3
	16	8	0	0	0		47	32	2	0	0
	75	62	5	12	0		52	38	5	0	1
	0	0	3	3	6	June 20	0	0	1	1	12
	100	30	(4)	0	0	June 22	0	0	0	0	25
	105	28	(4)	0	0		0	0	0	16	0
June 13	80	38	(4)	0	0	June 25	0	0	6	42	0
June 14	95	51	(4)	0	0		1	1	8	35	0
	40	29	(4)	0	0	June 27	0	0	0	0	50
	50	31	(4)	0	0	July 2	11	7	0	0	0
	27	9	(4)	0	0		11	6	1	0	3
June 16	399	199	90	18	5 45		2	2	0	0	0
	30	12	6	12	0	July 7	46	43	11	0	2
	0	0	3	15	0		45	30	7	0	1
June 17	28	17	10	16	0	July 10	9	7	2	10	0
	15	7	2	6	15	July 13	432	295	73	8	19
	4	3	0	0	1	July 16	93	48	25	9	14
	3	2	5	5	5		8	5	1	0	1
	10	5	0	10	16		20	9	6	0	2
June 18	38	16	18	19	20	July 17	26	18	2	0	0
	7	6	2	0	0		2	1	1	0	0
	1	0	3	4	2		9	6	3	0	0
	0	0	1	2	5						
	0	0	1	1	3	Total	2,493	1,231	385	306	283

[1] Includes unclassified yearlings and young bulls in some instances. The counts of cows were therefore somewhat larger than was representative.

[2] Bulls were not sufficiently represented in the counts because the main herds of males were missed.

[3] Young bulls often could not be identified from cows in the moving massed herds.

[4] Indicates that yearlings could not be distinguished from cows. In these cases yearlings were recorded in the column headed "Cows."

[5] Several bands.

extremes. The herd classified on May 24 had practically no calves, while one seen on June 12 had 75 cows and 62 calves, and another herd seen on July 7 had 46 cows and 43 calves. It is obvious that erroneous conclusions on the calf crop could be obtained by classifying only a few bands.

Of 2,493 cows in the herds classified, 1,231, or 49 percent of them, were followed by a calf. Since, as stated, some young bulls and yearlings are included in the figure for cows, the calf crop can be considered as being fully 50 percent.

1940 CALF CROP

The figures for the 1940 season are not extensive but they signify that the calf crop was about the same as that of 1939. Of the 735 cows classified, 379 were followed by calves, so that the calf-cow ratio was 51:100. Many general observations and partial counts of herds were in agreement with the figures listed in the table below.

TABLE 16.—*Classified Caribou Counts, 1940*

Date	Cows [1]	Calves	Year-lings	Bulls [2]
June 1	90	0	30	0
June 2	9	6	1	0
June 7	130	89	([3])	0
	30	17	([3])	0
	300	175	([3])	0
June 30	109	58	20	6
July 2	62	29	([3])	0
July 5	4	4	0	0
July 8	1	1	0	0
Total	735	379	51	6

[1] Includes unclassified yearlings and young bulls in some instances. The counts of cows were therefore somewhat larger than was representative.

[2] Bulls were not sufficiently represented in the counts because the main herds of males were missed.

[3] Indicates that yearlings could not be distinguished from cows. In these cases the yearlings were recorded in the column headed "Cows."

1941 CALF CROP

In 1941 I obtained but few figures on the calf crop. Many counts were attempted but were not accurate enough to tabulate. On June 28 two herds were classified. One consisted of 258 cows and 127 calves, the other of 29 cows and 17 calves. The calf percentage in these two herds was 50. From several partial counts my impression was that the calf crop was about the same as in the 2 preceding years.

It is interesting to compare the calf-cow ratio with that of elk, another herd animal. In Teton National Forest, Wyo., in the summer of 1935 O. J. Murie found that 38 percent of the cows were followed by calves and in Yellowstone National Park in 1937 I found 41 percent of the cows followed by calves. Darling (1937) states that the fertility of the hinds of the red deer in Scotland is about 60 percent and says it is the same as given by Cameron (1923) for red deer in the island forest of Jura. It would seem, from these figures, that the calf crop found in the caribou herds was about as expected.

Survival of Calves to Yearling Stage

It is difficult to learn what proportion of the calves survive to the yearling stage because not all yearlings are found with the cows. Many of them join the old bulls or the young bulls and cows. To get an accurate figure one would need a sample of a cross section of the herd and that is difficult to obtain, because many herds consist mainly of bulls and others of cows.

However, from the figures available we can perhaps get a fairly accurate idea of the percentage of yearlings. It will be noted that in 1939, in several bands, the yearlings were not classified separately from the cows. The counts for these bands have been eliminated in determining the ratio of yearlings to cows. In the bands in which yearlings were classified there were 1,727 cows and 385 yearlings. The ratio of yearlings to cows is 22 percent. Assuming that the count is a representative sample, and that the calf crop in 1938 was about the same as in the following 3 years, then it appears that a little more than half, or about 56 percent, of the calves succumbed during the first year. That, it would seem, is a satisfactory survival, although as yet we do not know how large a survival is needed to perpetuate the herd in the case of the caribou.

The figures for 1940, together with general observations, show about the same yearling ratio as was found in 1939, although the figures are meager. Ten small bands of cows were classified on May 12 with the following result: 160 cows and 34 yearlings, or a ratio of about 21 percent. That represents a survival of about 42 percent of the calves during the year. In June and July, bands were classified which contained 213 cows and 51 yearlings, which indicates a 48 percent survival of calves to yearling age.

In 1941 the survival of yearlings seemed less than during 1939 and 1940, but not enough figures are available to substantiate this impression. Certainly among the caribou wintering around Savage River there were few yearlings. Among three or four hundred cows there were only about 20 yearlings, or a yearling ratio of only 5 or 6 percent. However, the yearling ratio for the herd was considerably higher than this figure for in bands seen later yearlings were more abundant.

There is still much to learn about the mortality of young and the numbers necessary to perpetuate a herd. Different herds, due to many varia-bles, may require different degrees of survival among the young. In areas where there is heavy hunting by man there must be a higher survival of young to take the place of the adults shot. Under natural conditions, perhaps a much smaller survival is needed and desired. A too-high survival of young would increase the herds too rapidly, so that ranges would quickly be overgrazed. At the George Reserve near Pinckney, Mich., where some white-tailed deer were introduced in a fenced area, the survival of fawns for at least 7 or 8 years seemed to be complete. In the wild the survival of young is usually quite different. Under natural conditions a mortality of half of the young seems to be usual. However, we need more data to understand thoroughly the mechanics of wildlife population.

The number of yearling caribou, especially in 1939 and 1940, seemed adequate for the welfare of the herd when compared to the survival of yearlings in other large game animal populations.

Effect of the Wolf on the Caribou Population

It is difficult to determine the effect of the wolf on the caribou. Because the species has maintained itself through the centuries in the presence of the wolf we can expect it to continue to do so under wilderness conditions. The extensive predation on the caribou, especially on the calves, is apparently an important check on their numbers. It is not unlikely that at the present low human population level the wolves serve as a useful check on the caribou. If this check were entirely removed the caribou might increase in numbers to such an extent that vast areas of choice lichen range would be severely damaged. Those familiar with the overuse of many big game ranges in the States can readily appreciate the importance of this consideration.

In localities where hunting by man becomes extensive enough to be an important check on the caribou, as it may be in some parts of Alaska, some adjustment in wolf numbers may then be necessary to offset the reduction caused by man. Present information on these details is meager so that it is difficult to decide on management practices. But if man's hunting under the present wilderness conditions that exist over large parts of Alaska is insufficient to keep the caribou in check, then the value of the wolf in this respect should not be overlooked.

The effects of the wolf on the character of the caribou over a long period are also hard to evaluate. The wolves may be an important evolutionary force in changing or maintaining the caribou characteristics.

The Mount McKinley National Park herds appear to have held their own during the last 20 years. Although there has been heavy wolf predation in recent years, the caribou seem to be adjusted to withstand the losses. To care properly for the caribou herds and insure their perpetuation, regular observations should be continued so that their status, together with that of the range, may be known at all times.

CHAPTER FIVE

ᗕᗕᗕᗕᗕᗕᗕᗕᗕᗕᗕᗕᗕᗕᗕᗕᗕᗕᗕᗕ

Moose

ᗕᗕᗕᗕᗕᗕᗕᗕᗕᗕᗕᗕᗕᗕᗕᗕᗕᗕᗕ

Distribution

MOOSE (*Alces gigas*) occur over a large part of Alaska. Mount McKinley National Park lies along one edge of the vast interior moose range. In the park they are found inside the north and east boundaries, and for some distance up along the streams which are bordered by fringes of timber. The moose are not confined to the timber but are frequently found in willows far beyond timber.

In one trip along the north boundary in January 1941, I found tracks plentiful in each strip of spruces and willows bordering the streams and in the many draws between the main streams. Tracks also were seen in some draws grown up in willow above the spruce timber. On this trip 20 moose were seen between the railroad and Wonder Lake on the outward journey and 5 more were seen on the return trip through the interior of the park. There have been no extensive counts on which to base an estimate of the number of moose in the park. From my general observations I would estimate that they totalled somewhere between two and three hundred.

Usually the snow is not deep enough on the moose range to greatly hamper the movements of the moose or to encourage yarding. A few trails were noted, but generally the moose were found traveling where they pleased. They are often seen alone or in groups of two or three, but on one occasion in January seven bulls were seen together and three more bulls were in a group a short distance away, and in November four cows and a yearling were banded together. In 1932, during a period when the snow was exceptionally deep and crusted, groups of 15 and 18 were reported on McKinley River.

Breeding

The rut begins in early September and continues 3 or 4 weeks. In 1939, the first rutting activity was noted on

Figure 51: Bridge across Teklanika River. Cathedral Mountain on the left. Igloo Mountain on the right. The wooded area is permanent habitat for a few moose. [*September 1939.*]

September 5. On that date a lone cow which I was watching suddenly became alert and gazed intently southward toward a large bull which was approaching. His antlers were freshly cleaned of velvet and still bloody. The cow ran into the woods while the bull was still about 200 yards away and he followed her at a swinging trot.

The young are born in late May. Frequently there are twins. Of 16 cows, known to be different individuals, which were followed by calves, 9 were followed by a single calf, 7 by twins. This ratio is based on too small a sample to be taken as the average, but it shows that there is much twinning. The ratio of twins was much higher than at Isle Royale,

Mich. (Murie 1934), where few were observed.

Food Habits

The chief food of the moose in Mount McKinley National Park, winter and summer, is willow. In winter, twigs up to a quarter of an inch in diameter are eaten; in summer, the leaves are stripped off the twigs, but many twigs are also utilized. Some dwarf birch was regularly browsed in winter. Aspen and cottonwood are eaten but these species occur sparingly. White birch, a palatable moose food that is abundant in much of interior Alaska, is rather rare in the park and hence is not even a minor food item.

In Wyoming and in some of the Eastern States and Canada, moose in winter feed extensively on conifers such as Douglas fir, balsam, and ground hemlock, but in Mount McKinley National Park the only common conifer is the spruce and it is extremely low in palatability. On Isle Royale, Mich., some spruce was eaten by moose, undoubtedly because of the shortage of winter food. No spruce was found eaten in Mount McKinley National Park.

In summer, tender grasses and sedges are eaten to a certain extent, and no doubt various herbs are also taken at this time. Moose also seek the small ponds where they feed on submerged vegetation.

History of the Moose in Mount McKinley National Park

Moose are said to have been plentiful in the park prior to the period (about 1920) when the Alaska Railroad was being constructed. It is said that the moose in the eastern part of the park were reduced by market hunters who were at that time, and for a period preceding the coming of the railroad, hunting sheep and other game animals. Indians are reported to have hunted moose north of the park. I have no records indicating a reduction in moose numbers in the western part of the park at that time, although there may have been some decrease

there too. Hunting need not be especially heavy to reduce a moose population.

In 1922 and 1923 moose were considered scarce in the park. I saw none in the Savage River region at that time, although a few were known to be present between Savage River and the railroad. In 1927 they were considered scarce in the eastern section but more plentiful to the west. In 1928 a general increase of moose was reported in the eastern part of the park and along the north border.

The unusually deep and crusted snow in the spring of 1932 caused some reduction in the population. Ranger John Rumohr, who at the time was freighting mountain-climbing equipment and supplies to the base of Mount McKinley for a climbing party, told me that he found six or seven moose carcasses along the trail. Apparently the animals had died from malnutrition for they were exceedingly thin, "little more than skin and bones." One moose still alive was so weak that it could hardly stand and the next time Ranger Rumohr passed that way it was dead. The Superintendent's reports for that year tell of the hide being worn off the legs of the moose below the knees and that each track was covered with blood. The moose could probably have negotiated the deep snow but the hard crust was disastrous. That spring many moose must have succumbed to the elements. But in spite of these losses moose were still present in fair numbers and the next

Figure 52: A cow moose with newborn calf, which, in an unknown manner, had suffered a broken leg. [*Sanctuary River, June 3, 1939.*]

year were reported to be increasing.

During the last 10 years it appears that a satisfactory number of moose have been present in the park.

Moose-Wolf Relationships

Ranger John Rumohr reported that in January 1940 he had seen tracks in the snow which plainly told the story of an attack of five wolves on a bull moose. The snow was much trampled but no blood signs were observed. One prong of a horn had been broken off. The wolves had given up a bad job, for their trail pointed west while the moose had wandered off to the east.

Lee Swisher said that twice he had seen tracks in the snow which showed that wolves had worried a moose. In one case quite a large area had been trampled. He thought that the wolves had done this mainly in sport. Once a cow moose was seen in summer with hind legs bruised and wounded. He thought the moose may have fought off wolves. Her calf, however, was unhurt.

John F. Stanwell-Fletcher (1942) who made a number of observations on wolves in British Columbia, states that in December as the snow deepened, wolf trails were seen which "usually led through the forests to a moose-yard or its vicinity. But there was little snow under these trees, and the moose was seldom attacked, for its hoofs are sharp and deadly when it has firm footing. By the first of January, Indian trappers began to report small and large packs of wolves. All of these were seen traveling along the edges of lakes. They were in groups of from 4 to 31, moving slowly and in single file. By the end of January, with 6 to 8 feet of snow, the wolves began to hunt moose in earnest. Deeper snow beneath erstwhile sheltering trees forced the moose to travel farther for food, and in deep snow they were easy prey for the wolves. Within an area of 5 square miles just north of us, seven moose were killed by wolves during the winter of 1938–39. Only the moose, whose great weight forces him to travel with bent forelegs used as snowshoes, can be hunted successfully. That the wolf's food is not easily obtained even then, is evident when one follows a trail in the snow. We have the skull and skin of a large black dog-wolf which was found alive with broken ribs and leg bones, underneath a tree. Surrounded by moose tracks, blood patches and moose hair, the wolf had been crippled in a great battle. Similar cases were frequently reported by Indians and apparently usually occurred when the wolf had attacked the moose alone."

Apparently the moose killed in this area were under a great disadvantage because of the deep snow. Possibly food was also scarce or hard to get and the moose were consequently somewhat weakened. It would be highly significant to know the age and condition of the moose killed by the wolves, for possibly they were in a weakened state when killed. In the Mount McKinley National Park the snow depth is usually not great enough to hinder the moose as it does in the part of British Columbia referred to by Stanwell-Fletcher. But even in the latter region, where wolves which, were reported common, were killing the moose, it appeared that moose were not at all scarce.

Wolves perhaps worry many moose which fight them off with such vigor that they are unwilling to expose themselves to the deadly hoofs. However, if any sign of faltering is shown, due to old age, food shortage, or disease, the wolves would no doubt quickly become aware of it, and one would expect them to become more persistent in their attack in hope of wearing down the animal. Moose which are actually known to have been killed by wolves should be closely examined to determine their condition. Unfortunately in many cases the evidence is destroyed.

Granting that adult moose are difficult prey for wolves, one might suspect that young calves would be quite susceptible to wolf attack. However, a cow with a calf is a formidable creature and if molested by wolves would probably put up a vigorous fight to protect her young. I know of one case in which two Huskies, the size of wolves, attacked a cow with a calf. She held her ground beside her newly born calf and drove the dogs away. Nevertheless, we would expect that occasionally a calf would fall prey to wolves.

Although no precise data on survival of calves were obtained, it appeared that many calves were surviving in Mount McKinley National Park. More than half the cows seen, omitting known duplications, were followed by calves. Some interesting observations on calf survival in the ranges of the different wolf families were made.

In an area inhabited by a family of wolves on Savage River a cow and her twin calves were seen on August 14, 1940. She had raised them in an area where wolves traveled daily. During the winter tracks of calves were seen regularly in this general region.

At Igloo Creek a cow moose lived the year round in an area about 5 or 6 miles along the highway. Much of the time her wanderings were confined to an area about 2 miles across. On May 29, 1940, this cow was seen with two calves a day or two old. During the summer this family was frequently seen. It was seen in November and at various times during the winter and spring. The group often fed close to the the road which was used regularly as a highway by the 12 East Fork wolves. The wolves sometimes sniffed at the moose tracks on the road but did not follow them. On May 18, 1941, almost a year after their birth,

the calves were still with the cow. At this time they were feeding together, but the mother made frequent rushes at the yearlings to drive them away. They tried to remain near her but she no longer wanted them, for she was expecting another family. Later, on June 6, she appeared with her new single calf. The calf was still with her in August when I left the park, and the two yearlings were seen several times during the summer. Thus, in the heart of the wolf country along a much-traveled wolf highway the twins had survived, and another calf had passed the most critical stage in its life.

In 1940 another cow had a single calf on Teklanika River, not far from the point on Igloo Creek where the above-mentioned cow had her twins. Tracks of a cow and calf were seen as late as February, so here also a calf was surviving along the highway which was used by the wolves.

The relationship between wolves and moose is perhaps best shown by the fact that the moose increased in the park about the time the wolves became common, and have since held their own although the wolves have remained common. In the region north of the park, according to trappers, there has been a pronounced increase in moose in the last 4 years. This has been attributed to a decrease in hunting. In this region there are many wolves in winter. Greater numbers of moose also have been reported in sections east of the park on Moody Creek.

An old-timer stated that between 1898 and 1903 moose and wolves were abundant on Stewart River. He was sure that moose could survive in large numbers in the presence of a large wolf population. He said wolves were to be heard every night and that moose were so plentiful that people had all the meat they wanted.

In Mount McKinley National Park and adjacent areas a satisfactory moose population is maintaining itself in the presence of many wolves.

Condition of Moose Range

An examination of the moose range along Igloo Creek revealed that the browsing on the willows had resulted in a rather uniform condition of broomed tips. Since only a few moose live in the area, this amount of feeding sign was not anticipated. Although this range is in good condition, these observations suggest how readily a moose range can be overbrowsed. After viewing exceptionally overbrowsed ranges on Isle Royale, Mich., and in the Yellowstone region of Wyoming, it is especially gratifying to see a moose range not overutilized. The moose in Mount McKinley National Park could still increase somewhat without injury to the range, but a heavy increase of population would not be desirable.

C H A P T E R   S I X

≪≪-≪≪-≪≪-≪≪-≪≪-≪≪-≪≪-≪≪-≪≪-≪≪-≪≪-≪≪-≪≪-≪≪-≪≪-≪≪-≪≪-≪≪

Grizzly Bear

≪≪-≪≪-≪≪-≪≪-≪≪-≪≪-≪≪-≪≪-≪≪-≪≪-≪≪-≪≪-≪≪-≪≪-≪≪-≪≪-≪≪-≪≪

Description

ACCORDING to C. Hart Merriam (1918) there are two species of grizzlies in Mount McKinley National Park.[1] All but one of several bears collected in the park by Charles Sheldon were identified as *Ursus toklat* of the "*Alascensis* Group." Members of this group range to the west as far as Bering Sea. One grizzly which was shot and an old skull which was picked up were referred to *Ursus kluane*, a species belonging to the "*Hylodromus* Group" which ranges eastward from Mount McKinley National Park. (Sheldon, 1930, p. 379.)

There is considerable variation among the bears in their general appearance. Some are light in color, others dark. Large dark males were

[1] Black bears (*Euarctos a. americanus*) are occasionally seen in the lower wooded sections but are scarce. I never saw one. In 1969, all grizzlies and brown bears in North America were placed in a single species—*Ursus horribilis*. Some taxonomists place our grizzlies and the Eurasian grizzlies in the same species. When this is done the scientific name becomes *Ursus arctos*.

seen with light-colored females. In one case a light-colored female was followed by a large dark male and a light straw-colored male. A noticeable variation in color was present in three yearlings belonging to the same family.

Since various combinations of these bears were seen mating, all are believed to belong to the same species.

The bears are all darker in the late summer and fall when their coats are new and unbleached. Early in August, one bear was seen which was a rich chestnut color, quite different from that of the average bear. In the spring and early summer most of the bears are a light straw color over the back and their legs and faces are dark. Some of them are so faded that in the distance they may be mistaken (if casually observed) for mountain sheep.

Grizzlies were encountered in all parts of the park that I visited. They were generally found in the treeless terrain which seems to be their chosen habitat, but they were also frequently noted in the narrow strips of woods along the streams. They roam over the mountain slopes and valley bottoms in their foraging, climbing the mountains with surprising speed if disturbed. No counts were made but I estimate that there are from 50 to 75 grizzlies between Park Headquarters and Wonder Lake.

I found the grizzlies unusually well behaved. Many times they were encountered at relatively close quarters, that is close enough so that they became keenly aware of my presence. Once, while sitting on a rock watching sheep, I heard a loud snort close behind me. On turning I saw a mother and her yearling galloping up the slope about 100 yards away. One day my companion and I met a female with three cubs as we rounded the lower part of a ridge. We were about 100 yards from her, far from trees and unarmed; we continued walking but changed our course about 70 degrees. She stood placidly watching us and soon resumed her grazing. Once in the open tundra a bear, which had been hidden in a gully, loomed up 150 yards in front of me. It stood up on its hind legs for a half minute looking me over and then moved around to one side. When it had passed me it broke into a gallop, crossed a broad river bar, and hurried up a slope on the other side. In late August my companion and I found ourselves in an unexpected predicament. We were approaching the small relief cabin on Copper bar which is built in the open far from any trees. When 15 or 20 yards from the cabin we saw a grizzly about 60 yards behind the structure, standing on its hind legs looking for a ground squirrel. Then the ground squirrel broke forth from the clump of willows and scurried for the cabin. The grizzly came in hot pursuit. We did not know which way we should scurry, for obviously when the bear arrived at the cabin it would be almost upon us. Soon we also were dashing toward the cabin. When we arrived we found that the storm door was held rigidly in place by four bolts. Fortunately the bolts came out with a jerk and we found the inside door unlocked. I peeked around the corner of the cabin and the grizzly made two bluffing lunges toward me. It then walked away slowly, growling at intervals.

Some bears which were frequently seen became unafraid and permitted a close approach. One or two of them at garbage heaps became too tame. The chief danger to a person in the hills is in meeting a bear unexpectedly at close quarters. The grizzlies usually are peaceably inclined and run away when disturbed.

Food Habits

The Grizzly as a Vegetarian

The grizzly is for the most part a vegetarian, but by necessity rather than choice. There would be more meat in the diet if he were able to get it, as no opportunities to feed on meat are overlooked. Carrion is always relished but is largely obtained fortuitously. Mice are sometimes eaten as tidbits, but they are too small to be

Figure 53: A grizzly in fall coat feeding on buffaloberries. [*East Fork River, September 23, 1939.*]

relied upon for bulk unless they are very plentiful. Ground squirrels are sought to a certain extent at all times, but this food involves laborious digging, and even then, after much excavation, the squirrel often escapes. At long intervals a marmot is captured.

During the span of about 6½ months that the grizzlies are active in Mount McKinley National Park, their feeding habits pass through three marked phases. In the spring, up to early June, the chief food consists of roots. Then during June and July they feed mainly on green vegetation, chiefly grass (*Calamagrostis langsdorfi*) and horsetail (*Equisetum arvense*). In late July when berries become available, and during Au-

gust, September, and October, the bulk of the food consists of berries. Roots also become part of the late fall diet. These principal foods are supplemented by others. A few ground squirrels are caught and eaten at all seasons, and carrion is always highly acceptable.

The data on bear food habits were obtained during 3 years, and as the general pattern was the same each year it seems that the data presented depict the normal diet of the grizzlies. A total of 201 bear scats were analyzed in detail. Many others examined cursorily in the field corroborated the data obtained from those

TABLE 17.—*Results of food analyses of 201 grizzly scats collected in Mount McKinley National Park in 1939, 1940, and 1941* [1]

Food items	May (25 scats)			June and July (115 scats)			August, September, October (61 scats)		
	Times occur-ring	Percent [2]		Times occur-ring	Percent [2]		Times occur-ring	Percent [2]	
		Maxi-mum	Aver-age		Maxi-mum	Aver-age		Maxi-mum	Aver-age
VEGETABLE MATERIAL									
Grass (mainly *Calamagrostis langsdorfi*)	4	100	87	92	100	75	13	100	46
Roots (*Hedysarum* spp.)	6	100	85	2	100	60			
Blueberry (*Vaccinium uliginosum*)	3	100	67	9	100	68	41	100	60
Horsetail (*Equisetum arvense*)				26	99	57	3	75	49
Buffaloberry (*Shepherdia canadensis*)				5	95	40	28	100	23
Spruce cones (*Picea* sp.)	1	25	25						
Arctous sp	2	40	22	7	95	21	35	100	16
Herb, sp				6	50	10			
Sorrel (*Oxyria digyna*)				1	5	5			
Crowberry (*Empetrum nigrum*)	1	1	1	2	5	3	22	50	20
Cranberry (*Vaccinium vitis-idaea*)				4	10	3	9	85	10
Boykinia richardsoni				2	1	.5			
Dwarf Arctic birch (*Betula nana*)				1	Trace	Trace			
Saxifrage (*Saxifraga tricuspidata*)				2	Trace	Trace			
Sage (*Artemisia hookeriana*)							1	Trace	Trace
ANIMAL MATERIAL									
Hoary marmot (*Marmota c. caligata*)	1	100	100						
Caribou, adult (*Rangifer a. stonei*)				1	100	100			
Caribou, calf (*Rangifer a. stonei*)				13	100	54	2	100	100
Dall sheep, adult (*Ovis d. dalli*)	10	100	85	8	100	94	7	100	95
Dall sheep, lamb (*Ovis d. dalli*)							1	25	25
Ground squirrel (*Citellus p. ablusus*)	4	100	87	10	100	28	13	90	15
Mouse (*Microtine* sp.)				1	1	1			
Ptarmigan (*Lagopus* sp.)				1	1	1			
Wasp, sp				1	Trace	Trace			

[1] Scats have been segregated for different periods to show changes in grizzly diet as the season advances.

[2] The maximum percentage of the food item found in a scat and the average percentage of the food item in the scats in which it occurred.

studied minutely and listed in Table 17. The data secured from watching bears feeding were more extensive than those secured from the examination of scats and were highly important in corroborating the scat data and rounding out the entire food-habits picture.

The data from the droppings are segregated according to the periods in which the different food habits prevail, for to combine the data for the different periods would fail to show the shifts in food habits. Most of the droppings were accurately dated.

ANNOTATED LIST OF GRIZZLY FOODS

Roots.—Six of the 25 scats, gathered in May, contained roots of *Hedy-*

sarum. Many observations of the bears during May, however, indicate that this ratio does not give a true picture of the diet during this period. Of course, the number of scats are too small for a good statistical figure, but aside from that there are other reasons for the small proportion containing roots. The scats containing grass were from the previous year. The number of scats containing sheep is not representative because I spent much of my time searching for sheep remains and covered rather thoroughly the area where bears had fed on sheep. I would estimate that normally, during May at least, 75 percent of the food of the bears consists of roots.

Throughout May and into the first week of June the majority of the bears seen were digging for roots. Generally they seek the roots on the vegetation-covered bars or low slopes but at times they also seek roots far up on the mountains. Some of the favored spots, covering a few acres, had been dug so extensively that they suggested a plowed field. In some of these places bears were seen digging for roots day after day. I was interested in finding much sod turned over by bears just above some cliffs where the sod terminated. It apparently was easy to turn over the sod here where it lay like a carpet with an edge exposed. The bears' activity here had increased the erosion process.

Although roots are eaten mainly in the spring, I also found a number of places where they had been dug during September. Feeding on roots is probably resumed at this time because some of the other foods are either less available or less palatable.

It is difficult to identify the roots found in the scats and often it is not easy to determine the species of plant eaten at the diggings. One of the most sought plants is *Hedysarum*, including at least, *H. americanum* and *H. mackenzi*. It seemed to be the main plant sought in spring and fall. Dixon (1938, p. 145) mentions that *Anemone* roots were eaten. Former Ranger Harold Herning said he had found roots of dwarf birch eaten. Sheldon (1930) shot five bears during May and the stomachs of all of them were full of "pea vine" roots. There are two or three genera that he might have been referring to, but it is more than likely that it was *Hedysarum*.

To get at the roots the bear usually places both paws on the ground and thrusts back with the body until a chunk of sod is loosened. This is turned over, the free roots are devoured, and then, with a paw working slowly and lightly, more of the tender roots are uncovered and eaten. I have watched bears feeding in this manner for several hours at a time. The fleshy roots consumed range up to a half inch or more in diameter, and resemble dandelion roots.

Grass.—Grass was found in 92 of the 115 scats picked up in June and July. The average amount of grass in these scats was 75 percent. According to these data 60 percent of the food of the bears during June and July consists of grass and this combined with *Equisetum* makes up 73 percent of the food of the bears during this period. If it were not for the fact that some roots are eaten in early June and a considerable number of berries in late July when the berries begin to ripen, the percentage of grass in the scats would be even higher. There is a period of about 6 weeks (last 3 weeks in June and first 3 weeks in July) when grass and *Equisetum* probably make up more than 90 percent of the food consumed.

Many times I examined areas where bears had fed to determine what they had eaten. Only one species of grass, *Calamagrostis langsdorfi*, was found eaten, except that once a little sedge was also taken. In one scat I identified the seed head of blue grass and no doubt other grasses are at times consumed. But *Calamagrostis langsdorfi*, a tall juicy grass, is the species usually preferred. It is plentiful, as is also *Calamagrostis canadensis* which was not found eaten. In feeding on grass the bears graze steadily, like an ungulate.

Observations made of bears that were feeding substantiates fully the data obtained from the examination of the droppings, namely that during most of June and July grass is the main food of the grizzlies. Palmer (1941) reports grizzlies in the Mount Hayes region feeding on the flowers of *Dryas*, pods of alpine oxytrope, and willow, as well as on grasses and horsetail.

Horsetail.—Twenty-six of one hundred and fifteen scats gathered in June and July contained *Equisetum arvense*, and the average amount present in these scats was 57 percent, which indicates that large quantities of it are eaten when a patch is found. *Equisetum* is probably eaten as soon as it becomes available. It is also relished by mountain sheep and caribou. In August the place of *Equisetum* and grass in the diet is largely taken by berries.

Blueberry.—Blueberries (*Vaccinium uliginosum*) are widely distributed over the park. Some years the crop is better than in others, but it seems that each year there is a generous supply. The new crop of blueberries becomes available in late July, at which time feeding on them begins. One dropping, containing mainly blueberry, was found as early as July 12. During August, September, and early October, blueberries appear to be the most important single item in the diet. During August and September, 41 of 61 scats gathered contained blueberries, and the average amount in each was 60 percent. In this period, according to the data from the scats, they made up 40 percent of the bears' food. Nine droppings, containing an average of 68 percent blueberries, were gathered in July. Some blueberries of the previous year's crop are eaten in May. Three fresh droppings gathered in early May contained mainly blueberries. At this time most, if not all, of the blueberries have fallen to the ground.

Blueberries and other berries are grazed with great vigor. Berries, leaves, and twigs are all gobbled up together. The bears have too much eating to do to be finicky and selective in their berry eating. Even with their roughshod methods they are kept rather busy filling their paunches; furthermore, the food passes through them rapidly, judging from the slight digestion it seems to receive and the frequency with which scats are deposited. On one occasion I saw a bear leave four scats behind her during a single hour.

On August 1, 1940, part of a day was spent watching a mother and her cub feeding on blueberries. She fed continuously and hungrily from 9 a. m., when I first saw her, until 11 a. m. She lay down for half an hour, then fed steadily from 11:30 a. m. until 4 p. m. She lay down for 20 minutes and then commenced to feed. But in a half hour she lay down again and I left her. The cub picked at the berries only part of the time, and frequently rested while the mother fed.

Charles Sheldon, who hunted bears in the McKinley region in 1906, 1907, and 1908, and Joseph Dixon, who spent the summers of 1926 and 1932 in the park, agreed that grizzlies did not eat many berries. Sheldon (1930, p. 117) writes: "It is perfectly clear that many bears of this region do not go for salmon that ascend the rivers, nor do they feed much, if at all, on berries." Dixon (1938, p. 147) quotes Sheldon's statement and observes: "While black bears are notoriously fond of berries the grizzly does not appear to eat them to any great extent. In 1932, I found excellent blueberries growing abundantly in the region. However, only a very small proportion of the bear droppings which I examined showed that berries had been eaten."

In view of these statements about the bears in Mount McKinley National Park it may be well to summarize briefly my findings in this respect because they differ so strikingly from the conclusions of Sheldon and Dixon. According to the data from the scats, the five species of berries eaten by the bears made up 68 percent of their food supply during August, September, and October and formed an important part of their food in late July as well. A few berries were eaten in the spring. The berry eating was apparently as extensive in 1940 as in 1939, and although in 1941 I left the park soon after the beginning of the berry season, the bears were observed shifting their diet to berries as in the two previous years. My observations were made from Savage River to Wonder Lake so that the data are fully representative, and the many field observations were in full agreement with the data from the scats. Palmer (1941) found the grizzlies in the Mount Hayes area feeding in spring on berries of the previous season's crop.

Sheldon's conclusions seem to have been made from the stomach contents of 10 bears which he collected. Five of these bears were killed in May and the stomachs, as would be expected, contained mainly "pea vine roots" (probably *Hedysarum*). Along with the roots, one stomach contained a few mice; one, a ground squirrel; one, 2 mice; one, 1 mouse. Three bears—a mother and two cubs—were shot on August 24 after they had gorged on a sheep, so would be expected to have dined only on meat. A bear killed August 22 had three ground squirrels in its stomach, and the stomach of one killed August 5 contained grass, three ground squirrels, and a shrew. Only the two stomachs from the last two bears would be expected to contain berries. Data from two stomachs is inadequate for drawing general conclusions. Many of the scats examined by Mr. Dixon, which gave him the impression that few berries were eaten by bears, were no doubt deposited during the grass-eating period.

Buffaloberry. — Buffaloberry (*Shepherdia canadensis*) was found in 28 scats gathered in August, September, and October and made up, on the average, 23 percent of the contents. In July it made up 40 percent of the contents of five scats. On July 18, 1940, a mother bear and cub were observed feeding for about an hour on the berries. Most of them in this particular patch were ripe. In 1939 there was a bumper crop and bears were many times observed eating them. In feeding, the paw is sometimes used to lift the branches so the berries can be more easily eaten. This species is commonly found growing in the rocks and gravel along bars and creeks.

Arctous.—There are two species of *Arctous* (*A. alpina* and *A. rubra*) one having a red berry and generally growing in the woods, and the other a black berry, generally found on open, dry ridges. The latter seems most abundant. I do not know if the bear has any preference.

Arctous was found in 35 scats gathered in August, September, and October and averaged 16 percent of the contents in these scats. Seven July scats contained an average of 21 percent *Arctous*. It was found in two fresh scats collected in May. The shriveled berries remain attached to the dried stem over the winter.

Crowberry.—Crowberry (*Empetrum nigrum*) was found in 22 scats gathered in August, September, and October, in 2 collected in July and in 1 collected in May. It is at times eaten in large quantities. Once, in an area where crowberries and blueberries were both abundant, a bear fed mainly on crowberries.

Lowbush Cranberry.—Lowbush cranberry (*Vaccinium vitis-idaea*) is abundant on the slopes and produces heavy yields but it does not seem to be eaten to the extent other berries are consumed. Nine scats found in August, September, and October contained cranberry, averaging a content of 10 percent. One of the scats contained 85 percent cranberry, which shows it may be eaten in large quantities. In June and July, 4 scats contained cranberry. One was a fresh scat gathered in June and the berries in it were from the previous year. On June 12, 1941, a bear fed for a considerable time on cranberries of the preceding year's crop. Because cranberries survive the winter in fairly good condition, it is probable that they are eaten frequently in the spring.

Sorrel.—Sorrel (*Oxyria digyna*) was noted in only one scat, but since it disintegrates considerably in the digestive tract, traces of it in other scats may sometimes have been missed. On two occasions bears were observed feeding on sorrel. Once a large patch of it had been grazed.

Boykinia.—Small amounts of Boykinia were found in two scats. On July 15, 1939, for a period of 2 hours a grizzly was observed eating large quantities of Boykinia. The stems, leaves, and flowers were all consumed. It also ate much *Equisetum* later in the day. In feeding, the jaws were opened wide each time a mouthful was taken, and they worked steadily, chopping at the vegetation. There seemed to be an excessive amount of jaw action to accomplish the hurried mastication. This was the only time a bear was observed feeding on Boykinia. However, it is not as widely distributed as most of the food species, so usually it was not available where bears were seen feeding. On one occasion a bear was seen grazing on *Calamagrostis langsdorfi* and sorrel, and to pass up Boykinia.

Cow Parsnip.—The cow parsnip (*Heracleum lanatum*) was found eaten on July 15, 1939.

Angelica.—On June 10, 1940, a bear was surprised as he was eating a stem of *Angelica genuflexa* which had made about half its growth.

Dwarf Arctic Birch.—A trace was found in one scat. On May 28, 1941, a grizzly was observed feeding for a few minutes on the new leaves of dwarf birch, even though a portion of a calf caribou carcass was still available.

Saxifrage.—A trace of the basal leaves of what was apparently *Saxifraga tricuspidata* was found in two scats. Traces of this plant were also found in some sheep stomachs, so it is apparently a generally palatable species.

Spruce Cones.—Spruce cones, together with dirt and debris, were present in a scat found in May.

Sage.—A trace of sage (*Artemisia hookeriana*) was found in one scat gathered in September.

Willow.—On May 4, 1940, a yearling was observed feeding on willow catkins. In the Mount Hayes region L. J. Palmer (1941) found willow eaten in June.

Ground Squirrel.—Ground squirrels are eaten at all times. This is the one animal, aside from mice, which the bear can hunt methodically with some success. The spring, summer, and fall diets are all supplemented with ground squirrels, but usually in small amounts.

Although grizzlies are often seen digging out and eating many ground squirrels, other foods make up the bulk of the diet. In May, 4 out of 25 scats contained ground squirrels, in June and July, 10 out of 115 scats contained them, and in August, September, and October they were found in 13 of the 61 scats gathered. According to the data secured from the analysis of the scats, 16 percent of the bears' diet in May consists of ground squirrels, 2 percent in the June and July period, and 3 percent in the August-September-October period. These low percentages are consistent enough to show that ground squirrels actually make up a small but probably important part of the diet.

Much time and energy is generally used in seeking squirrels. Sometimes luck is with the bear, and ground squirrels may be captured in two or three successive excavations, but more frequently a bear may dig out or prospect two or three holes without success.

On August 8, 1939, I came upon a mother bear who had dug a trench 15 feet long and was still digging near the middle of it. Her three cubs were digging in various parts of the trench, perhaps in imitation. In typical fashion the mother would place both front paws on the sod and push downward until the piece gave way. Dirt was pawed out and frequent sniffs taken at the mouth of the hole where she was working. Once she reached into the hole with her arm, lying down on her side so she could reach in farther. At this point the cubs all crowded close in expectation. The mother then moved to another entrance above where she had worked and as she was pressing down the sod with her front paws to loosen it, the ground squirrel scurried forth from the hole. The bear jumped

for it but it dodged to one side and managed to escape from four pounces, the last time leaving the bear flat-footed off to one side. But with the next pounce the squirrel was captured. The cubs sat close by watching the mother chew the squirrel but she made no offer to share it with them. One cub did get a morsel which dropped from her jaws. More than half an hour was expended in catching this squirrel.

On July 21, 1940, a grizzly discovered a squirrel under a large snow drift perhaps 25 feet across. There was an entrance on the upper edge of the drift and one on the lower side. The bear kept going back and forth from one entrance to the other. In going from the upper hole to the lower one he often slid down the drift. He would poke his head into the upper entrance to sniff the squirrel, then return to the lower hole to continue digging into the snow. He dug into the drift so far that he was completely hidden. Once while the bear was in the lower hole digging, the squirrel came out through the upper hole, sat up straight to look around, then scurried away from the drift. The bear made a few more trips up and down the drift after this, then lost interest, seeming to realize that the squirrel was no longer there. He stood on the drift hesitatingly, appearing, to me, to be deeply disappointed. A whole half hour of strenuous work, all for naught! He walked off to a patch of grass and grazed, a meal perhaps not as tasty but one more certain.

On October 9, 1940, I saw a female bear wandering over a snowy slope examining a half dozen ground squirrel burrows with her nose. Finally she poked her nose through the snow into the entrance of the burrow and sniffed hard. One could tell by her actions that the scent was hot. She tore away some sod and dug down through the dirt. It took her only a few minutes to reach the squirrel nest, out of which she removed a ground squirrel already in hibernation 20 inches below the surface. Only the upper 2 inches of the ground was frozen at the time. Her cub sniffed about while the mother chewed, and did some digging of its own in the loose dirt pawed up by the mother. The mother examined another squirrel hole, dug into it a little, then wandered off to feed on blueberries.

On August 4, 1941, what appeared to be a lean bear hurried up the slope of a basin, then turned and followed a contour line in search of ground squirrels. It investigated a number of burrows with its nose as it hurried along, intent, it seemed, on finding a squirrel at home. Once it broke into a gallop but stopped abruptly at some holes and began to dig. At first it dug with one paw, at the same time keeping a watch on other holes where the squirrel might emerge. The dens usually have several entrances, and the bear is aware that the squirrels may escape by any of them. Later, both forepaws were used in digging but the bear stopped at intervals to look around for the squirrel. After much digging with no success it moved on, again breaking into a gallop. It stopped at another burrow, where it made a large excavation, still with no success. A magpie sat on a willow nearby watching it dig, waiting for scraps. The bear wandered away from this failure and fed on blueberries which on this particular slope were not abundant that year. This bear had spent about 45 minutes seeking squirrels with no success. It could not afford to gamble further on the ground-squirrel hunting so returned to the staple diet. After filling up on berries the bear would probably again try its luck and dig after ground squirrels for it seemed hungry for a taste of meat.

These incidents show somewhat the nature of ground-squirrel hunting. If there was not considerable uncertainty in this hunting the bears would no doubt devote more time to it. But there is a limit to the amount of gambling they can indulge in, and even if successful they must return to foods which are available in quantity to fill their rapidly emptying paunches. The ground squirrel has been referred to as the staff of life of the grizzly, but it is only a "side dish."

Hoary Marmot.—Marmot remains were found in only one scat. As a rule, marmots have their burrows among rocks where they cannot be dug out by other animals. Bears travel slowly and are large and easily seen, so perhaps they seldom surprise marmots away from safe retreats. The capture of a marmot is no doubt accidental.

Mouse.—Mouse remains were found in only one dropping. Mice are picked up when available but are too small to be hunted with profit unless very abundant. In years when mice are plentiful they probably are frequently eaten. Sheldon (1930, p. 170–171) found a bear catching mice in the snow on October 9, 1907, at a time when mice were unusually plentiful. He describes its actions as follows: "The bear, evidently scenting a mouse in a tunnel, would plunge its nose into the snow, its snout ploughing through, often as far as 10 feet, until the mouse had gone down into its hole in the ground; then the bear would dig it out and catch it with a paw." In the summer of 1939 mice were scarce, and the following two summers they were present in only moderate numbers. They had been unusually numerous in the fall of 1938 but had died off the following winter. On July 7, 1941, I saw a bear pouncing in a grassy swale, apparently catching mice, the only time a bear was seen engaged in this activity.

Porcupine.—Porcupines are probably not often eaten by bears. However, two porcupine quills were found stuck in a bear's nose, which indicated a too close approach.

Caribou.—Adult caribou are eaten when found as carrion. Six carcasses were seen which had been eaten by bears. Two of these were untouched and putrid when first found by me and were later cleaned up by bears.

A grizzly would be unable to catch a healthy caribou unless he came upon one in an unusually deep sleep, or had some other special advantage.

Caribou calves form a part of the grizzly diet during the calving period. Grizzlies which happen to be ranging where the caribou have their calves no doubt kill some of them, and pick up others which are found as carrion. After the first few days the calves probably are able to escape the bears. In 1941 three different bears were noted on the calving grounds near Sanctuary River feeding on calves. On May 28, 1941, two bears were seen feeding on calf caribou remains, and another lone bear was surprised at a carcass of which only the legs remained. It galloped away and when again seen it was carrying the carcass of another calf. This was carried into a swale where the bear fed on it while keeping a close watch for me. Later in the season, especially in 1940, bears fed on caribou calves which wolves had killed. There did not seem to be any general movement of bears to the calving grounds.

In Table 17 (p. 192) no calf remains are tabulated for May. However, in both 1940 and 1941 some of the bears were eating calves during that month. Probably some of the scats, containing calf, recorded for June and July, were deposited in May. In May 1939, calves were not available to the bears in the eastern part of the park since the caribou calved at the McKinley bar region and westward.

Dall Sheep.—The Dall sheep eaten almost certainly represent carrion. Most of this consists of winter kills and remains of sheep killed by wolves. Sheep make up a smaller part of the food of the bears than the food table indicates because, as already stated, in searching for sheep carcasses, I covered the area well where most bear droppings containing sheep were likely to be found. If the wolves fail to crunch the bones surrounding the brain cavity of a sheep skull, the grizzlies come along later and chew up the skull to eat the brains. On two occasions in the fall when wolves killed sheep, a grizzly was on hand soon after and helped eat the carcass. In one case the bear buried parts of three sheep after feeding on them.

Lamb remains were found in one dropping. This food was probably picked up as carrion. Lambs can avoid bears soon after birth so are probably rarely captured unless diseased. Perhaps more lamb would be eaten as carrion if it were not for the fact that eagles, wolves, and foxes are also on the lookout for it, and there is so little meat in a lamb that whatever animal finds the carrion disposes of it before any others appear.

Ptarmigan.—Remains were found in one scat. Ptarmigan and other birds are picked up as carrion or possibly captured sometimes in a nestling stage.

Wasp.—Parts of three wasps were found in one scat. Bears in Jackson Hole, Wyo., frequently dig out wasp nests that are in the ground, probably chiefly for the larvae.

Garbage.—Grizzlies quickly learn to frequent garbage pits. In 1941 a female with cubs formed the habit of visiting the hotel garbage pit; another bear visited various outlying camps in the park; and a female with three yearlings visited a road camp garbage pit regularly. Arrangements should be made as soon as possible to dispose of garbage so that it will not be available to bears. Obviously, bears lose much of their attractiveness when spoiled by garbage eating. They also become a destructive nuisance to camps and a source of danger to visitors. In a great wilderness area such as Mount McKinley National Park it seems especially incongruous to see grizzlies feeding on garbage.

Breeding Habits

Bears presumably mate every 2 years, although possibly the interval is sometimes longer. A female with three yearlings, observed regularly during the mating season, was not seen with a mate, so in her case it would seem the interval would be at least 3 years. The young follow the mothers during two summers. Grizzlies have from one to three cubs, and perhaps occasionally four. Three young are common and several such families were seen.

Breeding takes place in the spring and early summer. In 1939 two large grizzlies, probably a pair, were seen together on June 23. On June 10, 1940, an exceptionally large dark grizzly was seen following a small straw-colored grizzly. Two bears of this description, reported together about a week before, may have been the same as the two I saw. The large dark one was probably the male. Ranger Harold Herning and Frank Glaser reported seeing a pair of bears mating on June 18, 1940.

On May 15, 1941, two grizzlies were seen together digging roots. When I approached them one ran away and the other came toward me. A short bluffing run of about 10 feet was followed by a swipe in the air with the paw. The grizzly then went into the woods and later was seen with the other one a half mile away. On May 28 two bears that appeared to be these same ones were seen where the caribou were calving about 10 miles from the place where they had been on May 15. When I first saw them at 10:30 a. m. they were sleeping a few feet apart. Soon they started to wrestle and play. They stood up on their hind legs, hugged, pushed, rolled over each other, and then did it all over again, first one on top, then the other. When they saw me they stood erect, then moved on down the slope and played for half an hour. They then traveled to some calf caribou remains near me. Both of them fed together on the same piece at times. Sometimes the remains were shaken and waved in the air to tear them apart. Later both bears moved off together, stopping to wrestle at intervals. One of them, probably the female, took the initiative in the play. An hour later

these bears were seen some distance up a slope, still at play. On the following day they were again seen wrestling about 2 miles from the spot where they had been seen the previous day. These two were apparently paired.

About May 10, 1941, a female grizzly was seen at Toklat River near a small road camp. She spent most of the day digging roots, and fed on garbage thrown away near the camp. About a week later she was joined by a lighter-colored male, noticeably smaller. They were seen breeding on May 20. They were together most of the time and were often seen playing together and hugging much like the two bears referred to above. On May 22 it became a triangle affair, for a huge dark male appeared on the scene. He endeavored to drive the small male away, chasing it far up the mountainside, back to the bar, and up the mountain a second time. When the large male followed the female she also ran away from him. On May 23, at 9 a. m., the female was seen digging roots. A little later, a half mile away, the large male was following the small male across the broad river bar. The large male grunted at intervals. The bears climbed up a slope where they fed on roots, the smaller one keeping an eye on the rival. Later he descended to the bar and started across to the female. But the observant bigger male hurried down the slope and on the bar came up within 200 yards of him. Both bears then galloped away, disappearing behind a patch of woods, and then reappeared four or five hundred feet up the slope on the other side of the bar. The small male returned to the bar, started to cross it, but changed his mind and came back to the female. The big bear, seeming to be winded by the exertion rested high on the slope for a long time, then came down and was lost to view in the trees. The female and small male wrestled, then fed close together on roots. Later they wrestled again and the male grabbed the female back of the ear and tried to mount her but she rolled over. They continued to wrestle and play for some time, then resumed feeding on roots. When I left at 2:30 p. m., the pair was crossing the bar. The big male was not seen after he came off the mountain and disappeared in the woods. It appeared that the female was being true to her first love and that the strongest bear was unable to win her affections.

On May 24 the small male was in the woods. Later he was joined by the female which apparently had been chased, for not long after she arrived the large male came through the woods on her trail, grunting and bawling loudly at intervals. At his approach the other two bears ran away together. On June 2 the small male was again seen mating with the female.

The large male continued following the pair of bears at Toklat. On June 8, when the three were seen moving toward Mile 66, the large male was chasing the female. On June 9 I saw the three bears 2 miles from Mile 66, 14 miles from Toklat. All three were sleeping only a few feet apart, on a point of rock. They lay sprawled on their backs, stomachs, and sides, occasionally changing positions or stretching a leg. Most of the time they lay on their sides. When I returned 3 hours later they had moved to the gravel bar where they were sleeping on their sides on the wet mud. The persistence of the large male had been rewarded to the extent of sharing the female. It was reported that the large male mated with the female on June 10. Soon after this date the mating activities of the bears apparently terminated.

These grizzlies had mated over a period of several weeks. The small male and the female were together for at least 23 days. All observations indicated that breeding generally takes place during May and June.

Home Range

According to the data gathered the grizzlies have a rather definite home range. Possibly these ranges shift, but for periods the bears' activity is restricted to certain areas. The mother and three yearlings observed in 1940 ranged over an area about 10 miles across. Their movements, however, were restricted by the road camp garbage pit which they visited nearly every evening during the summer.

Another female with a cub did not frequent any garbage pit, but ranged throughout the summer of 1940 between the cabin on Igloo Creek and

East Fork River over an area about 9 miles across. Only once did I see them beyond this area, and then they had wandered 4 miles westward. They were easily identified because of the runty appearance of the cub. On May 25, 1941, I saw what I took to be these same two bears in their range used the previous year. On June 14 I saw the yearling alone, and after that did not see either of them. Other bears were sometimes seen in the range of this female. A small dark bear, about a 2-year-old, was seen several times at one end of this range. Once the female discovered the small bear and ran a few yards toward it. The small bear climbed far up the mountain, watched for a time, then circled widely and went deeper into the range occupied by the female.

A "spoiled" bear which frequented garbage pits was known to range from Mile 66 to Mile 42 on the highway. This distance of 24 miles was, at least on one occasion, traveled in one day.

Denning

Grizzlies in Mount McKinley National Park go into hibernation in October and emerge in early April. Tracks were seen in late October. In 1939 I saw bear tracks on April 17—the first day I was in the field— and in 1941 the first bear track was seen on April 8.

On October 11, 1939, when there was a foot of snow on the ground, a grizzly was seen digging a den on a steep slope far up a mountain. In

digging, the bear disappeared in the hole, then came out tail first pawing the dirt out of the entrance. At intervals the pile of dirt at the entrance was pawed back and it rolled far down the slope on the snow. The entrance was just large enough to permit the bear to enter. The following spring I saw fresh tracks leading away from the den so it was undoubtedly used by the bear for his winter sleep. When I climbed to the den later in the summer the chamber had caved in, so.it could not be used a second year. The chamber was 4 feet from the entrance and was about 5 feet in diameter. The burrow led upward to it at an angle of about 10 degrees. Where the den was dug the mountain sloped upward at a 45 degree angle. Another den, also caved in, was seen in a similar situation.

Grizzly-Wolf Relationships

As a rule grizzlies and wolves occupy the same range without taking much notice of each other, but not infrequently the grizzlies discover wolf kills and unhesitatingly dispossess the wolf and assume ownership. This loss is usually not a serious matter to the wolves, for if food is scarce the kills will generally be consumed before the bears find them. In the relationship existing between the two species, the wolves are the losers and the meat-hungry bears are the gainers.

When the bears take possession of a kill in the presence of wolves they are much harassed, but they are so powerful that the wolves must be careful to avoid their strong arms. The wolves must confine their attack to quick nips from the rear. But the bears are alert, so usually the wolves must jump away before they come near enough for even a nip.

At the East Fork wolf den, two encounters were observed. The first one, which took place on June 5, I did not see, but it was reported to me by Harold Herning and Frank Glaser. A female with three lusty yearlings [2] approached the den from down wind. They lifted their muzzles as they sniffed the enticing smell of meat, and advanced expectantly. They were not noticed until they were almost at the den, but then the four adult wolves that were at home dashed out at them, attacking from all sides. The darkest yearling seemed to enjoy the fight, for he would dash at the wolves with great vigor, and was sometimes off by himself, waging a lone battle. (On later occasions I noticed that this bear was particularly aggressive when attacked by wolves.) The four bears remained at the den for about an hour, feeding on meat scraps and uncovering meat the wolves had buried. During all this time, the bears were under attack. When the pillaging was complete the bears moved up the slope.

The following morning I was at the wolf den a little before 8 o'clock. The female grizzly and the three yearlings were on a snowbank about

half a mile above the den. The yearlings were inclined to wander down to the den when the bears started for the river bar, but the female held a course down a ravine to one side. On the bar the bears fed on roots, gradually moving out of view behind a hump of the ridge I was on.

At 10 o'clock the black male wolf returned to the den, carrying food in his jaws. He was met by four adults and there was much friendly tail wagging. While the wolves were still bunched, a dark object loomed up in the east. It was a grizzly and it appeared to be following a trail, probably the trail of the female grizzly with the yearlings, for they had come along that way the day before. The bear was in a hurry, occasionally breaking into a short gallop. It is possible that this was a male interested in the female with the yearlings. As it came down wind from the den it threw up its muzzle and sniffed the air, no doubt smelling both meat and wolves. It continued to gallop forward. The five wolves did not see the grizzly until it was a little more than 100 yards away. Then they galloped toward it, the black male far in the lead. When the bear saw the approaching wolves, it turned and ran back over its trail, with the black wolf close at its heels. The bear retreated a few jumps at a time but had to turn to protect its rear from the wolves which tried to dash in and nip it. When all the wolves caught up with the bear they

---

[2] The three cubs were 2-year olds rather than yearlings.

surrounded it. As it dashed at one wolf another would drive in from behind, and then the bear would turn quickly to catch this aggressor. But the wolves were the quicker and quite easily avoided its rushes. Sometimes the lunge at a wolf was a feint and in the sudden turn following the feint the bear would almost catch a wolf rushing in at his rear. In lunging at a wolf both paws reached forward in what appeared to be an attempt to grasp it. There was no quick slapping at a wolf with its powerful arms. The target was perhaps too distant for such tactics. After about 10 minutes the two female wolves withdrew toward the den and shortly thereafter the wolf identified as Grandpa moved off.

The black male and the black-mantled male worried the bear for a few minutes and then the latter lay down about 75 yards away. A few minutes later the black father also departed. Left alone, the bear resumed his travels in a direction which would take him a little to one side of the den, but not for long. The black-mantled male quickly attacked and the other four wolves approached at a ga lop. After another 5 minutes of worrying the bear, the wolves moved back toward the den, the black male again being the last to leave. The bear turned and slowly retraced his steps, disappearing in a swale a half mile or more away. It did not seem that the wolves actually bit the bear. The bear did not touch any of the wolves, although once the black-mantled male escaped from the bear's outstretched arms only by strenuous efforts. On this occasion, at least, the wolves had surely discouraged the bear with their spirited attack.

Figure 54: **"The fight with the grizzly."**

soon after it was killed by a wolf. Two of the five wolves present attacked the bear, but after being chased a few times they retired. Having killed three other calves and eaten their fill, they probably did not have a strong desire to attack the bear.

At a road camp garbage dump the female with the three yearlings,[3] and the wolves often met in their common search for choice bits. Here the wolves walked about within a few yards of the bears. One evening the bear family approached the pit four abreast as the black-mantled male and the black male wolf fed. The black one moved off a few yards to one side and the other wolf looked back at the bears a few times as they came, but fed with tail toward them until they were 8 or 9 yards away. Then he easily avoided a charge made by one of the yearlings. The two wolves maneuvered among the bears, who brought their food out of the pit to eat. Frequently the yearlings chased the wolves but the latter easily avoided the rushes. Once a wolf walked between two bears which were only 7 or 8 yards apart, but in doing so he watched them closely. After a half hour of this activity the wolves lay down to wait for the bears to depart.

On September 22, 1940, the bear family and the wolves met not far from the garbage pit. On this occasion the black male chased one of the yearling bears for a short distance, then the yearling turned and chased the wolf. Variations of this were repeated several times. These particular bears and wolves had more frequent contact than usual because of the road camp garbage pit which attracted them. These bears were seen robbing the wolf den only once.

Effect of the Grizzly on the Fauna and Flora

The influence of the grizzly on the fauna and flora appears to be moderate. Its effect on the mountain sheep and caribou populations is negligible. As grizzlies are relatively scarce they have little effect on the vegetation, their principal food. Their root digging is sometimes concentrated so as to cause the ground to be torn up over a small area, but usually this is not at all harmful. At times the bear may have some influence on plant distribution, for the seeds of the grasses and berries eaten are scattered widely by means of its droppings. It thus tends to increase its own food supply. But the plant associations are probably adjusted so that the bear as a rule has little influence on them.

---

[3] These incidents took place when the cubs were 2-year olds rather than yearlings.

CHAPTER SEVEN

⫷⫷⫷⫷⫷⫷⫷⫷⫷⫷⫷⫷⫷⫷⫷⫷⫷⫷⫷⫷

Red Fox

⫷⫷⫷⫷⫷⫷⫷⫷⫷⫷⫷⫷⫷⫷⫷⫷⫷⫷⫷⫷

THE RED FOX (*Vulpes kenaiensis*) is widely distributed throughout Alaska and is an important fur resource. In Mount McKinley National Park it is numerous and prospering. Along the north boundary trappers take many, some of which probably have drifted out of the park.

There seem to be an unusual number of silver and cross foxes in the park. I knew of six different adult silver foxes and three pups of this color phase. Cross foxes were frequently seen; in places they appeared to be as numerous as the red ones. The percentage of the different color phases varies in different areas. North of Wonder Lake a trapper captured three or four silver foxes in the winter of 1940–41; on lower Savage River a trapper had taken 15 or 20 reds and no silvers; and a trapper farther east had three reds and four crosses. In 1940 at Sable Pass a pair of cross foxes with blackish faces and more black hairs in their coats than usual had a litter of three pups—one cross and two sil-

vers; and in 1941, in the same den they had four pups—two cross, one silver, and one red. In this general area there were some adult silver foxes too, so that it appears that here a strong strain of this color phase had been developed.

Home Range

Some information on home range was gathered incidentally. A male fox, easily identified because of a missing lower canine tooth, was first seen on April 24, 1939, near the cabin on Igloo Creek. During the summer the fox was rarely seen, but in September and October he often came to the building and became rather tame. He learned to come to me when I whistled, and once followed me a mile from the cabin when coaxed with tidbits. In 1940 I lived elsewhere so had less opportunity to watch this fox, but he was seen twice, on June 21 and November 17. While I stopped a few days at Igloo Creek in February 1941, the fox appeared, looking for scraps.

During the summer of 1941 he was seen regularly in the same vicinity. This fox, then, lived in the neighborhood continuously for at least 2 years and 3 months. No information on the extent of his range was secured; when seen he was always within a few hundred yards of the cabin.

At Sable Pass a pair of unusually colored cross foxes used the same den in two successive years. The same foxes, apparently, were seen in the area in winter.

Near the cabin on Toklat River a cross fox lived for at least 3 or 4 years. The building was vacant most of the year but whenever occupied, summer or winter, the tame fox made its appearance for scraps. It

Figure 55: The red fox is plentiful in Mount McKinley National Park. The silver and cross color phases are common. [*Igloo Creek, October 6, 1939.*]

was not fed regularly enough to restrict its movements.

An unusually beautiful silver fox lived on the east side of Sable Pass. I first saw him on April 23, 1939. He discovered me when I was only 7 yards away, looked at me with eyes which, in the bright sunlight, were only slits, then continued unhurriedly on his way. I was often close to him but this was one of the few times he ever deigned to look directly at me. Usually he went about his affairs as though I did not exist, even when I was near him. He was always seen in an area about 3 miles across, south of the draw where I suspected he was denning. In 1939 he was seen during the summer and again in late October shortly before I left the park. In the summer of 1940 I continued to see him at frequent intervals. In November he was seen on two successive days near the same spot. In the spring and summer of 1941 he was frequently seen. Twice he was carrying food, apparently to his den. This fox was known to occupy a definite range over a period of 2 years and 3 months. Since this fox lived some distance from any cabin and was never fed any scraps, he was existing in an entirely natural environment.

Although some foxes seem to live all year in a restricted home range, there may be, at times, general movements of foxes. A trapper told me that during a mouse epidemic on his trapping ground there seemed to be an influx of foxes from other areas. This was correlated with a scarcity of foxes reported by other trappers some distance away where mice were scarce. The increase noted may of course have been due to a good fox crop as a result of a large carry-over of breeders and an abundant food supply. Little was learned concerning the dispersal of the young each year. They probably wander about considerably and fill in unoccupied territories.

The proximity of some of the occupied dens suggests the size of the home ranges but of course there may be a deep overlap of territories. Two dens were 5 miles apart. Two others were 6 miles apart. About half way between the latter two I was sure there was a third den, which would place these dens about 3 miles apart. The ranges of these foxes overlapped to an unknown extent.

Home Life

Dens were found in various situations—in the open and in the woods, on sunny knolls far up the slopes, and on the flats. Most of them were dug in sandy loam, but a few were located in hard clay. Generally they were found on south-facing knolls where the soil was somewhat loose. A typical den has from 6' or 7 to 19 or more entrances. In one instance there were 19 entrances over an area 10 yards across and 25 yards long.

Ten occupied dens were found without making a special search for them. In 1940 five were located along a 32-mile stretch of the highway. In this same stretch the approximate location of four other dens was known. This gives some indication of the abundance of the foxes in the park.

The parents at one of the dens, which I kept under observation, both participated in feeding the pups. There was no difficulty in supplying the required food, for uneaten remains of mice and ground squirrels were frequently seen about the den. Sometimes when there was a surplus, the food was cached by the foxes on the premises. In caching food, a shallow hole is dug with the paws, and the food is covered with dirt by making forward strokes with the nose.

The pups rested most of the day, usually inside the den, but not infrequently on a mound at one of the entrances. In the daytime the pups behaved as though they were tired and sleepy. Most activity was noted in the evening and in the early morning, which was perhaps the beginning and the ending of their nocturnal activity. At these times the pups played together vigorously.

On July 9 at 4 p. m. an adult brought a ground squirrel and dropped it near one of the entrances. After lying down a few moments the adult returned to the ground squirrel and dropped it in front of one of the pups. Two other pups suddenly appeared and there was a scramble for the squirrel; one of the pups dove into a hole with it. Later a pup was seen playing with a dead mouse. The parent lay down at one side of the den on a favorite spot. She licked one of the pups thoroughly with her tongue. Two other pups appeared and they all trailed after the mother as she moved about the den, playing among themselves when she sat on her haunches. She left them and hunted mice on a slope while they watched her intently from the den. This activity at the den was typical when a parent was with the pups.

I do not know how long the young remained at the den. In one case the pups were still at a den on September 21. On September 28 a black pup was seen alone half a mile from this den

so it appeared the pups at this time were wandering widely. During the summer the foxes sometimes changed dens; in two instances changes were made when the foxes were undisturbed so far as I knew. There sometimes are several vacant dens near an occupied one.

The same dens are sometimes used in successive years just as is the case among the wolves.

Injuries and Disease

Only two crippled foxes were seen. One was not using a front leg, the other, a silver fox, was limping badly on a hind leg.

No foxes definitely known to be sick were noted, but a fox seen on June 14, 1940, behaved as though it might have been ailing. It would not move from a clump of spruces where it was lying until I crawled in after it and then it ran out and stopped only 20 yards away. When I walked toward it, it returned to its bed. I approached it again and it moved over to another clump and lay down. It may not have been sick but only behaving toward me as it would toward a caribou that disturbed its rest. Possibly it had not seen a human being before.

In the spring of 1922 a trader told O. J. Murie that foxes had been unusually abundant in the lower Kuskokwim country in 1907, and that they had died of a disease which was thought to be rabies, since several dogs bitten by the foxes had died.

In early June of 1939 I found a dead female fox at Stony Creek which had not been touched by anything. It was an old fox with well-worn teeth so it may have died of old age. In the stomach was a ground squirrel.

Food Habits

The information on the food habits of foxes was largely secured by the analysis of scats. In the summer months most of them were gathered at eight fox dens; in winter they were picked up along the roads and trails. It is felt that sufficient data were secured to give a satisfactory picture of the food habits under existing conditions. Snowshoe hares were extremely scarce where the scats were gathered so consequently there were few remains of hares. If the hares had been numerous they would no doubt have been well represented in the diet.

DISCUSSION OF FOOD ITEMS

Field Mice.—Four species of *Microtus*, a *Lemmus*, and a *Clethrionomys* are available to the fox. At least some of the species are subject to definite cyclic fluctuations. In 1938 mice were extremely abundant; rangers reported seeing them frequently scurrying about in the open. They died off in large numbers sometime during the winter of 1938–39 so were quite scarce in the late spring of 1939. In 1940 and 1941 mice were more plentiful than in 1939 but had not by any means reached a peak of abundance. They were common enough, however, to furnish good hunting for the foxes. Species of the genus *Microtus* were most abundant.

Mice were found in 415 or in almost two-thirds of the summer

TABLE 18.—*Classification of 827 summer food items found in 662 red fox scats gathered in Mount McKinley National Park from June 1 to October 1 in 1939, 1940, and 1941.*

Food item	1939 (218 scats)		1940 (102 scats)		1941 (342 scats)		Total (662 scats)	
	Occurrence	Percent	Occurrence	Percent	Occurrence	Percent	Occurrence	Percent
Field mouse (Microtine)	197	90.3	44	43.1	174	50.8	415	62.6
Ground squirrel (*Citellus p. ablusus*)	78	35.7	41	40.1	188	54.9	307	46.3
Dall sheep, adult (*Ovis d. dalli*)	13	5.9	2	1.9			15	2.2
Dall sheep, lamb (*Ovis d. dalli*)	11	5.0					11	1.6
Caribou, adult (*Rangifer a. stonei*)					1	.3	1	.1
Caribou, calf (*Rangifer a. stonei*)	12	5.5	3	2.9	2	.5	17	2.5
Hoary marmot (*Marmota c. caligata*)	2	.9	1	.9	1	.3	4	.6
Porcupine (*Erethizon epixanthum*)	3	1.3			1	.3	4	.6
Snowshoe hare (*Lepus a. macfarlani*)	1	.4					1	.1
Birds (unidentified)	8	3.6	16	15.6	8	2.3	32	4.8
Egg shell	2	.9					2	.3
Large bone fragment					1	.3	1	.1
Wasp	2	.9	3	2.9	1	.3	6	.9
Snail	2	.9					2	.3
Blueberry (*Vaccinium uliginosum*)	3	1.3	2	1.9	3	.8	8	1.2
Grass	1	.4					1	.1

TABLE 19.—*Classification of 178 winter food items found in 124 red fox scats gathered in Mount McKinley National Park between October 2 and May 31 in 1939, 1940, and 1941.*

Food item	Number of scats in which each item occurred	Percent
Field mouse (Microtine)_____	94	75.8
Dall sheep, adult (*Ovis d. dalli*)__	19	15.3
Ground squirrel (*Citellus p. ablusus*)_____	4	3.2
Caribou (*Rangifer a. stonei*)_____	2	1.6
Bird_____	2	1.6
Cony (*Ochotona collaris*)_____	1	.8
Porcupine (*Erethizon e. myops*)__	1	.8
Blueberry (*Vaccinium uliginosum*)_____	52	41.9
Bearberry (*Arctostaphylos uva-ursi*)_____	3	2.4

scats. In some of them, remains of two or three mice were found, but generally remains of only one mouse were identified. Most of these scats were gathered at various dens so that the majority of them were from pups. Possibly the diet of adult foxes includes an even higher proportion of mice than does the diet of pups, since odd mice captured while hunting for the pups probably are eaten more often than ground squirrels. Parent foxes seemed to prefer to carry to their pups the bulkier ground squirrels rather than the much smaller mice. Such a practice would be efficient.

The scats gathered in 1939 when mice were scarcest showed a predominance of mice in the diet. This may be due to the location of the den at which the majority of the 1939

scats were gathered. It was in a grove of trees at Teklanika Forks, surrounded by flats, where ground squirrels were less abundant than they were near the other dens located on mountain slopes and passes. Even though mice were scarce at the 1939 den they may have been more conveniently secured than ground squirrels.

During the winter and in the absence of hares, mice usually form the staple diet. Meadow mice are easily captured even when their activity is carried on under moderate depths of snow. The fox locates the mouse by scent or hearing, then pounces so as to break through the snow directly over the mouse and pin it down. Even if the first pounce fails it may block runways so that escape is shut off and the mouse is captured in the ensuing scramble.

Ground Squirrel.—Ground squirrels are abundant and much used. They hibernate in winter but are obtainable from April to October. Their remains were found in 307 of the 662 summer scats.

On June 17, 1941, a silver fox was seen moving steathily along a ditch beside a road, hunting for squirrels. At intervals he stopped to look. Meanwhile, the squirrels from surrounding points were calling sharply and disappearing into their holes as he neared them. After moving along slowly with no success, the fox made a quick dash of 200 yards through some hummocks, apparently to get into new territory where his presence was not widely advertised. After making this long spurt he stood still, watching, then moved out of my view among the hummocks. When hunting mice, no attempt is made to hide, but while hunting ground squirrels the fox keeps hidden as much as possible.

On July 2, 1941, this same silver fox was again observed hunting. He captured three mice in 10 or 15 minutes. I then had to leave, but when I returned an hour later the fox was carrying a ground squirrel. Three times he laid it down in order to pounce for mice. Once he lay watching a hummock for several minutes waiting for a mouse to come out. Then, weary of waiting, he picked up his ground squirrel and trotted homeward.

A fox appeared at the Mount Eielson tent camp and quickly captured three of the ground squirrels which had been tamed by feeding (a good example of one effect of domestication). After catching the three squirrels he piled them so that the second squirrel crossed the first, and the third crossed the second. Then he seized all three where they crossed each other and left for his den with the heavy burden.

On October 14, 1939, a red fox appeared at our cabin looking for food scraps. He was about to feed on some morsels we had tossed to him when he suddenly turned, crouched, ran forward a few steps, and pounced. We did not know what he had pounced upon until he lifted his catch—our pet ground squirrel which had not been out of its burrow for several days and this day was probably taking its last look around before the long winter's sleep. My assistant and I looked at each other open-mouthed, and then Emmet said, "Well, that's Nature."

The fox with this treasure would not trust us so galloped away to feed in security.

Once a fox chased a ground squirrel into a hole and spent considerable time digging for it. Another fox ran for 15 yards and pounced at a ground squirrel but missed him. He put so much energy into his pounce that he rolled over. As this fox continued on his way the squirrels in the neighborhood sat on their hind legs and scolded him loudly, and sparrows darted at him.

Hoary Marmot.—Remains of marmot were found in four scats only.

Porcupine.—Porcupine remains were found in four summer scats and one winter scat.

John Colvin and Lee Swisher, trappers along the north boundary of the park, both told me that on skinning foxes they frequently found porcupine quills lying against the inner side of the hide. One fox trapped by Swisher had festered sores over its throat and shoulders caused by the presence of numerous quills. Swisher once found the remains of two or three porcupines at a fox den. A road crew once captured a half grown fox at Savage River with eight or nine quills in its face. The fox was weak and easily run down but after the quills were removed it regained its strength in a few days.

Like the coyote and wolf, it appears that foxes occasionally kill porcupines.

Snowshoe Hare.—Remains of snowshoe hare were found in only one scat, but hares were extremely scarce in the region studied. Dixon (1938, p. 161) found remains of 25 hares at a single den at a time when hares were abundant. Hares are no doubt an important food when they are available.

Cony.—Remains of cony (*Ochotona collaris*) were found in but one scat. The cony is probably rarely captured.

Caribou.—Remains of adults and calves were found in 20 scats. Probably all caribou eaten is carrion, although on rare occasions I suppose a very young calf might be killed. I have no record of such predation, however.

Dall Sheep.—Adult remains were found in 34 scats. Leg bones were found at one den. Sheep are frequently eaten as carrion.

Remains, representing at least three lambs, were found in 11 scats. It is of interest to note that lamb remains were found only in the 1939 scats, the year that the wolves preyed to some extent on lambs. This suggests that foxes were feeding on what the wolves left.

Shrew.—Although very abundant, no shrews (*Sorex* sp.) were found in any of the scats. A dead one, uneaten, was found at one of the dens. In Michigan I found that foxes often killed shrews but scarcely ever ate them (Murie, 1935).

Birds.—Ptarmigan remains were identified in only one scat but some of the remains classified only as "bird" may have been ptarmigan. Feathers of ptarmigan were found at one den. On May 15, 1939, a fox was seen carrying a female willow ptarmigan it had just captured. After playing with it, he ate most of it, then carried the remainder off through the woods. While he fed, some magpies watched from the willows, and two or three gulls, attracted by the kill, lit on a nearby gravel bar. During the course of the study willow ptarmigan were relatively scarce, especially near the particular . dens studied. This accounts for the few remains in the scats. At a time when ptarmigan were abundant, Dixon (1938, p. 161) reports finding remains of 20, mainly males, at a den.

Small birds are picked up incidentally. Several of the scats contained remains of small birds, two of which were identified as sparrows. At one den a pup captured a nestling sparrow which fluttered on the ground nearby.

Egg shells were found in two scats at one of the dens. The shells possibly were those of ptarmigan eggs.

Snails—Traces of snails were found in two scats.

Wasp.—Wasps were found in six scats. There were at least five wasps in one of the scats.

Blueberry.—Blueberries were found in 52 of 124 scats picked up in winter and in 8 of the summer scats. The volume of blueberries in these scats generally varied from 50 to 100 percent of the contents. Blueberries are common over the fox range and are a highly important winter food. They began to appear in the droppings as early as September 13, and the foxes fed on them throughout the winter and into April. Mice during this time were present in moderate numbers. When foxes were first noted feeding on this berry, mice were available in sufficient quantity to furnish the foxes food, which would indicate that they are especially fond of blueberries. But no doubt the blueberries are at times eaten from necessity. Lee Swisher said that in the winter of 1939-40, when mice were scarce, foxes were living almost entirely on blueberries. They dug down through the snow for the berries lying on the ground. That winter, probably because of the scarcity of mice, foxes captured in traps were eaten more than usual by other foxes.

Bearberry.—One fresh dropping picked up in February, and two collected in March, contained mainly bearberries. This plant is not abundant in the park.

Bear-Fox Relationships

I do not know of any significant relationship between the fox and the grizzly bear. Both feed considerably on ground squirrels and blueberries but there is enough of this food for all. On June 28, 1940, a grizzly digging out ground squirrels was closely followed by a fox. While the grizzly excavated, the fox lay on the grass nearby. Sometimes the grizzly followed the fox, which retreated slowly before it. The fox remained near the bear for the 1½ hours that I watched them. Knowing that the fox had a den somewhere in the vicinity, I wondered if it were trying to lead the bear away. Shortly before I left, the fox was sitting some distance up the hill, tall and straight, watching the bear below it. Then it trotted over a knoll out of sight.

Coyote-Fox Relationships

There were so few coyotes present in the park that there was no opportunity to learn much concerning the relationships between coyotes and foxes. Former Park Ranger Lee Swisher said that there never were many coyotes in the park and that is the general consensus. In the locality where I saw a coyote three times there were several foxes. Among others was the silver fox which I saw there at intervals for more than 2 years.

On October 10, 1939, a coyote was seen on the east side of Sable Pass. As I walked up the road toward it, it circled up the opposite slope and doubled back. A half mile down the stream a silver fox stood for a time watching the coyote approach, then galloped easily to the steep slope of Cathedral Mountain and climbed to a low rocky promontory. Here he sat and watched the coyote find his trail and begin to follow it. Previously the coyote had scented or seen the fox for he trotted forward expectantly. When the coyote commenced to climb, the fox galloped rapidly upward to the next prominence where he stopped to watch it following laboriously. Farther up the slope the fox frequently stopped to bark at the coyote until it was quite near. After the animals had disappeared near the top of the mountain, the barking of the fox could still be heard. The fox escaped, for I saw him the following spring. The incident suggested that the coyote might be in the habit of chasing foxes and perhaps capturing them at times in certain types of terrain. It showed too that in the rocky slopes the fox need not be afraid of the coyote.

The food habits of foxes and coyotes are similar in many respects, so where they both inhabit an area there is a certain amount of competition. However, this competition is probably not serious. To determine the degree to which coyotes are harmful to a fox population the study would have to be made in an area where both animals were present in sufficient numbers.

Eagle-Fox Relationships

No fox remains were found in any of the 632 eagle pellets collected. There was no evidence that the eagle affects the fox population.

Foxes are so numerous and spend so much time traveling in the open, treeless areas during daylight that the eagle would have many opportunities to prey upon them if it were so inclined. The lack of any remains in the pellets indicates that foxes are rarely, if ever, eaten by the eagle. There is some possibility that young eagles sometimes attack foxes with serious intentions but they probably learn that it is a dangerous venture. Perhaps a fox is occasionally captured by an eagle but such an incident would be exceptional.

Eagles have been observed swooping at foxes just as they swoop at almost every other mammal in the park, including grizzlies. Many of these maneuvers are in sport. On May 14, 1939, an eagle was seen soaring 30 or 40 feet over a fox which stood in the open looking grim and tense, his tail straight up in the air. (Foxes often assume this pose when excited. I have seen one holding his tail in this manner after pouncing on a mouse which he still searched for, and have seen pups at a den take this stand.) When the eagle saw us it flew away, and the fox relaxed and trotted slowly over the tundra. The pose taken by the fox is apparently one of readiness to ward off an attack. If the fox should run, it would give the eagle an opportunity to strike.

Dixon (1938, p. 45) describes an incident in which he saw an eagle swoop at a fox which was crouching in the open. A second fox was driven out of a culvert nearby and when it galloped away the eagle attacked it as it ran, but the fox avoided its swoop and went into a cleft in a rock. The fox possibly would have behaved differently—probably would not have run—if he were not escaping from humans as well. To avoid humans he must run; to avoid an eagle he must stand ready for attack or discreetly retire to cover. The same maneuver was not suitable for both enemies. The incident must be interpreted in the light of this knowledge. Its significance, as I see it, lies primarily in showing that the fox can avoid the stoop of an eagle.

On June 7, 1941, an eagle was seen standing beside the entrance of one of the burrows of a fox den. I am not sure just what was taking place. The eagle would reach into the entrance with its beak and then withdraw as the fox's head emerged from the hole, its jaws wide open and snapping. When the fox's head would disappear, the eagle would stoop over the hole, only to draw back quickly as the fox's open jaws appeared again. This was repeated four or five times before the eagle flew away and the fox came out to lie on the grass. Possibly the eagle had first been attracted to the den by the presence of a dead ground squirrel or some other scrap of food.

In September 1941, a combat between a fox and an eagle was reported to a ranger. Upon investigation it was found that the animal was near an eagle with a broken wing. Examination of the eagle after it was collected disclosed no evidence that the fox had injured it. (Wildlife Report, September 1941, Mount McKinley National Park.) Apparently the fox had appeared after the eagle had broken its wing and was curious, or perhaps was aware that the eagle was a potential source of food.

It is of interest to compare the relationships between the golden eagle and the red fox in Mount McKinley National Park with the relationships between the bald eagle and the blue fox on the Aleutian Islands as reported by O. J. Murie (1940, p. 198–202). The food remains of 28 eagle nests were examined and the remains of only one fox pup were found at a nest. This might even have been carrion for several dead foxes were found on the beaches. I quote (p. 201) to give the general situation and conclusions: "Depredation on blue foxes has been charged to the eagle, and this was cited by many with whom we talked. Here is a problem particularly applicable to the Aleutian Islands, since most of the islands have been leased for raising foxes. The blue foxes run wild, forage for themselves, and are usually trapped at 2- or 3-year intervals. They would seem to be vulnerable to eagle attack, living as they do on the beaches of treeless islands. Also, Aleut natives told us that eagles do take young foxes. Accordingly we gave special attention to the eagle-fox relationship. Although most of the eagle nests examined were on islands occupied by foxes, we found a fox pup in only one nest, on Rat Island. . . .

"On Amchitka Island, within 200 yards of an eagles' nest containing no fox remains, a family of young foxes was living unmolested. There was another fox family at a somewhat greater distance in the opposite direction. Foxes were seen on the beach within easy reach of eagles on Kavalga Island. Many such instances could be cited . . .

". . . At any rate, the evidence shows that eagles are not a serious menace to the blue foxes in the Aleutian Islands. An excellent fur crop is generally harvested on islands with suitable productive beaches."

The results of the bald eagle-blue fox study in the Aleutians are similar to the results of the golden eagle-red fox study in Mount McKinley National Park. The considerable data available indicate that neither the bald eagle nor the golden eagle is a serious enemy of foxes.

Wolf-Fox Relationships

I was especially interested in the relations between wolves and foxes because the statement has frequently been made that wolves are destroyers of foxes. It soon to me became obvious that a large fox population could maintain itself in a territory inhabited by several wolves, for foxes were unusually numerous over all the north side of the park east of Wonder Lake. The area west of Wonder Lake was not investigated. In the range of the wolf family on East Fork I observed one fox den in 1939, two in 1940, and five in 1941. So far as I know none of the foxes was destroyed by wolves. Only one of the 1,174 wolf scats examined contained fox remains.

Foxes seem to have no fear of wolves. On July 23, 1940, a red fox sat watching a wolf 60 yards below

it. Later the fox trotted along parallel with the wolf as the latter traveled across the slope. When the wolf descended the slope, the fox followed it a short distance down. The actions of the fox showed a confidence in its ability to evade the wolf.

On July 19, 1941, some members of a road crew saw a black wolf sniffing about the vicinity of a fox den. An adult fox followed the wolf closely and barked at it from a distance of a few feet. Once the fox ran off as though it were trying to entice the wolf away but returned when the wolf did not follow. The wolf paid no attention to the fox. It was searching for cached food items. Wolf scats at the fox den showed that the wolves had visited the den previously. Mr. Brown of the Alaska Road Commission told me about the incident, but though I hurried to the den the wolf had gone before I arrived. However, I saw the wolf about 2 miles beyond the den and later saw it catch a calf caribou and photographed it as it fed and then cached the remains. The incident again illustrated that foxes have full confidence in their ability to run away from or avoid a wolf. I have observed magpies and short-billed gulls (*Larus canus brachyrhynchos*) searching for morsels at a fox den. The den is a source of food which many animals know about.

At Teklanika Forks in 1939 a gray wolf was observed sniffing about a fox den, perhaps looking for food. Wolves probably visit many fox dens in search of scraps, especially if their food supply is a little scant.

The relationship between the wolf and the fox seems to be one of mutual gain. The wolves benefit by having available a large number of old fox dens which they can enlarge for their own use. It is a simple matter for the wolf to enlarge a burrow and much easier than digging a new one. Although the fox burrows are too small for the adult wolves, the pups can use the entire system of burrows. So far as I know, all the wolf dens found in Mount McKinley National Park were renovated fox dens.

Although the fox loses a few food items when a wolf ransacks its den site, the loss is insignificant. If there is food present it is a surplus which can be spared, whereas if food is scarce there will be none lying around.

Generally when a wolf makes a kill of a large animal it is shared by the fox, for after the wolves have eaten there is usually some of the carcass remaining. Signs at a great many of the carcasses examined in the field showed that foxes had shared in the spoils. Much of the food supply is made available to the foxes in winter when their food is scarcest. Here the fox's large gain is the wolf's small loss. Since the fox eats much less than the wolf, the loss is usually not serious and to a degree represents a surplus, although at times of course this surplus may be later needed by the wolf.

Wolves often cache the remains of a carcass after eating their fill, and the foxes commonly track down the wolves and rob the stores. Such an incident took place on October 4, 1939. A wolf had killed a lamb on Igloo Creek in the morning and, after feeding, had removed a part of the carcass and carried it away with him. The ground was covered with 2 or 3 inches of snow, sufficient for good tracking. The first indication I had that the wolf was carrying a load was the blood and hair on the snow where he had placed it on a knoll when he had stopped to look around. At two other little prominences he had laid the meat on the snow. Although the wolf track was only a few hours old a fox was ahead of me on the trail. He probably had gotten the scent of the sheep meat from the vegetation along the way. In one place the wolf had back-tracked for 15 yards, had jumped off the trail 8 feet to one side, and then had wandered about in several loops. At this point the fox tracks circled about as though the fox had been having some difficulty in unraveling the trail. The wolf resumed his direction northward through some wet tundra, walking in shallow puddles of water apparently by choice to destroy his scent. After passing through some woods he came to Igloo Creek and there his trail disappeared. The fox had come to the stream and had stood with front feet on a snow-covered rock in the shallow water beside the shore, apparently sniffing for the scent. In two other places, tracks of the forefeet on a rock showed that the fox had stood facing the stream looking for the lost trail. The wolf had walked in the water for 15 yards and had come out on the same side of the stream again. The fox and I both followed down the stream until we came to his tracks. Down the bar 300 yards the tracks led directly across the shallow stream. Here the fox, without hesitating, had also crossed the stream. After following the bar a little farther the wolf went into the woods where his trail made an S. And there beside a tree was the cache, already raided. Here I caught a glimpse of a cross fox carrying something, probably sheep meat. All that was left at the cache was much loose sheep hair. The cache had been covered with lichens and snow. Beyond this point the wolf and fox tracks continued for 150 yards to a second cache beside a hummock. The wolf apparently did not believe in having all his eggs in one basket.

But both baskets had been robbed for the second cache was also raided. The wolf tracks continued through the woods and led up a long mountain slope. Blueberries on the ground, which he squashed as he walked, colored many of his footprints purple. The fox tracks stopped at the second cache. The fox probably knew that the wolf had cached all his load. The behavior of the wolf seemed to show that he was aware that he would be followed by foxes for it seemed he made deliberate attempts to throw them off his trail.

All the data gathered on the wolf-fox relationships strongly support the conclusion that the fox population has not been harmed by the presence of the wolves in Mount McKinley National Park and the adjacent region north of the park, and that both species can subsist in the same region in good numbers.

CHAPTER EIGHT

Golden Eagle

THE GOLDEN EAGLE (*Aquila chrysaëtos canadensis*) is one of the conspicuous members of the Mount McKinley National Park fauna. There are probably 25 or more pairs breeding in the mountain sheep hills. They arrive in March and depart in October, and rarely one may winter there. Because of the abundance of this bird it was possible to get quantitative data on its food habits and information concerning its relationships to the sheep and other animals.

Nesting

All of the nests that were found were built in cliffs, which were located at various altitudes from the base of a ridge to near its summit. Some nests placed on perpendicular rock walls I was unable to reach, but others were easily accessible. A nest in a tree was reported but I did not see it. Frequently the rock surrounding a nest is orange colored because of the presence of a foliose lichen. Probably the moisture held by the nest favors the growth of this lichen.

These orange-colored patches on the rocks on a few occasions first attracted my attention to the nest.

The same nest may be used in successive seasons, or it may be deserted a year or more and then used again. A nest in use in 1939 was vacant in 1940 and again in use in 1941, and another nest vacant in 1939 and 1940 was used in 1941. Sometimes a nest is deserted and a second one is built nearby. A nest occupied in 1939 and 1940 was deserted in 1941 and a new nest was built on a ledge a little lower on the slope. The addition of some branches of heather and dwarf birch to the old nest showed that the owner still took a little interest in it. In 1940 a new nest was built only a few yards from an old one which had been built up quite high and seemed in danger of falling off the ledge.

In 1939 five occupied nests were found; in 1940 three, and in 1941 five. Two nests used in 1939 were not visited the following two seasons, and one nest used in 1940 was not visited in 1941. During the 3 years 10 dif-

Figure 56: An eagle nest in a typical location on a cliff. [*Polychrome Pass, June 3, 1939.*]

ferent nest sites were found in use. Thirteen other nests were found which were not in current use. The approximate location of several nests was known but there was not time to search for them.

In the nests observed, two young occurred more frequently than one. In five of them there were two young; in another one young and an unhatched egg; in another one egg, and in each of two nests there was a single young. In four nests it could not be determined how many young there were. A complete record of the survival of the young was not kept, but in at least two cases two young in a nest survived until fully feathered. A dead young one,

just getting a few feathers, was found near one of the nests.

The eggs generally hatch in June, often in the latter part of the month. At one nest the egg did not hatch until about the middle of July and the young one was still in the nest on August 24. In a nest at Beal's Cache near McCarty in interior Alaska, O. J. Murie found a golden eagle egg hatched May 26. This is considerably earlier than any hatching date I noted, but possibly some eagles do nest that early in Mount McKinley National Park.

Home Range

In 1939 two occupied eagle nests were only about 1½ miles apart, and in 1941 two pairs of eagles were nesting on the same slope of a ridge only about 1 mile apart. The distance between other occupied nests was sometimes less than 5 miles. With the nests so near one another it is obvious that there is considerable overlapping of ranges. Probably eagles nesting so near one another cruise over the same areas, although each pair may have favorite slopes over which they glide in search of ground squirrels. However, I would guess that eagles nesting near each other hunt indiscriminately over the slopes in the general region except perhaps close to a nest.

It is of course difficult to determine the size of the hunting area of a nesting pair. I have seen eagles fly off 4 miles from the nest site in a few minutes. It would seem highly improbable that the eagles confined their activities to an area less than 10 miles in diameter and I expect they may cruise considerably farther afield at times, especially when carrion is available. On June 16, 1940, near a wolf den, 7 eagles were gathered at carrion in one spot, and three others were feeding not far away. The nearest nest to the spot where they fed was almost 5 miles away. On June 28, 1941, 9 eagles were assembled at a carcass, and on July 2 there were 14 at a carcass.

Some of those eagles may have been nonbreeders but most of them appeared to be adults. (The 14 eagles were sitting in the rain. When the sun came out they half spread their wings to dry.) These assemblages during the nesting season indicate that many eagles feed over a common territory and that their ranges are quite extensive.

Food Habits

The food habits of the eagle were studied principally by examining the pellets they had regurgitated. The food remains at the nests were also noted, with special effort to find remains of lambs.

At the nests, both occupied and unoccupied, the following items were found: ground squirrel, 14; marmot, 6; snowshoe hare, 3; ptarmigan, 2; calf caribou, 2; lamb, 4. In two cases the lamb bones were found near the base of the slope under the nest and were old and weathered. These data on food habits are in general accord with those secured from the examination of pellets.

Eagle pellets collected over a 3-year period totaled 632—83 in 1939; 330 in 1940; and 219 in 1941. They were gathered from widely separated areas over the mountain sheep range so should be representative. A few were found at the eagle nests, some near the nest on prominent points used by the adults, and others along the ridges, generally on promontories used as perches. Above one nest there was a knife-edged ridge, with a rock escarpment on one side and a steep

Food item	Number of pellets in which each item occurred			
	1939 (83 pellets)	1940 (330 pellets)	1941 (219 pellets)	Total (632 pellets)
Ground squirrel (*Citellus p. ablusus*)	60	284	200	544
Marmot (*Marmota c. caligata*)	6	18	13	37
Mouse (*Microtine* sp.)	7	17	8	32
Caribou, calf (*Rangifer a. stonei*)	6	17	1	24
Ptarmigan (*Lagopus* spp.)	11	4	6	21
Small bird (including sparrows)		3	9	12
Bird, sp.		8	1	9
Dall sheep, adult (*Ovis d. dalli*)	1	6	2	9
Dall sheep, lamb (*Ovis d. dalli*)	2	2	2	6
Snowshoe hare (*Lepus a. macfarlani*)	3			3
Hawk, sp.		1		1
Muskrat (*Ondatra z. spatulata*)		1		1

grassy slope on the other. More than 40 pellets were found along this ridge on grassy points used by the eagles. Prominent grassy knobs, sometimes far down the ridges, are favorite feeding perches and therefore good places to search for pellets. Sometimes as many as a dozen or more pellets were found together. The pellets contained the hair and bones of the animals eaten. Sometimes the entire foot of a ground squirrel was present. Some pellets were as large as 4 inches long and 1¾ inches thick, but usually they were slightly smaller.

Because of the large size of the eagle pellets and the great scarcity of hawks and owls in the sheep hills, there was little danger of any pellets being misidentified.

Table 20 gives the number of pellets in which each species was found in each of the 3 years. Except in the case of mice, only one individual of a species was found in a pellet. In the 632 pellets there were 699 occurrences, so that not more than 67 pellets contained more than one species. The findings during the 3 years are similar, so that it seems that a true picture of the food habits of the golden eagle in the park has been secured.

Annotated List of Animals Eaten by the Golden Eagle

Ground Squirrel.—The staff of life of the eagles in Mount McKinley National Park is the ground squirrel. In 1939 it was found in 72 percent of the pellets, in 1940 in 86 percent, and in 1941 in 91 percent. Of the 632 pellets gathered during the 3 years, 544 or 86 percent contained ground squirrel.

Ground squirrels are widely distributed over the sheep hills inhabited by the eagles, and occur from the river bars to the ridge tops. They are plentiful on the slopes where eagles may often be seen hunting for them, sailing along a contour close to the ground. In passing over sharp ridges one wing sometimes almost scrapes the ground as the eagle pivots to skim over a new slope. Its sudden appearance over a ridge probably is quite a surprise to many a ground squirrel.

Ground squirrels come out of hibernation in April and remain active until late September. One was seen as late as October 20. During most of the time that eagles are in the park ground, squirrels are available to them.

Hoary Marmot.—Marmot remains were found in 37 or 6 percent of the 632 pellets. If ground squirrels were not so readily available there probably would be a heavier toll on the marmots. On July 3, 1939, an eagle was seen eating an adult marmot, freshly killed, which showed that the old as well as the immature are taken.

Mouse.—There are four species of field mouse, a lemming, and a red-backed mouse in the park. During my stay, the field mice were by far the most numerous, so that most of the microtine remains probably belong to the genus *Microtus*. Mice were found in 32 pellets. The greatest number of individuals found in any one pellet was five. Once an eagle pounced on something in the grass which I took to be a mouse since a ground squirrel or bird could probably have been seen. When he struck he slid along for about 6 feet. He laboriously flapped away over the ground and after flying about

150 yards struck again at something in the grass, apparently another mouse. Mice were, in general, very scarce in the summer of 1939, but in 1940 and 1941 some species were again common.

Caribou.—Remains of adult caribou were not noted in the pellets, but I have several times seen eagles feeding on carcasses. The eagles assemble at any carrion they happen to find.

Calf caribou remains were found in 24 pellets. In 1941 only one pellet contained caribou. The scarcity of calf caribou remains in 1941 was correlated with the rapid passage of the cows through the park after they had calved. They were available as food in most of the area for a relatively short period. If a thorough search near the calving ground had been made more pellets containing caribou calf would, of course, have been found. Although some calves are killed by eagles, it is thought that these are generally stray animals which have lost their mothers. It was known that many of the calf caribou eaten by eagles were wolf kills. Predation of eagles on the calves seems insignificant. The relations between eagles and caribou have been discussed in the section dealing with caribou beginning on p. 162.

Ptarmigan.—Three species of ptarmigan are available. The willow ptarmigan (*Lagopus lagopus alascensis*) is usually the most abundant species but is subject to definite cycles so that its availability as a food supply varies over a period of years. From 1933 to

Figure 57: Male willow ptarmigan in breeding plumage. [*Igloo Creek, May 11, 1939.*]

1941 it was relatively scarce. In 1939 it showed some increase in numbers which continued during the following 2 years. The rock ptarmigan (*L. rupestris kelloggae*) seemed less numerous than the willow ptarmigan, and the white-tailed ptarmigan (*L. leucurus peninsularis*) was scarce.

Ptarmigan remains were found in 21 or 3 percent of the pellets. Some of the unidentified feathers found in pellets may have been those of ptarmigan, but the percentage would not be changed much regardless. When ptarmigan are more abundant, especially when at the peak of their cycle, they probably constitute a larger percentage of the food supply. On two occasions eagles were seen feeding on a freshly killed ptarmigan which was still warm.

Other Birds.—Twelve pellets contained remains of small birds, including sparrows, and the remains of a hawk were found in one pellet. In nine pellets the bird remains were too meager to indicate the species or the size of the bird eaten. Nesting birds were plentiful, so that there was considerable bird life available. The effect of the eagle on bird life is insignificant.

Dall Sheep.—Nine pellets contained adult sheep which were eaten as carrion. Lamb remains were found in only six pellets. Although eagles are plentiful in the sheep hills, it is apparent that their predation on sheep is negligible. No authentic case of an eagle killing a lamb came to my attention. The relationship between eagles and sheep is discussed in Chapter III, (p. 97.)

Snowshoe Hare.—Snowshoe hare remains were found in only three pellets. Hares were extremely scarce within the area occupied by the eagles. When hares are abundant they will of course be a more important source of food.

Muskrat.—Muskrats (*Ondatra zibe-*

Figure 58: Male rock ptarmigan in winter plumage. This species is generally found at higher elevations than the willow ptarmigan. The latter is most plentiful along streams. [*Sanctuary River, May 20, 1939.*]

thica spatulata) are scarce in the region studied and probably are generally scarce where the golden eagle nests. Remains were found in only one pellet.

Relationship of the Golden Eagle to the Park Fauna

The extensive data gathered on the food habits of the golden eagle from an examination of pellets, and the many observations made on habits, manifest that the eagle's relationship to the fauna is satisfactory from all viewpoints. Its effects on the other animals with which it is associated are all moderate, even on the ground squirrel which it hunts diligently.

Its predation on lambs and calf

caribou is negligible. As pointed out in the chapter on caribou (p. 162), two calves were found which almost certainly had been killed by eagles. It appears, however, that there would be slight opportunity for an eagle to kill a calf accompanied by its mother. No case was found of an eagle killing a lamb, and observations indicate that such predation is rare.

The eagle has frequently been accused of being destructive to red foxes. A fox pup or even an adult might be taken occasionally but predation on foxes in Mount McKinley National Park is slight. This is shown by the absence of fox remains in the eagle pellets, also by the large flourishing fox population where the eagles are abundant.

Ptarmigan are preyed upon, but when they are scarce few are taken, and when they are numerous the species can stand a heavy predation.

The eagle often feeds on animals killed by wolves, but such robbing does not seriously affect the wolf. The amount eaten by eagles is probably directly related to the abundance of food available to the wolf.

The chief food of the eagle is the ground squirrel. If the ground squirrels were scarce the extensive predation on them by the eagle might be considered detrimental to the fox, bear, wolf, and other species which also prey on them. But there are enough for all, so that the eagles'

feeding on them is perhaps useful in helping to curb their increase and maintain some sort of balance. It is likely that predators take the equivalent of the yearly increase among the ground squirrels, thus leaving an ample breeding population to transform vegetation into flesh for the meat-eaters in succeeding years. The continued high population level of the ground squirrels suggests that the predation is such as to maintain them at a high level by preventing their numbers from pyramiding and then going into a tail spin; also, the steady pressure maintained on them by the eagle and other predators may be sufficient to destroy the ailing animals should the species here be subject to disease. To a limited extent the ground squirrels do compete for food with the sheep, but at present such competition is not important. Should the ground squirrel become excessivly abundant perhaps the competition with sheep would be significant, especially on many of the wind-blown ridges. To summarize, we might say that the predation of the eagle on the ground squirrel, its chief food, tends to be beneficial to the general interrelationships existing.

To us, the greatest value of the eagle consists in the pleasure of seeing it, or hoping to see it, in its mountain home. It is fortunate that the bird's economic status is also favorable.

CHAPTER NINE

Conclusions

ONLY THOSE CONCLUSIONS involving major considerations are discussed here. It is hoped that the factual findings in this study will be useful not only in administering the National Park System but also lands having other objectives.

First, it seems apparent that the wolf is the chief check on the increase of the Dall sheep in Mount McKinley National Park. This conclusion is based on historical evidence, on the absence of indications that other factors such as disease or poor range operated sufficiently to curb the population, and on the fact that wolves spent much time hunting sheep successfully. Because of the limited survival of lambs during some winters, it appears that the predation on lambs is the most important limiting factor in stabilizing sheep numbers. Furthermore, it was found that the sheep preyed upon, other than lambs, were generally old or diseased and therefore already doomed to an early death.

During the period of this investiga-tion the size of the sheep population was satisfactory from the standpoint of their survival as a species in the park. They were also present in sufficient numbers so that even from the highway many could be seen. Because there are so many fluctuating factors the future status cannot be predicted with certainty. The status of the so-called "buffer species," whether these be snowshoe hare or caribou, may change; also the effect of human activities within the park and adjacent to it cannot be predicted.

It appears that wolves prey mainly on the weak classes of sheep, that is, the old, the diseased, and the young in their first year. Such predation would seem to benefit the species over a long period of time and indi-cates a normal prey-predator adjust-ment in Mount McKinley National Park. These conclusions are based on a study of 829 sheep remains, mainly skulls, gathered on the range. Field observations of hunting methods and freshly killed animals support the con-clusions drawn from the skull studies.

The caribou is the main food of the wolf, and a heavy toll of the calves is taken. Yet the park herd of between 20,000 and 30,000 animals is apparently maintaining its numbers. After the first few days in the life of the calves the hunting of them by wolves necessitates a chase which usually eliminates the slowest and weakest. Since the caribou and the wolf (and also the sheep and the wolf) have existed together for many centuries, it is not surprising that under wilderness conditions the two species are well adjusted to each other. The status of the caribou should be watched because the herds spend much time outside the park where they are in territory open to hunting. In respect to the sheep, the caribou is an important buffer species.

The moose in recent years, in the presence of a high wolf population, has increased conspicuously in Mount McKinley National Park and adjacent territory. This increase is generally attributed to a decrease of moose hunting by man.

The effect of the wolf and the eagle on the red fox appeared to be negligible. The fox was found to be flourishing in the presence of high wolf and eagle populations. All information indicates that seldom is the fox preyed upon by these two forms.

The coyote was so scarce in the sheep hills that it was not a factor. It seems to seek areas where the snowshoe hare is available, a fact in itself significant.

The predation of the golden eagle on the Dall sheep is negligible. During my 3 years of field work the eagles lived mainly on ground squirrels. Authentic studies in other regions also show that the golden eagle seldom preys on mountain sheep. The popular contrary impression probably arises from the fact that eagles have been known to kill mountain sheep lambs on some occasions and that they often swoop low over sheep, just as they may frequently be seen swooping low over wolves and grizzlies.

Sheep and caribou eaten by grizzlies are largely in the form of carrion. A very few young caribou may be killed by bears that happen to be living on the calving ground, but after the calves are a few days old they are generally too speedy to be caught by the grizzlies.

It is likely, judging from experience with the Mount McKinley wolves over a period of 3 years and from other information, that the Alaska wolf population has been at the saturation point for some time. It would not be surprising if, in the course of the little-understood population cycles, the Alaska wolf again declines. What the course of events will be during the next decade cannot be predicted with certainty because many fluctuating biological influences are at work. But Mount McKinley National Park is a small part of Alaska (half of 1 percent) and wolves are plentiful in many parts of the territory. It becomes obvious therefore, that whatever policy is practiced in the park will have an insignificant effect on the wolf and other wildlife populations in Alaska as a whole.

In considering the wolf and the general ecological picture in Mount McKinley National Park it must be emphasized that national parks are a specialized type of land use. Wildlife policies suitable to national parks—areas dedicated to preserving samples of primitive America—obviously may differ from those applicable to lands devoted to other uses.

References

→≫❖≪←

ANDERSON, R. M. Investigation into wild-life conditions in national parks (Waterton Lakes, Banff, and Jasper) in the Province of Alberta, 1938.

BAILEY, VERNON. A biological survey of North Dakota. U. S. Department of Agriculture, Biological Survey, 1926. 416 p. (North American Fauna No. 49.)

BEEN, FRANK. Memoranda to Director of National Park Service, dated February 3, 1942 and April 14, 1942. Manuscript.

BLAIR, W. REID. Actinomycosis in the black mountain sheep. Eleventh annual report of the New York Zoological Society, 1907.

CAMERON, A. G. The wild red deer of Scotland. Edinburgh, Wm. Blackwood & Sons, 1923. 248 p.

CAPPS, S. R. The eastern portion of Mount McKinley National Park. U. S. Geological Survey, 1932. (Bulletin No. 836-D, p. 219-300.)

DARLING, F. FRASER. A herd of red deer. A study in animal behavior. London, Oxford University Press, 1937. 215 p.

DIXON, JOSEPH S. Birds and mammals of Mount McKinley National Park. U. S. Department of the Interior, National Park Service, 1938. 236 p. (Fauna Series No. 3.)

FORSLING, C. L. Saving livestock from starvation on southwestern ranges. U. S. Department of Agriculture, 1924. 22 p. (Farmers Bulletin No. 1428.)

GOBLE, FRANS C., and MURIE, ADOLPH. A record of lungworms in Ovis dalli (Nelson). Journal of Mammalogy, 23: 220-221, 1942.

HADWEN, S., and PALMER, LAWRENCE J. Reindeer in Alaska. U. S. Department of Agriculture, 1922. 74 p. (Bulletin No. 1089.)

HENRY, ALEXANDER and THOMPSON, DAVID. New light on the history of the greater Northwest. The manuscript journals of Alexander Henry and of David Thompson, 1799-1814. Edited by E. Coues, New York, F. P. Harper, 1897, 3 vols.

HIBBEN. FRANK C. A preliminary study of the mountain lion (Felis oregonensis sp.). The University of New Mexico, 1937. (Bulletin No. 318; Biological Series, Vol. 5, No. 3, p. 3-59.)

HONESS, RALPH F. and FROST, NEDWARD M. A Wyoming Bighorn Sheep Study. Wyoming Game and Fish Department, 1942. 127 p. (Bulletin No. 1.)

MARSHALL, ROBERT. North Doonerak, Amawk and Apoon. New York. Privately printed, 1939, 31 p.

MERRIAM, C. HART. Review of the grizzly and big brown bears of North America (genus Ursus) with description of a new genus, Vetularctos. U. S. Department of Agriculture, Biological Survey, 1918. 136 p. (North American Fauna No. 41.)

MURIE, ADOLPH. The moose of Isle Royale. Museum of Zoology, University of Michigan, 1934. 44 p. (Miscellaneous Publication No. 25.)

—— Following fox trails. Museum of Zoology, University of Michigan, 1936. 45 p. (Miscellaneous Publication No. 32.)

—— Ecology of the coyote in the Yellowstone. U. S. Department of the Interior, National Park Service, 1941. 206 p. (Fauna Series No. 4.)

MURIE. O. J. An epizootic disease of elk. Journal of Mammalogy, 11:214-22, 1930.

——— Alaska-Yukon caribou. U. S. Department of Agriculture, Biological Survey, 1935. 93 p. (North American Fauna No. 54.)

—— Food habits of the northern bald eagle in the Aleutian Islands, Alaska. The Condor, 42: 198–202, 1940.

NELSON, E. W. Report upon natural history collections made in Alaska between the years 1877 and 1881. Washington, D. C., Government Printing Office, 1888. 337 p. (No. 3, Arctic series of publications issued in connection with Signal Service, U. S. Army.)

OLSON, SIGURD F. A study in predatory relationship with particular reference to the wolf. The Scientific Monthly, 46: 323–36, 1938.

PALMER, LAWRENCE J. Progress of reindeer grazing investigations in Alaska. U. S. Department of Agriculture, 1926. 37 p. (Bulletin No. 1423.)

—— Progress report Dall sheep in the Mount Hayes region, 1941. 27 p. Manuscript.

PIKE, W. The barren ground of Northern Canada. London, The Macmillan Co., 1892. 300 p.

PREBLE, E. A. A biological investigation of the Athabaska-Mackenzie region. U. S. Department of Agriculture, Biological Survey, 1908. 574 p. (North American Fauna No. 27.)

SDOBNIKOV, V. M. Relations between the reindeer (*Rangifer tarandus*) and the animal life of tundra and forest. Transcript of the Arctic Institute, Leningrad, 24: 5–60, 1935. (English summary, p. 61–66.)

SETON, E. T. The Arctic prairies. New York, Charles Scribner's Sons, 1911. 415 p.

——Lives of game animals. Garden City, N. Y., Doubleday, Doran and Co., 1929. (4 vols.)

SHELDON, CHARLES. The wilderness of Denali: explorations of a hunter-naturalist in northern Alaska. New York and London, Charles Scribner's Sons, 1930. 412 p.

SOPER, J. DEWEY. Mammals of Wood Buffalo Park, northern Alberta and District of Mackenzie. Journal of Mammalogy, 23: 119–45, 1942.

SPENCER, CLIFFORD C. Notes of the life history of Rocky Mountain bighorn sheep in the Tarryall Mountains of Colorado. Journal of Mammalogy, 24: 1-11, February 1943.

STANWELL-FLETCHER, JOHN F. Three years in the wolves' wilderness. Natural History, 49: 136—47, March 1942.

SUPERINTENDENTS' MONTHLY REPORTS, Mount McKinley National Park, 1925–42. Manuscript.

SWISHER, LEE. Personal letters.

YOUNG, STANLEY P. The war on the wolf. American Forests, 48: 552–55, 572–74, December 1942.

Index

U.S. GOVERNMENT PRINTING OFFICE : 1978 O—277-686